LOVE LIVES

CAROL DYHOUSE

LOVE LIVES

From *Cinderella* to *Frozen*

OXFORD
UNIVERSITY PRESS

OXFORD

UNIVERSITY PRESS

Great Clarendon Street, Oxford, OX2 6DP,
United Kingdom

Oxford University Press is a department of the University of Oxford.
It furthers the University's objective of excellence in research, scholarship,
and education by publishing worldwide. Oxford is a registered trade mark of
Oxford University Press in the UK and in certain other countries

First Edition published in 2021

Impression: 1

Published in the United States of America by Oxford University Press
198 Madison Avenue, New York, NY 10016, United States of America

British Library Cataloguing in Publication Data

Data available

Library of Congress Control Number: 2020945654

ISBN 978-0-19-885546-0

Printed and bound in Great Britain by
Clays Ltd, Elcograf S.p.A.

CONTENTS

LIST OF ILLUSTRATIONS

1

INTRODUCTION

Lives, Loves, and Fairy Tales

It is commonly believed that fairy tales live on because they express essential truths about the human condition, but cultural historians might question this. These tales aren't fossilized in amber. Their motifs and meanings shift and evolve in response to the societies which retell them. Some stories have particular relevance in specific historical settings. As such, they lend themselves to looking like 'tales for the times'.[1]

The story of Cinderella was rich in meaning for women in Britain and North America during the post-war years. There were impressive numbers of retellings of this story in popular culture and the children's literature of the time.[2] In particular, the Walt Disney animated film *Cinderella* (1950) was a runaway success, effectively restoring the fortunes of the studio at a time when it was plagued by debt and even on the verge of bankruptcy. Walt Disney's personal insights into the relationship between animated cartoons and contemporary fantasy were shrewd. In an oft-cited memorandum to animation artist Don Graham in 1935, he suggested the need 'to picture on the screen things that have run through the imagination of the audience', and thus 'to bring to life dream fantasies and imaginative fancies' that the audience would recognize, but also to 'make fantasies of things we think of today'.[3] The process is essentially two-way: cartoons both tap into, and at the same time help to spin, dreams.

The Disney film version of Cinderella was all about dreams. The story resonated, particularly, with the dreams of women in Britain in the 1950s who were fed up with austerity and the deprivations of wartime. Many of these women were exhausted by the 'double shift' of factory work during the daytime and domestic chores during the evening. Fathers and husbands had often been absent during the war, and the desire for romance, an escape from drudgery, and a more settled family life could be strong. Women yearned for prettier clothes: hence the appeal of Christian Dior's celebrated *ligne corolle* or 'New Look' dresses with their tiny waists and fullblown, flower-like skirts.[4] Many dreamt of being courted by romantic, princely lovers who would turn into faithful, loving husbands. Even if new brides didn't get to live in fairy-tale castles or palaces, they certainly dreamt of living in nice homes.

If dreams of romance and happy marriages were potent in the 1950s, so too were the gender scripts of that decade. An ideal family life was envisaged in terms of a partnership between a strong male provider and an economically dependent, domestically skilled housewife. Opportunities for women's education and work were limited at the time, and a woman's most promising route towards achieving her dreams lay via marriage rather than through her own career efforts.[5] Marriage was the major determinant of the quality of female lives: you could scarcely envisage having a house, let alone children, without a husband. Banks and lending companies commonly threw up their hands in horror at the idea of making loans to single women without a male guarantor (husband or father), even if these women were among the tiny and unrepresentative proportion of high-earning female professional or managerial types.[6] As for single motherhood, the social stigma attached to illegitimacy was powerful. 'Normal' sexual experience was supposed to be strictly heterosexual and confined within marriage. Homosexuality was still a criminal offence. Both unmarried motherhood and divorce were shameful.

Fast-forward sixty years or so and the changes have been remarkable. For some, this has been an exhilarating story of liberation; for others, one marked by a worrying erosion of values and certainties. Today, marriage itself need no longer be considered a life sentence, and as an institution it counts for less than it once did. Social historian Stephanie Coontz has suggested that the upheavals in romantic and family life that have taken place over the past half-century or so have transformed the ways in which people conduct their personal lives as thoroughly and as permanently as the Industrial Revolution transformed working lives two hundred years ago. Marriage, she points out, 'is no longer the main way in which societies regulate sexuality and parenting or organise the division of labour between men and women'.[7]

This book sets out to explore ways in which social change since 1950 has reshaped women's aspirations and dreams, and how these changing dreams impacted upon society. The focus is mainly on Britain and to some extent North America, and I look mostly at heterosexual women whose lives and loves were so often subjected to media and social scrutiny. (Lesbian, bisexual and trans women were less visible in mainstream media, although their lives would make for a fascinating comparison, as would the experiences of women in other parts of the world.) Within its focus, this book is concerned with social transformations, and whether women's lives can be said to have got better or worse.

Most historians and social theorists have highlighted the ways in which a culture based on the values of individualism and personal fulfilment has weakened or washed away many traditional social strictures and controls.[8] But we should beware of assuming that human beings have become irredeemably selfish as a consequence, and that they are now less able to form lasting relationships with others. The presumption that a decline in the importance of marriage has necessarily led to weaker and less effective forms of parenting, for instance, is unproven, and has been contested by British historian Jane Lewis. In her book *The End of Marriage?* (2001), Lewis reminds us that the business of living together, sharing resources, running a home, and raising children requires careful negotiation between couples. Cohabiting couples can demonstrate levels of responsibility and commitment in these matters quite equal to those demanded in the past by marriage.[9]

British historian Jeffrey Weeks gave a fundamentally optimistic account of the way lives were transformed between 1945 and 2005 in his history of *The World We Have Won: The Remaking of Erotic and Intimate Life* (2005).[10] Weeks pointed to reforms in laws affecting the rights of homosexuals, sexual citizenship, and gender relations since the Second World War as a cause for celebration, although he was careful not to imply that we should take liberalization for granted. *The World We Have Won* was published shortly after the Civil Partnership Act of 2004 came into effect in Britain, allowing same sex couples to legalize their relationships on terms which were similar to marriage. Gay couples were finally allowed to marry in Britain in 2013, although in Northern Ireland they had to wait until 2020. Campaigns for same sex marriage have had a protracted and strongly contested history in the United States, where the Supreme Court ruled in favour of same sex couples having a right to marry in 2015. This reshaping of public attitudes towards homosexuality and gender diversity since the 1950s constitutes one of the most dramatic social changes of our time. Along with feminism, these changes have transformed the ways in which we think about men, women, and heterosexuality, as well as social and family relationships.

Observers of a more pessimistic frame of mind, often on the political right, tend to deplore what they regard as a weakening of moral values governing family life. But wallowing in nostalgia for a time when stable marriages and moral certainty prevailed is unwarranted and difficult to defend. As Coontz and other historians have emphasized, marriage systems in the past rested on kinship structures and property rights. The idea that romantic love should generate lasting unions is essentially a modern one. This belief in love and the associated quest for a soulmate, along with the con-viction that individuals are likely to find their ultimate fulfilment through love and sex, can be held to have actually *destabilized* marriage. Marriage became weighed down with a burden of unreal expectation. Coontz explains:

> The origins of modern marital instability lie largely in the triumph of what many people believe to be marriage's traditional role— providing love, intimacy, fidelity and mutual fulfilment. The truth is that for centuries marriage was stable precisely because it was *not* expected to provide such benefits. As soon as love became the driving force behind marriage, people began to demand the right to remain single if they had not found love or to divorce if they fell out of love.[11]

Hence the subtitle Coontz chose for her book *Marriage: A History*, first published in 2005, was the succinct *How Love Conquered Marriage*.[12]

In *The English in Love* (2013), Claire Langhamer argued that an 'emotional revolution' preceded what we generally understand as 'the sexual revolution' in twentieth-century Britain.[13] Drawing upon her intensive research in Britain's Mass Observation Archive,[14] she has shown how people's ideas about romantic and emotional attachment gradually changed in the first half of the century. Love came increasingly to be seen as the major justification for marriage and commitment. The importance of material considerations or the values of pragmatism were less likely to be seen as 'authentic' than was the case in the past: true love was what really counted. In mid-century Britain, marriage might have *looked* stable. British historian Pat Thane has spoken of how some have nostalgically pictured the 1950s as 'a golden age' of marriage: a period of near-universal, long-lasting unions.[15] Most people married, divorce rates were low, and life expectancy was increasing. But far from representing a normal or usual state of human affairs from which we then departed, Thane has shown how this period represents something of 'a historical blip'. Marriage rates were lower in preceding decades, people married later in life, and they died earlier. And the impression of stability we often associate with the 1950s can be deceptive: it was a decade in which social ferment bubbled beneath and often erupted through the surface. Rates of premarital conception were high, as were 'shotgun marriages' among pregnant teenagers, and even though stigmatized, lone motherhood wasn't uncommon.[16] The prohibitive difficulties and expense attached to getting a divorce meant that many couples chose to cohabit, quietly, even if they guiltily thought of this as 'living together in sin'.[17] There was a great deal of secrecy, deception, and shame around family affairs.[18] As more and more came to be expected of a 'happy marriage', the ideal itself became unrealistic. It was unlikely that one partner could provide everything for another over fifty-plus years. But the institution was sustained by the fact that birth control was still unreliable, and by the harsh treatment of illegitimacy. A tide of break-ups was held in check by women's economic dependence on men, and the difficulties, costs, and social stigma attached to divorce. All of this was to change radically in the 1960s and 1970s.

The immense changes of the 1960s and 1970s, commonly referred to as 'the sexual revolution', unsettled society by demonstrating how things previously assumed to go together could so easily come apart: love and marriage, for instance; sex and love, sex and parenting, marriage and parenting; sex and gender, gender and social role. Technology—in particular, the development of an oral contraceptive pill—played a key role in the 'liberation' of women during these decades.[19] The ability to control reproduction allowed women to think quite differently about their education and careers, and their aspirations and their goals in life started to change accordingly.[20] Sex before marriage went from being risky behaviour to being accepted as normal, no longer shocking. The age at which most people married had been falling: now it began to rise again, sharply. Young people began to postpone getting married until their late twenties or thirties; some opted to cohabit with lovers or to live alone, eschewing marriage altogether. The availability of safe contraception massively impacted on the 'sexual politics' of relationships between men and women. A newly confident generation of young people—young women as well as men—were increasingly questioning the wisdom and authority of their elders. The challenges posed by civil rights activism, feminism, and gay liberation were profound and to some observers their combined agenda threatened to destabilize society from its core. A backlash against liberal demands and 'permissiveness' in both North America and Britain was fierce. Feminists and gay liberationists came in for a great deal of vilification for their demands, and were often scapegoated by those alarmed by the pace and direction of change.[21]

Although feminism has certainly had a huge effect on women's lives and dreams, feminists themselves have not always been popular, and have regularly been caricatured as man-haters. Representations of those who fought for women's suffrage in the early twentieth century commonly depicted suffragists as harridans with whiskery chins, their bodies and features contorted with rage, brandishing umbrellas at cowering males. In the second half of the century, 'women's libbers' were similarly pictured as hags, often woolly-hatted, with unforgiving features and stringy hair.[22] Feminists were dismissed as Cinderella's ugly sisters, unable to find husbands, bristling with anger and resentment, and conspicuously lacking in femininity. By the 1990s many young women had become diffident about identifying as feminists because they didn't want to appear hostile to men.[23]

Feminism has consistently challenged patriarchy, but clearly this is not at all the same thing as a blanket hostility or an aversion to all men. Understandings of how best to challenge patriarchy have varied according to social context and personal and political outlook: different issues have sometimes called forth different strategies. At root, feminism is about equality and justice. By the end of the twentieth century, many people in the West had come to accept and even take for granted rights which feminists in the past had to fight for, including women's rights to hold property, to have access to education, to vote, to make decisions about their own bodies, to have custody over their children. It is unlikely that a return to the inequalities and oppressions of the past would have popular appeal. Even so, when Susan Faludi published *Backlash: The Undeclared War against American Women* in 1991, she found plenty of evidence to show that virulent anti-feminism was still very much alive.[24]

The suspicion that feminism is somehow responsible for undermining romance and damaging family life dies hard. Feminism may have offered a robust critique of family forms based on inequality, but there is a long tradition of feminist thinking about how greater equality between men and women would foster respectful and loving partnerships and thereby *strengthen* the family.[25] This way of thinking can be traced back to the feminists of the late nineteenth and early twentieth centuries, such as the South African writer Olive Schreiner. Schreiner's seminal text *Woman and Labour* (1911) argued that the Industrial Revolution had reduced white middle-class women to 'parasites', socially and psychologically powerless because economically dependent on their husbands.[26] Seventy years later, writers such as Colette Dowling were still identifying over-dependence on the male as a major obstacle to feminism, even if more at a psychological than an economic level.[27] Dowling called this 'the Cinderella complex'. But things had changed a great deal over the course of the previous century. Sometime after the sexual revolution, more and more women stopped looking to princes for survival and began to live their own lives.

In some ways, the demise of the male breadwinner/dependent female ideal in the last quarter of the twentieth century might be seen to have restored elements of what Olive Schreiner, and the early feminist historians who followed her, represented as a preindustrial model of the family as working partnership, where both

9

husband and wife were economically active or even wage-earners.[28] We should remember that among less privileged sections of the population (such as working-class and/or non-white families) women had never really had the option of material dependency. They had always had to earn their own living. But circumstances after the 1970s were different in that more women (though still by no means all) had choices. In terms of rights as citizens, they were in a much stronger position than their forerunners.

After the 1970s, gendered differences in sexual behaviour narrowed. Reliable contraception allowed women a freedom to experiment sexually in ways which had previously been envisaged as only available to men. The age-old and deeply entrenched 'double standard' of sexual morality began to fade.[29] That more people came to judge men's and women's behaviour similarly helps to explain a significant change in attitudes to sexual fidelity and adultery. Traditionally, expectations of sexual fidelity focused on women, who were expected to be pure and faithful not least because this meant that their husbands could be sure of their progeny. Male infidelity, on the other hand, might be looked upon much more leniently. Men, popularly assumed to be driven by uncontrollable urges, were almost expected to 'stray'. By the end of the twentieth century, attitudes had changed, and this double standard had become much less defensible.[30] Men were more and more likely to be judged by the same standards as women. American sex advice columnist Dan Savage has dubbed this a disaster for marriage.[31] He contends that, rather than extending to women the same latitude and licence that men had previously enjoyed 'as a pressure release valve' in marriage, the feminist revolution has extended the fetters that women have endured historically to men. In Savage's view, both sexes are now penned into expectations of sexual fidelity that are unrealistic over the course of increasingly long lifetimes. He sees this as leading to difficulties in both heterosexual and same sex marriage.

If attitudes to adultery have hardened, at least publicly, the evidence suggests that a great deal of it goes on. Some estimates now suggest that around half of married individuals, women as well as men, will stray.[32] Exactly how many is hard to say, of course, and not only because people aren't always honest or upfront about their sexual behaviour. The very word 'adultery' has an out-of-date, Old Testament ring to it.[33] At a time when more and more couples opt for cohabitation rather than marriage it is more appropriate to think in terms of sexual fidelity as one component of commitment. But it is something to be negotiated, perhaps, rather than a necessary component. As women's ideas of happiness change, and women as well as men come to question one-partner, marriage-is-for-life models, attitudes to infidelity become more complex.

Any consideration of sex and commitment touches on one of the major fault-lines of our culture. The advantages, difficulties, and drawbacks of monogamy and sexual fidelity are much discussed today. Esther Perel, a Belgian psychotherapist now living in New York, has racked up impressive sales for her two books, *Mating in Captivity: Sex, Lies and Domestic Bliss* (2006) and *The State of Affairs: Rethinking Infidelity* (2017). Her associated TED talk, 'The Secret to Desire in a Long-Term Relationship' (2013), had been translated into thirty-six languages and been viewed more than 14.5 million times by 2019.[34] Perel writes and speaks engagingly about the often contradictory human needs for security and commitment on the one hand, and for new experience on the other. She offers suggestions on how to reconcile the domestic and the erotic. Her global popularity suggests that these problems are widely experienced and that a very large number of people are grappling with them.

Some thinkers go further, questioning whether monogamous arrangements can ever suit everyone. Christopher Ryan and Cacilda Jetha's *Sex at Dawn: The Prehistoric Origins of Modern Sexuality* (2010) challenged the assumption that human beings had evolved to be monogamous.[35] Though reviews were mixed, the book attracted a great deal of attention. Dossie Easton and Janet Hardy's *The Ethical Slut*, first published in 1997, had originally been subtitled *A Guide to Infinite Sexual Possibilities*. A second edition, in 2009, carried the subtitle *A Practical Guide to Polyamory, Open Relationships and Other Adventures*. In a third edition, which appeared in 2017, the authors anticipated a younger generation of readers less hidebound than the previous one in respect of ideas about gender.[36] They considered that the word polyamory was now much more widely understood to suggest ethical and consensual non-monogamy, and they were confident that they could now employ a non-binary gender language that hadn't been common usage when they were first writing in the 1990s.

Guides to what to expect from relationships, and how to negotiate them, abound. We live in what Stephanie Coontz has called 'uncharted territory', where much of what was taken for granted about the relationship between men and women no longer applies.[37] Meg-John Barker's insightful *Rewriting the Rules* (2013) gained a loyal following not least because of its absence of dogmatism. Barker insisted that individuals should try to embrace uncertainty rather than to follow rules, and that they should try to work out how best to organize their lives and relationships for themselves.[38]

Feminism and the socio-cultural changes of the past half-century have worked together to bring about more equality between men and women. There are signs that men as well as women are benefiting. Coontz is guardedly optimistic, suggesting 'a steady convergence' between men and women in their 'support for mutual respect, fidelity, honesty and shared tasks'.[39] As women have acquired more social and economic options, men have been freed from some of their previously often burdensome responsibilities as providers. They too may dream differently.

Has feminism killed romance? Some recent research in both Britain and North America suggests quite the opposite. In the United States, a study by Laurie Rudman and Julie Phelan at Rutgers University found that both men and women seemed to benefit from relationships which were more feminist in character and outlook.[40] In Britain, social psychologist Viren Swami of Anglia Ruskin University similarly emphasized the ways in which gender equality was affecting gender scripts, allowing young women to experience a stronger sense of agency in sexual relationships, rather than seeing sex as something which 'just happened to them'. This, Swami suggested, could lay the basis for more satisfying and healthy partnerships.[41]

Anthony Giddens, one of the most influential theorists who has set out to chart the ways in which our experiences and understandings of intimacy have been transformed in modern times, has argued that the momentous changes of the second half of the twentieth century made possible new forms of 'confluent' love and 'pure relationships'. At the time he was writing (*The Transformation of Intimacy* was published in 1992), Giddens conceded that relationships between men and women were difficult: that 'an emotional abyss has opened up between the sexes and one cannot say with any certainty how far it will be bridged'.[42] Even so, he was hopeful about the potential of new forms of relationship, where men and women would come together solely for emotional fulfilment and pleasure. These relationships were only possible with what he called 'plastic sexuality', where sex could be separated from reproduction, and where women had achieved a high degree of autonomy. 'Pure' relationships would become part of a reflexive project of the self, Giddens suggested, because in modern society people were able to craft their own biographies rather than being shaped by custom and tradition.

Social inequalities moderate opportunity: people vary in the power and capacity they have to shape their own lives. Gender, social class, and ethnicity still load the dice when it comes to the exercise of freedom and personal autonomy. But many in the West do enjoy a great deal of choice regarding how to live their lives, compared to previous generations. As Giddens and many others have noted, this can be both liberating and troubling; exciting but also scary.[43] Who we are can depend on the choices we make: whether to live with someone or to live alone, whether to marry, whether to have children, whether to commit to a lifetime of monogamy, or whether to embrace the risks and rewards of new relationships and experiences. We must decide for ourselves and negotiate with partners the value of fidelity, when to stay in existing relationships or when to pursue desires that lead elsewhere. Identity may reside in the capacity to construct a coherent story about the self, to commit to a narrative about one's life and to keep it going.

On the whole this may be harder for women than for men. Women's lives were sometimes so constrained in the past that finding a man to marry could appear one's best option: less of a romantic dream than a practical strategy. Only it wasn't 'feminine' to look too determined about this. It paid to be discreet about 'man-hunting': to appear passive and demure and to try to make it look as if the man had found and pursued *you*. The fairy-tale narrative of feminine helplessness and masculine salvation was essentially a story of *closure*. Once you had true love's kiss that was it. All you had to do was to live happily ever after. Fairy tales and romantic fiction conspired to make a woman believe that true love would be forever. Cinderella's life was transformed when she met her prince. A man was an ending.

Women writers have long challenged this narrative and its tropes, especially since the 1950s. The challenges have come about from changing social conditions as well as from feminism. Writer Edna O'Brien was never comfortable about identifying as feminist: she once claimed, somewhat unconvincingly, that feminists found her fiction unpalatable because it dealt with themes of love and longing. Yet she found herself embroiled in bitter controversy in her Catholic Irish homeland because her novels showed young women bent on pleasure and self-fulfilment and failing to find these in marriage.[44] Interviewed by Nell Dunn in the early 1960s for Dunn's book *Talking to Women* (1964), O'Brien insisted that 'what blights friendships and marriage and everything…is this little Cinderella dream that you get one man and one woman and that it lasts, you know, they live happily ever after'.[45] Women were frightened of being abandoned by men, she thought, and especially of 'being stranded with babies'. Wouldn't it be marvellous, she asked, if a woman in love could simply say to herself: 'It is beautiful for this moment and I'm with this man and the moon is round and tomorrow—God knows.'[46]

It hasn't been easy for women to let go of the Cinderella version of romance, centring on fantasies of rescue and transformation, the idea that the right man would complete them and make their lives perfect. Even today, high-achieving women can still feel as if they are failing if they don't meet the right man by the time they reach their mid-thirties, especially if they want children. Samhita Mukhopadhyay, former executive editor of Feministing.com, records that she came to write her book *Outdated: Why Dating is Ruining Your Love-Life* (2011) out of frustration with what she felt were still the dominant narratives of romance pedalled in mainstream media.[47] Described as 'not so much a hopeless romantic as a romantically hopeful feminist', Mukhopadhyay dismissed any notion that feminism was destructive of romance but insisted that young women needed to focus on their development as individuals, rather than assuming that their identity depended on finding the perfect relationship.[48] In an interview published in the online magazine *Salon* she was quoted as having observed that 'This friction has come up between the reality of how we're living our lives and the romantic story that hinges on gender relationships that don't exist anymore'.[49] There was a pressing need, she thought, for new narratives.

The trials and tribulations of young women, mostly city-dwellers, wrestling with relationships, love, and romance have been a staple of countless popular novels and television series over recent decades. The great appeal, to female readers and viewers, of Helen Fielding's *Bridget Jones's Diary* (1996), or of Candace Bushnell/HBO's *Sex and the City* (1998–2004) is in itself testimony to the ways in which deep-seated social changes have left women uncertain about romantic dreams and life ambitions. A few pages into Fielding's novel, a somewhat discombobulated Bridget arrives at a New Year party ('Turkey Curry Buffet') given by friends of her parents.[50] She has not been looking forward to it. She is greeted by her avuncular but rather lecherous host who gives her an inappropriate hug, proffers a drink, and immediately asks her about her love life. She cringes with resentment. Throughout the book, the intrusive 'How's your love life, Bridget?'—whether from friends or mere acquaintances—is guaranteed to raise her hackles and destroy her equanimity.

For many young women the issues of whether they will meet the right partner and whether they will have children remain pressing concerns and can be a source of anguish. This may be exacerbated by recurrent media scare stories about 'biological clocks' ticking away for those who over-invest in their careers. Expanding options and freedoms can generate uncertainty. In 2014 a short video entitled 'Tinderella: A Modern Love Story', produced by comedy website College Humor, circulated widely on YouTube, quickly attracting more than four million viewers (by 2019 it had been viewed more than eleven million times). It was a clever parody of Walt Disney's animated screen version of Cinderella, showing her modern-day equivalent as dreamily absorbed in texting and swiping away on dating websites. After hooking up and enjoying passionate sex, Tinderella and her 'prince' go their separate ways, without fuss, promises, or commitment. The more than four thousand comments on the video show a global audience much divided on issues of sexual ethics, gender, and morality—and perplexed about the possibilities of true and lasting love.[51]

This book is a social and cultural history, and as such it looks back rather than forwards. I have tried to take stock of the massive changes in women's lives since the Second World War, and to consider how these changes have reshaped the landscape of largely heterosexual intimate relationships. I have chosen to frame the story between two chronological markers or bookends. The account begins with the screenings of Walt Disney's animated cartoon version of *Cinderella* in 1950, and it ends with the same studio's spectacularly successful film *Frozen* in 2013. It is necessarily a story of changing hopes and dreams.

Notes

1. There is an extensive literature on the development, use and interpretation of fairy tales. Useful starting points are Bettelheim, Bruno, *The Uses of Enchantment: The Meaning and Importance of Fairy Tales* (London: Thames and Hudson, 1976; Penguin edition, 1991); Warner, Marina, *From the Beast to the Blonde: On Fairy Tales and Their Tellers* (London: Vintage, 1995); Warner, M., *Once Upon a Time: A Short History of Fairy Tales* (Oxford: Oxford University Press, 2016); Zipes, Jack, *Why Fairy Tales Stick: The Evolution and Relevance of a Genre* (Abingdon: Taylor and Francis, 2006), and the same author's *The Irresistible Fairy Tales: The Cultural and Social History of a Genre* (Princeton: Princeton University Press, 2012).

2. In the UK the Ladybird children's reader versions of Cinderella and other fairy tales proved extremely popular. A 1944 illustrated version was published by Wills and Hepworth in Loughborough (Ladybird series 413) with text by Muriel Levy, illustrated by Evelyn Bowmar. It sold for 2/6 and had gone through seventeen editions by 1957. A Wonder Book version, with text by Evelyn Andreas and illustrated by Ruth Ives, appeared in 1954 and (with a slightly different cover illustration) in 1956. This was published by Grosset and Dunlap in the USA. Another Ladybird version (by Vera Southgate, illustrated by Eric Winter) appeared in 1964.

3. Memorandum, Walt Disney to Don Graham, 23 December 1935, included in Usher, Shaun, ed., *Letters of Note*, http://www.lettersofnote.com/2010/06/how-to-train-animator-by-walt-disney.html, accessed 05/04/2019.

4. The appeal of Christian Dior's New Look in Britain after the War is discussed in Dyhouse, C., *Glamour: Women, History, Feminism* (London: Zed Books, 2010), chapter 4.

5. See for instance Eisenmann, Linda, *Higher Education for Women in Postwar America, 1945–1965* (Baltimore: Johns Hopkins University Press, 2006) and 'Wasted Investments and Blocked Ambitions: Women Graduates in the Postwar World', in Dyhouse, C., *Students: A Gendered History* (Abingdon: Routledge, 2006), 34–60.

6. Hennessy, Kathleen, 'You've Come a Long Way, Jenny', *Observer Money*, 18 April 2004, https://www.theguardian.com/money/2004/apr/18/womenandmoney.observercashsection, accessed 14/05/2019; Council of Mortgage Lenders (CML), https://www.cml.org.uk/news/news-and-views/429/, accessed 14/05/2019.

7. Coontz, S., 'For Better, For Worse', *Washington Post*, 1 May 2005, http://www.washingtonpost.com/wp-dyn/content/article/2005/04/30/AR2005043000108.html, accessed 27/07/2018.

8. See for instance Giddens, Anthony, *The Transformation of Intimacy: Sexuality, Love and Eroticism in Modern Societies* (Cambridge: Polity Press, 1992); Bauman, Zygmunt, *Liquid Love: On the Frailty of Human Bonds* (Cambridge: Polity, 2003); Illouz, Eva, *Cold Intimacies: The Making of Emotional Capitalism* (Cambridge: Polity, 2007) and *Why Love Hurts: A Sociological Explanation* (Cambridge: Polity, 2012); Beck, Ulrich and Beck-Gernsheim, Elisabeth, *The Normal Chaos of Love* (Oxford: Polity, 1995).

9. Lewis, Jane, *The End of Marriage? Individualism and Intimate Relations* (Cheltenham: Edward Elgar, 2001).

10. Weeks, Jeffrey, *The World We Have Won: The Remaking of Erotic and Intimate Life* (London: Routledge, 2007).

11. Coontz, 'For Better, For Worse', 1.

12. Coontz, S., *Marriage, A History: How Love Conquered Marriage* (New York: Penguin (USA), 2006).

13. Langhamer, Claire, *The English in Love: The Intimate Story of an Emotional Revolution* (Oxford: Oxford University Press, 2013).

14. Mass Observation was established in 1937 by a group of intellectuals who wanted to explore 'an anthropology of ourselves'. The archive went to the University of Sussex in the 1970s, and a new 'Mass Observation Project' continues to carry out research into the lives and attitudes of 'ordinary' British people. For the history of Mass Observation see Hinton, James, *The Mass Observers: A History, 1937–1949* (Oxford: Oxford University Press, 2013) and Hubble, Nick, *Mass Observation and Everyday Life: Culture, History, Theory* (Basingstoke: Palgrave Macmillan, 2005).

15. Thane, Pat, 'Family Fortunes: The British Family', in *History Today*, vol. 60, no. 12, December 2010; Langhamer, C., 'Love and Courtship in Mid-Twentieth Century England', *Historical Journal*, 50, 1, 173–96, http// sro.sussex.ac.uk/23963/, accessed 27/07/2018.

16. Kiernan, K., Land, H., and Lewis, J., *Lone Motherhood in Twentieth Century Britain* (Oxford: Clarendon, 1998), 35.

17. On single motherhood, see Thane, Pat and Evans, Tanya, *Sinners? Scroungers? Saints? Unmarried Motherhood in 20th-Century England* (Oxford: Oxford University Press, 2012); on cohabitation and the difficulties of divorce, see p. 8.

18. Cohen, Deborah, *Family Secrets: Living with Shame from the Victorians to the Present Day* (London: Viking, 2013).

19. See *inter alia* Cook, Hera, *The Long Sexual Revolution: English Women, Sex and Contraception, 1800–1975* (Oxford: Oxford University Press, 2004); Tyler May, Elaine, *America and The Pill: A History of Promise, Peril and Liberation* (New York: Basic Books, 2011).

20. Dyhouse, *Students: A Gendered History*, chapters 4 and 5.

21. Faludi, Susan, *Backlash: The Undeclared War Against American Women* (London: Vintage, 1992).

22. LaFrance, Adrienne, 'The Weird Familiarity of 100-Year-Old Feminism Memes', *The Atlantic*, 26 October 2016, https://www.theatlantic.com/ technology/archive/2016/10/pepe-the-anti-suffrage-frog/505406/, accessed 30/07/2018; Florey, Kenneth, *Women's Suffrage Memorabilia: An Illustrated Historical Study* (North Carolina: McFarland, 2013); McDonald, Ian, *Vindication! A Postcard History of the Women's Movement* (London: Bellew, 1989).

23. Angela McRobbie has written about the ways in which feminism was invoked as 'a censorious voice' in popular culture at the end of the twentieth century: see her 'Postfeminism and Popular Culture', *Feminist Media Studies*, vol. 4, no. 3, 2004, 255–64, https://www.tandfonline. com/doi/abs/10.1080/1468077042000309937, accessed 30/07/2018.

24. Faludi, *Backlash*.

25. See for instance Dyhouse, C., *Feminism and the Family in England, 1880–1939* (Oxford: Blackwell, 1989).

26. Schreiner, Olive, *Woman and Labour* (1911; London: Virago, 1978).

27. Dowling, Colette, *The Cinderella Complex: Women's Hidden Fear of Independence* (New York: Simon and Schuster, 1981).

28. See, for instance, Clark, Alice, *The Working Life of Women in the Seventeenth Century* (first published 1919; reprinted with an introduction by Amy

Louise Erickson, Abingdon: Routledge, 2006). More recently, historians such as Amy, Erickson, *Women and Property in Early Modern England* (Abingdon: Routledge, 1993) and Laura, Gowing, *Gender Relations in Early Modern England* (Abingdon: Routledge, 2012) have critically reassessed ideas about gender, work, and the pre-industrial family. For a detailed consideration of women's economic participation in the pre-industrial economy see Shepard, Alexandra, 'Crediting Women in the Early Modern English Economy', *History Workshop Journal*, vol. 79, no. 1, Spring 2015, 1–24.

29. Still a classic on the origin of the double standard of sexual morality is Keith, Thomas, 'The Double Standard', *Journal of the History of Ideas*, vol. 20, no. 2, 1959, 195–216.

30. See for instance Langhamer, C., 'Adultery in Post-War England', *History Workshop Journal*, vol. 62, no. 1, 2006, 86–115.

31. Savage, Dan, quoted in Oppenheimer, Mark, 'Married, with Infidelities', *New York Times Magazine*, 30 June 2011, https://www.nytimes.com/ 2011/07/03/magazine/infidelity-will-keep-us-together.html, accessed 30/07/2018.

32. See for instance, https://www.divorcemag.com/articles/frequently-asked-questions-about-infidelity/, accessed 30/07/2018; Miles, Rosalind, 'Current Affairs', *Prospect Magazine*, 20 January 1996, https://www.prospectmagazine.co.uk/magazine/currentaffairs, accessed 30/07/2018.

33. See for instance Annette, Lawson, *Adultery: An Analysis of Love and Betrayal* (Oxford: Blackwell, 1989). Data used in this study (for the period 1920–83) is archived at the University of Essex (UK Data Service, SN 4858). Lawson's book offers insights while also illustrating many of the difficulties confronting those who would investigate this topic.

34. Perel, Esther, *Mating in Captivity: Sex, Lies and Domestic Bliss* (New York: HarperCollins, 2006); *The State of Affairs: Rethinking Infidelity* (New York: HarperCollins, 2017). See the same author's TED talk, 'The Secret to Desire in a Long Term Relationship' (TED/Salon NY 2013).

35. Ryan, Christopher and Jetha, Cacilda, *Sex at Dawn: The Prehistoric Origins of Modern Sexuality* (New York: HarperCollins, 2010).

36. Easton, Dossie and Liszt, Catherine A. (Janet W. Hardy), *The Ethical Slut: A Guide to Infinite Sexual Possibilities* (Emeryville, CA: Greenery Press, 1997); Easton, D. and Hardy, J., *The Ethical Slut: A Practical Guide to Polyamory, Open Relationships and Other Adventures* (Berkeley California: Celestial Arts, 2009); *The Ethical Slut: A Practical Guide to Polyamory, Open*

Relationships and Other Freedoms in Sex and Love (3rd edn, Berkeley, CA: Ten Speed Press, 2017).

37. Coontz, Stephanie, *Marriage: A History*, chapter 17.
38. Barker, M., *Rewriting the Rules: An Integrative Guide to Love, Sex and Relationships* (Abingdon: Routledge, 2012).
39. Coontz, *Marriage: A History*, 298–99.
40. Rudman, L. A. and Phelan, J. E., 'The Interpersonal Power of Feminism: Is Feminism Good for Romantic Relationships?' *Sex Roles*, vol. 57, no. 11, December 2007, 787–99, https://www.researchgate.net/publication/225145092_The_Interpersonal_Power_of_Feminism_Is_Feminism_Good_for_Romantic_Relationships, accessed 30/7/2018.
41. Swami, Viren, 'Is Feminism Killing Romance?' *The Conversation*, 1 December 2016, https://theconversation.com/is-feminism-killing-romance-69676, accessed 30/07/2018.
42. Giddens, Anthony, *Transformation of Intimacy*, 3.
43. See particularly Beck and Beck-Gernsheim, *The Normal Chaos of Love*.
44. Cahalan, James M., 'Female and Male Perspectives on Growing Up Irish in Edna O'Brien, John McGahern and Brian Moore', *Colby Quarterly*, vol. 31, no. 1, 2009, 4.
45. Dunn, Nell, *Talking to Women* (London: Silver Press, 2018), 70–1.
46. Ibid.
47. Mukhopadhyay, Samhita, interviewed by Emily, McAvan, 'Negotiating Love', *Global Comment*, 19 November 2011, http://globalcomment.com/negotiating-love-an-interview-with-samhita-mukhopadhyay/, accessed 05/04/2019.
48. Ibid.
49. Samhita Mukhopadhyay, interviewed by Tracy Clark-Flory for *Salon*, 2 October 2011, 'She's Just Not That Into Dating', https://www.salon.com/2011/10/02/shes_just_not_that_into_dating/, accessed 30/07/2018.
50. Fielding, Helen, *Bridget Jones's Diary* (London: Picador, 1996), 11.
51. https://www.youtube.com/watch?v=bLoRPielarA, accessed 08/01/2019.

2

CINDERELLA DREAMS

When Men Were an Ending

The American Dream, as envisaged by James Truslow Adams in 1931, was a heady mix of political idealism and faith in prosperity and progress.[1] Rather than a simple gospel of consumerism, it was a belief in a new social order, a 'dream of a land in which life should be better and richer and fuller for everyone'. Dreams of happiness feed social purpose. As Gloria Steinem is widely alleged to have remarked some decades later, 'without leaps of imagination, or dreaming, we lose the excitement of possibilities', reflecting further that 'dreaming, after all, is a form of planning'.[2]

In the exhausted, bomb-scarred Britain of post-war years, dreams counted for a great deal. At the level of policy and social provision, dreams inspired planning for a better society: for happy families, for national health needs, for housing, for schools, and for 'ideal homes'. At the personal level, and particularly for women, dreaming could incorporate profound longings for comfort and safety, for colour and romance.

Popular music of the 1950s and 1960s was full of references to dreams, love, and longing. 'All I have to do is dream/dream dream dream' sang the Everly Brothers in 1958, in a song written by

American songwriter Boudleaux Bryant which rose quickly to the top of the charts. This same song was recorded many times: by Bobby Darin (1957), Paul Anka (1960), Richard Chamberlain (1962), Roy Orbison (1963), and Glen Campbell (1969). Bobby Darin also serenaded his 'Dream Lover', Perry Como sang 'Dream on Little Dreamer', and British pop singer Billy Fury offered 'Once Upon a Dream', sung in tones which tugged at female heartstrings, in Michael Winner's movie *Play It Cool* (1962). Billy Fury's wistful rendition of the song was filmed in a setting of what was then cutting-edge modernity: the departure lounge in London's Gatwick Airport. Air hostesses clutched clipboards to their hearts and gazed at Billy dreamily.

Among the most memorable of the dream-songs of the time was Ilene Woods' rendition of 'A Dream Is a Wish Your Heart Makes' from Walt Disney's *Cinderella*. The story of Cinderella had huge appeal in the post-war years, even before the first screenings of Disney's blockbuster. A trawl through the British Library Catalogue shows that an impressive number of retellings of the early version by Perrault were published between 1945 and the end of the 1960s.[3] A much-loved Ladybird version for children, *The Story of Cinderella*, written by Muriel Levy and illustrated by Evelyn Bowmar, first appeared in in Britain in 1944 and had gone through seventeen editions by 1957.[4] Theatrical and pantomime productions of Cinderella were crowd-pullers in the late 1940s. The ballet version of Cinderella, with a score by Prokofiev and choreography by Frederick Ashton, was first performed at the Royal Opera House on 23 December 1948. Margot Fonteyn had injured a ligament, so Moira Shearer danced that night in the title role. A production of 'Cinderella on Ice' featured at the same time at the Empress Hall in London: this show was broadcast live on British television by the BBC a year later.[5] After 1950, though, the massive success of Disney's Cinderella inevitably shaped popular understandings and representations of the story.

There are many reasons why this story should have resonated so much with audiences in Britain and North America after the War. In Britain, the story offered a dream vision of an escape from austerity. Cinderella in the 1944 Ladybird version wears a white crinoline dress, suggestive of fairy tales and anticipating Christian Dior's New Look. Her hair is curled in the then fashionable sausage-roll style. She looks like a princess: no trace of wartime penny-pinching or the 'make-do-and-mend' campaigns which had seen women contrive wedding dresses out of recycled parachute silk or old curtains. Disney's version of Cinderella is of course even more sparkly: she keeps the sausage-roll hairdo, and her crinoline is garnished with panniers, thus accentuating the tiny waspy waistline. An extra level of class is signified by her ladylike long white gloves.

One of the most appealing aspects of Cinderella in these postwar years is that she manages to escape from household drudgery. In the Disney cartoon, bluebirds help her to get dressed in the morning, and cute little mice do lots of the domestic work. Bullied by her sadistic stepmother into endless floor-cleaning, Cinders weeps into buckets, but rescue is near at hand through the magic of a fairy godmother and *bibbidi bobbidi boo*.

Before she meets her prince, Cinderella is a domestic servant. Her name (*Aschenputtel* in German, *Cendrillon* in French) associates her with smuts on the skin from lugging coals, cleaning out ashes, and the blacking of lead grates and fireplaces. In the Disney animation, her life is shown as tortured by the incessant ringing of the servants' bell. Yet all over Britain in the 1950s, servants' bells were falling silent. For the middle classes, 'the servant problem'—that is, the business of finding and holding on to servants—was a chronic headache which went back a long time. Indoor domestic service had been the largest single employment category for women in Victorian times and this remained the case at least until the First World War. But many people had hated and resented being 'in service', with its restricted freedoms, backbreaking chores, and everyday assaults upon dignity.[6] As soon as girls could find other occupations—even if unprepossessing-sounding, such as working in canned foods or pickle factories—they voted with their feet. Between the wars, some girls had been driven back into service through a lack of alternatives, and the sector continued to absorb large numbers of women. But the end of the Second World War marked something of a watershed in the organization of household work and labour in the United Kingdom. Slowly and painfully, over the first half of the new century, the middle classes had to adjust to managing their households with minimal 'help'. This had left former mistresses of large households facing the perceived indignity of answering their own doorbells, worrying about whether or not to use soap in the scrubbing of carrots and potatoes, and squeamishly contemplating greasy sinks full of dirty dishes.[7]

The vision of a life without such drudgery had a powerful appeal to British women of both the middle and working classes. To achieve it required efficiency: kitchen gadgetry and labour-saving devices, and/or marrying someone very rich. Britain lagged behind North America in terms of the diffusion of new labour-saving devices designed for modern homes.[8] In *The Glass Slipper*, MGM's 1955 screen version of Cinderella starring Leslie Caron and Michael Wilding, a slightly petulant, smutty-faced Cinderella

1. Billy Fury, *Once Upon a Dream*

irritates everyone around her by boasting that one day she'll escape from drudgery by living in a palace. Where Disney had shown furry creatures taking on household tasks, *The Glass Slipper* featured a ballet sequence set in the palace kitchens. A cast of winsome, cheerful serving maids and handsome chefs in pastel-coloured tights choreograph domestic tasks made light by fairground-like machines. Rodgers and Hammerstein's 1957 TV special version of Cinderella for CBS attracted the largest TV audience in history—more than one hundred million viewers are estimated to have watched the show in black and white.[9] Julie Andrews plays Cinderella: neat as a new pin and not remotely servile. She inhabits a kitchen, but it's small and quite modern. Andrews, fresh from playing the spirited Eliza Doolittle on Broadway, is said to have found *My Fair Lady* 'the best Cinderella-story, really'.[10] With different—and maybe less ossified—attitudes to class distinctions than in Britain, what appealed strongly in North America was the 'rags to riches' motif, based as much on a sense of inherent personal worth and pulling yourself up by your own bootstraps as on any fairy godmother's magic.[11]

In spite of this appeal of self-help and suggestion of meritocracy in American versions of Cinderella, the allure of European princes and British royalty remained strong. It was strengthened further in the early 1950s with widespread public interest in the coronation of the young Princess Elizabeth as Queen of the United Kingdom and Commonwealth. In Britain, both the wedding of Princess Elizabeth and Philip Mountbatten in 1947, and the coronation in 1953, drew on elements of the fairy tale. Elizabeth was no scullery maid, but she certainly exemplified romantic transformations, wore unforgettable fairy-tale gowns, and appeared at Westminster Abbey in a golden coach, sparkling with diamonds.

In culture and commerce, images of fairy-tale princesses were everywhere. Cosmetic manufacturers marketed lipstick in 'Cinderella's Pumpkin' shades of orange (Revlon) and perfume packaged in a faux-glass slipper (Coty). Even Shell Petroleum joined in, with an advertisement showing a fashionable young lady in a boxy-cut suit stepping down from a pumpkin-shaped coach, while liveried footman bowed homage.[12]

Young girls growing up in the post-war world could scarcely escape the Cinderella story, which suffused popular culture and exemplified the dominant romantic narrative of the time. The Disney merchandising was ubiquitous: from Cinderella wristwatches to picture books and wind-up clockwork toys. Young women might long to meet their own version of Prince Charming, ideally strong, handsome, and rich enough to ensure them a life of comfort and protection. The dream could linger into maturity. Historian Carolyn Steedman has recalled her mother's lasting disappointment in life: she attributed this in part to an early immersion in fairy tale, stories where a humble goose-girl, good as gold, might capture the heart of a king.[13] How were young women to meet, select, and make sure of their future husbands and protectors? The fairy tale suggested that they didn't have to do much: if they were innocent, pure, and good enough, a prince would seek them out, they would fall in love, and that love would last forever. Real life, of course, wasn't quite like that.

Patterns of courtship and 'boy-meets-girl' were changing, as young people asserted a new independence after the war. Signs of this new assertiveness, and the roots of what came to be labelled 'the teenage revolution', were strengthened by economic recovery in the 1950s and by new opportunities for leisure, earning, and spending. Social historian Beth Bailey has described how in

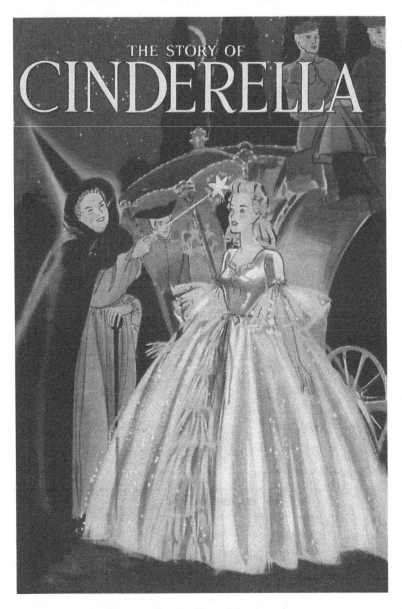

2. *The Story of Cinderella*, Ladybird Books, 1944

America, an earlier pattern of boys 'calling on' girls, and visiting them in their family homes under the watchful eye of parents, had given way to the practice of boys asking girls out on dates.[14] She suggests that after 1945, girls became less concerned with building up a reputation for popularity and the capacity to attract a large number of beaux than with 'going steady' as soon as possible, with one particular boyfriend. In Britain, although young heterosexual couples met in diverse and often haphazard ways, after the 1920s the dance-hall and the cinema became increasingly important as venues for picking up partners and looking for romance.[15]

By the 1950s, most towns in Britain boasted several picture houses—large towns such as Birmingham or Manchester boasted a couple of hundred—and a range of facilities for dancing, from large, commercially run ballrooms ('The Ritz' or 'The Palais') to less formal facilities in pubs, clubs, church halls, restaurants, and even department stores.[16] As in North America, courtship was increasingly happening outside of the parental home and away from the supervision of parents. This was especially the case, on both sides of the Atlantic, where young women were privileged enough to attend colleges and universities away from home. In Britain, only a small proportion of eighteen-year-olds (about 4–5 per cent) made it to university at this time, and young women's behaviour in college environments was still carefully supervised. However, the strict prohibitions against heterosexual 'mixing' and rules about 'chaperonage' which had been common in British higher education before the Second World War were increasingly—and often effectively—challenged by students in the 1950s.[17] It became common for young women to meet their future partners in these college settings. Dances held in college or student unions could range from the informal jazz evening or weekend 'hop', through to formal college balls. The latter were often occasions where female students agonized for weeks over who to invite, or what to wear.

Dulcie Groves, an English undergraduate living in Florence Boot Hall at the University of Nottingham in the early 1950s, remembered how keen she and her fellow women students had been to meet men of their own age. They had mostly been educated in single sex schools, and a combination of protective parents and years of dutiful attention to homework meant that many were gauche in male company, painfully aware that 'it was not done to be seen to be "chasing" the opposite sex'.[18] Describing Saturday night 'Hops' in the Student Union brought back memories of how the women students used to stand against the wall in a long line while the men hung about awkwardly, ignoring them. Many of the women hated and felt humiliated by these 'cattle-markets'.[19]

It could be hard for the young men, too. Malcolm Stevens, an undergraduate at Nottingham in the 1950s who later became a professor at the same university, recalled that 'meeting girls was problematic: the few girls at university in the late 1950s were locked up each night in Florence Boot and Florence Nightingale Halls'.[20] Returning home after 'gate hours'—a 10.30 pm curfew—could threaten a girl's reputation and even her career. The best hope one had of meeting someone was for a boy to escort a girl home, or back to halls, after the student dance, when they could maybe suggest a trip to the pictures later in the week. Stevens remembered that 'town girls' were easier to deal with than female students: the town girls were not subject to the watchful eye of lady wardens, moral tutors, and other university authorities.

3. Julie Andrews as Cinderella admiring her crown

University authorities were responsible for student discipline, being then *in loco parentis* in regard to students under twenty-one years of age. Responsibilities for supervising the conduct of female students might be taken very seriously. From the man's point of view, meeting young women was also difficult because of the business of buying drinks. Here, fellow students could be easier than the town girls, because they understood the penny-pinching necessary to subsist on a student grant. Stevens recalled that 'whereas town girls preferred to drink expensive martini cocktails or disgusting Babychams in funny glasses', Val, a fellow student whom he met at a college hop and eventually married, 'was no great burden on the pocket, as she would make a half of the local Shipstone's bitter ("Shippos") last the whole night'.[21]

Formal college dances could be worrying for women students because they were expected to invite suitable young male partners. Brothers and other male relatives might do if you were short of ideas and social contacts. What to wear when going to the ball required careful thinking and planning. Dulcie Groves recorded her outfit for a Hall party in a letter home. It was 'apple green water-wave silk' with a full skirt and could be worn strapless (although she decided not to risk that). The dress cost £7-17-6 and another 16 shillings for alterations—a substantial outlay at the time. She accessorized the dress with silver shoes and long red net gloves, borrowing her mother's diamanté necklace for the occasion.[22]

Balls, hops, and dance halls loomed large in the romantic scripts of the 1950s, across class divides. They were places of fantasy and romantic imagining for men as well as women. Actor and writer Steven Berkoff vividly recalled his youthful experiences in Tottenham's Royal dance-hall in the 1950s, when, spruced up 'in drapes and rollaway Johnnie Ray collar', he 'spraunced' onto the dance floor, 'into the expectations of a dream'.[23] Young men experimented with clothes and demeanour. In the Palais 'you were who you wished to be—warrior, lover, Jimmy Cagney, Tony Curtis, villain, spiv, leader, loner, heavy, Beau Brummell'. One

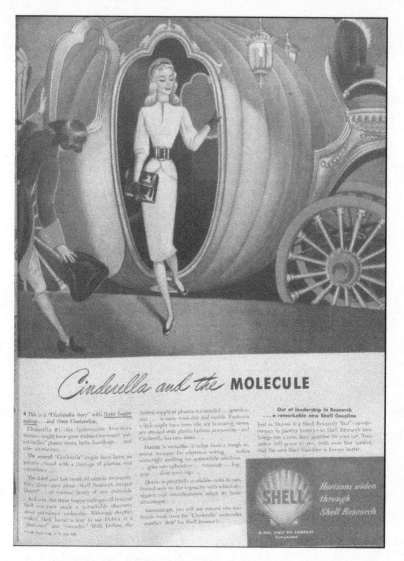

4. Advert for Shell Petroleum, 1946

5. Clacton Carnival, 1966

could flick through identities to the glancing light of the glitter-ball. Both sexes could be tortured with sexual longing. Men might start off sprauncy—'this was the mating game and the locking of horns', remembered Berkoff—but at eleven o'clock, rather than Cinderella's midnight curfew, the band would stop playing and the magic would be over. There was a scramble, then, for the last dance. Berkoff, like others, recalled that 'you became more and more desperate for someone you could take home', this opening the possibility of goodnight kissing, maybe some clandestine sexual fumbling, and, more realistically, an opportunity to arrange a date in the future.[24]

Parents often worried about what went on in the dance halls. Injunctions to be back home by midnight were commonplace. British social worker Pearl Jephcott considered the importance of the craze for dancing. She emphasized that it had become perhaps the most important way for girls 'to meet and look over men, with

6. Disney's Cinderella, enraptured by her Prince

an eye to selecting a husband'. 'To say that you will go dancing implies that you are going man-hunting, in a perfectly reputable sort of way.'[25] This didn't mean that all the men a young girl might encounter in these places would be reputable, of course, and girls had to watch out. Just as upper-class young women used code for more predatory types of young men who you might be ill-advised to allow to take you home after a dance (NSIT, for instance, meant 'Not safe in taxis'), there were attractive, unreliable types in the commercial venues with the potential to turn a girl's head and sully her reputation. Such themes were interestingly explored in the British film *Dance Hall*, directed by Charles Crichton in 1950, where four girl factory workers seek romance in the local Palais. One of the girls, Eve, is shown as very torn between her steady and decent boyfriend (and subsequently husband) Phil (Donald Houston) and Alec (Bonar Colleano), a more wolfishly glamorous American lothario who drives a flash sports car. This kind of predicament would have been readily understandable to British girls, who had come in for a great deal of criticism for having fallen for the handsome, confident American servicemen they had come into contact with during the war. Tight-lipped critics had been quick to label them 'good-time girls' who would barter their virtue for chewing gum and nylons.[26]

The problems of choice, of knowing which boy to go for, and of what 'true love' really felt like preoccupied many young women at a time when it paid to be prudent and to think hard about your prospects, because *who* a girl married certainly mattered: the choice of boy was one likely to determine the shape of your future life.[27] These were common themes in the pages of the American and British romance comics which proliferated in the 1950s. North American publishers led the way, with publications like *Young Romance* and *Young Love*. By the early 1950s there were some 150 similar titles on the North American news-stands.[28] *Cinderella Love* (Ziff Davis/St John Publications) ran between 1950 and 1955 and offered fairly standard fare, with stories titled 'My Prince Charming' or 'Rustic Cinderella'. Many of these were rescue fantasies where put-upon girls found their lives transformed by meeting Mr Right. In these stories, rich men were shown fairly commonly as defensive, keeping quiet about their massive fortunes. Girls had to learn to sift out promising types from no-good bounders; wealthy men had to avoid falling into the hands of gold-diggers. The criteria here were uncertain, since few girls would turn their noses up at riches. *Cinderella Love* featured cartoons entitled 'Man Hunt' showing simplified predicaments. A 'Correspondence Club' offered lists of lonely-hearted servicemen who girls could write to in their quest for romance.[29]

In the UK, magazine publishers were less sure of their market. *Housewife* (1954–68) was ostensibly aimed at 'go-ahead young wives', but nonetheless offered features on how to meet your man: 'Go where the men are', urged Alice Hooper Beck, recommending that hopeful girls set up camp in university towns or the neighbourhood of a military or naval base.[30] British offerings in terms of romance comics were fewer than across the Atlantic, and most of these came into existence in the later 1950s. Examples were *Marilyn*, *Mirabelle*, *Roxy*, *Romeo*, and *Valentine*. *Date* appeared in 1960, incorporating the previous cinema magazine *Picturegoer*, and much influenced by American prototypes. Its early issues dealt with 'going steady' and 'the dangers of petting'. A regular feature, 'Manhunt', asked 'Who Makes the Best Husbands?' and pop star Adam Faith cautioned readers with warnings about how much he loathed girls who put on 'an act of being equal to a man'.[31] *Boyfriend*, launched in 1959, was similar in tone, suggesting coffee bars in university towns as a setting for meeting boys, and wooing readers with the offer of an inexpensive 'going steady' ring. The British romance comics, established in the main five years later than the American examples cited, were infused with a new awkwardness about rock music and teenage culture. In a May 1959 issue of *Mirabelle and Glamour*, for instance, a very young Cliff Richard introduces himself—and a new serial dubbed 'Riverboat Romance'—with 'Hi Cats! This is Cliff speaking and we're off down Old Father Thames on a riverboat shuffle. There'll be singing and jiving to the hottest beat you've ever heard.'[32]

What all these magazines have in common is a powerful message about the importance of pouncing on the right boy as soon as possible. This finding of someone to 'go steady with' was represented as a supremely urgent task: if a girl left it until she was out of her teens it might already be too late. 'Is seventeen too young to marry?' asked a feature writer in *Date* magazine, and most of the romantic comics sported similar articles on 'Teenagers in Love'.[33] Parents might have their doubts about daughters marrying young, it was conceded, but true love carried its own imperative. An issue of *Mirabelle* in 1956 ran a story about a young woman who was driven to desperation by not having found her man by the ripe old age of twenty-nine.[34] This agitation about finding Mr Right was a message drilled into girls while still at school in the 1950s. Publishers had originally targeted papers such as *Mirabelle* at girls aged eighteen upwards, but were later to discover that they enjoyed most popularity with 13–16-year-olds.[35] These publications were heavy with advertisements for inexpensive engagement rings. Kathleen Ollerenshaw, a mathematician and educationalist writing about girls' schools in post-war Britain, expressed concern that it had become fashionable to get engaged while still at school, and that it was increasingly common 'for a girl to step from the school choir to the church altar, and to discard her prefect's badge for a wedding ring'.[36]

In both England and America the age of marriage had been falling. This had been a long-term trend since the 1890s in North America; in Britain the tendency to marry younger had become apparent in the 1930s and was most clearly marked after the Second World War.[37] In America, data from the Census Bureau show that between 1890 and the mid-1950s the median age of first marriage for men fell by roughly three years, and that for women by two. As in Britain, teenage engagements and marriages following liaisons made in high school became common.[38] In 1921 in Britain, only 14.9 per cent of brides had been under twenty-one years of age; by 1965, this proportion had risen to 40 per cent. Whereas only 11.4 per cent of girls under twenty years of age had been married in 1936–40, the proportion had risen as high as 26.4 per cent by 1960.[39]

British social investigator Michael Schofield, researching for his book *The Sexual Behaviour of Young People* (1965), found more than a third of the younger women in his sample were keen to marry before the age of twenty-one.[40] Without their parents' permission this was not at the time possible: in England the age of majority was not reduced from twenty-one to eighteen until the end of the decade.[41] As well as marrying young, women were becoming mothers earlier than before: in each year of the 1950s, around 27 per cent of all teenage brides were pregnant at their weddings.[42] Schofield emphasized that alongside 'the tremendous prominence of marriage as an immediate goal in the lives of many teenage girls', many of these girls were reluctant to use contraceptives, nor did they generally insist on their partners doing so.[43] There were several explanations for this. Historian Kate Fisher has shown how men, rather than women, tended to take responsibility for contraception before the 1960s.[44] Contraceptives were not easily available to the unmarried in the 1950s and early 1960s. Sex education in schools was often woefully minimal or non-existent: Schofield urged that schools should seek to remedy this as soon as possible. And young women were often heavily invested in seeming innocent about sexual matters.[45] To look too knowledgeable, or to prepare oneself for safe sexual encounters, could seem brazenly unfeminine, or might indicate worldly experience, which would be even worse.

Some families coped pragmatically with unwanted pregnancies. In working-class communities, particularly, grandmothers or married sisters might step in to raise the babies of young unmarried women. Respectability was sometimes preserved through deception, and the maintenance of family secrets around adoption and real parentage.[46] Even so, there are many sad stories about unwanted pregnancy among young people in the 1950s. Unmarried mothers were widely stigmatized as bringing shame upon themselves and their families. They might be discreetly sent off to give birth in secluded homes, 'reformatories', or hostels, or bullied into giving up their babies for adoption soon after these were born.[47] Students who became pregnant were likely to be thrown out of college. The more sexually adventurous or unguarded female student often lived in a permanent state of anxiety about her menstrual cycle, anxiously checking off the days in her diary or on the calendar to calculate whether her period was late and at what point she should start to panic.[48] Some women resorted to desperate attempts at abortion when first discovering unwanted pregnancies, and in an era of botched self-help and illegal, 'back-street' operations, the cost, in terms of physical damage, septic complications, haemorrhage, and accidental death, was frighteningly high.[49]

Education didn't offer many glittering prizes to girls in the 1950s. In Britain, although the Butler Education Act had extended secondary education, three-quarters of all girls still left school at the age of fifteen.[50] The question of what girls should be taught in school had become highly vexed. Many teachers and educationalists battled to improve girls' academic performance and to extend their horizons beyond the idea of marriage. But they had to contend with an increasingly vocal strain of public opinion which claimed that this was a waste of time. Exam performance didn't matter in the case of girls, it was argued: very few would go on to university, and, quite frankly, sending them there was tantamount to pouring money down the drain.[51] Boys didn't like scholarly girls, and these bluestocking, bespectacled types were a bit of a throwback to times when there weren't enough men to go round. Feminists ground their teeth while educational authority John (later Sir John) Newsom argued that women needed to be schooled in the cookery and domestic skills that would turn them into good wives.[52]

It was often asserted that many girls fretted and fidgeted through their last years in school, finding lessons irrelevant and boring, school rules irksome and infantilizing. At a time when they wanted to look attractive and grown-up they might be forced into unfashionable school uniforms; their interest in boys and romance denounced by unmarried women teachers, their curiosity about sex viewed with some distaste or even seen as pathological.[53] Some contemporaries found it unsurprising when girls rebelled against all this, keen to leave their school years behind and to begin to earn money and be treated as adults. A series of government reports on the education of young people highlighted the trend to early marriage and considered how schooling and social provision should adjust to this.[54] The Crowther Report, *Fifteen to Eighteen* (1959), emphasized the importance of treating adolescent girls more as students than as schoolgirls, insisting that it was not 'calf-love, but the kind of love that leads to marriage' that fuelled their interest in boys.[55] The authors of the report pointed out that 'marriage looms much larger and nearer' in girl pupils' eyes than ever before, estimating that nearly nine times as many girls as boys would marry before reaching the age of nineteen. They recommended that schools should aim to shape curricula more around personal relationships, dress, and creative homemaking, particularly in the case of the less able girls.[56]

This was all something of a vicious circle. Confusion over the aims and purposes of girls' education was echoed in and exacerbated by confusion over their future roles in the workplace. If a girl was fashioned for domestic life, destined to marry in her teens and play happy families thereafter, there didn't seem much point in her entertaining ambitions for a serious career. To be 'a career woman' suggested those bluestocking bespectacled types and implied something of a failure. Too much slogging away at the schoolbooks would probably mean you'd wake up in your early twenties to find yourself left on the shelf. The best thing to do would be to leave school as soon as they'd let you, and to find a job to fill in the time until you married. Any job would do, really, although it would be nice to find something that was fun or reasonably glamorous (such as air hostessing, or being a smart secretary) or feminine (nursing, care work), particularly in a field where you might come across eligible men. Historian Stephanie Spencer has described how a popular series of 'career woman' novels with titles such as *Air Hostess Ann* or *June Grey Fashion Student* conveyed some excitement about work while confirming that a girl's real happiness would come through romance, at which point she'd abandon the workplace.[57]

Even families with a strong respect for education and self-help could prove surprisingly accepting of the idea that marriage was the best career for their daughters. Journalist Lynn Barber, for instance, a high-achieving pupil at an academic girls' school in London in the 1950s, had been brought up by parents with a fervent belief in social betterment and personal achievement. Lynn confidently set her sights on going to Oxford. At the age of sixteen she was coming home from school when she was picked up by a much older man in a posh car. He seemed glamorous and sophisticated and she was soon embroiled in a relationship with him. It later turned out that he was a liar and a con-man who already had a wife and children. What shocked Lynn most, however, was the rapidity with which her parents had abandoned their ambitions for their daughter to go to university when marriage loomed. It seemed that even they valued hooking a potential spouse above an Oxford degree—at least in the case of a daughter.[58]

It couldn't be denied, though, that teenage marriages often failed. Young people carried away by fizzing hormones and frothy romance weren't always realistic about their future, as many observers and parents knew. Given that young people were increasingly likely to meet prospective partners in commercial settings, and that parents were in many ways losing control over courtship, it was inevitable that there would be conflict. Parents of daughters worried about whether the boys their daughters fell for would make steady husbands. Parents of sons worried about whether their boys' ambitions—particularly if these involved working towards a professional career—would be compromised by falling for a predatory girl's wiles. Would the girl turn out to be a gold-digging hussy? What if she 'trapped him' into marrying her by getting pregnant?

Conflict over these issues rose to new levels in post-war Britain and was reflected in a worrying surge of applications by parents who felt they had lost control over 'wayward' daughters to make these daughters into wards of court.[59] This meant handing over ultimate responsibility for the supervision and protection of these girls to the High Court, and in particular invoking the full force of law against what were considered unsuitable relationships or marriages. In England, with the consent of their parents, young people could marry at sixteen years of age. Without this consent they had to wait until the 'age of majority', which was then twenty-one. Where there was conflict over a daughter's choice, or parents feared that young people were behaving imprudently, there was the concern that the lovers would elope to Gretna Green, in Scotland, where the law allowed marriages from sixteen without the need for their parents' agreement. Dramatic stories of elopements among thwarted lovers featured large in newspapers of the day.[60] The courts claimed to be overwhelmed by applications for wardship in the 1950s and early 1960s, and lawyers complained that the system was no longer workable. High Court judge Sir Jocelyn Simon pointed to a newly emerging pattern whereby parents—mainly fathers—would petition the courts to take responsibility for daughters deemed to be associating with undesirable men and whose behaviour was seen as out of control, only to have the same parents returning shortly afterwards pleading for the order to be revoked.[61] This was commonly because the daughter in question had become pregnant in the meantime, and even a less than perfect son-in-law seemed better than criminal proceedings and a bastard grandchild.

The trend towards early marriage, and the many problems associated with this, were a major concern of the Latey Committee, set up in 1965 by the government to consider the age of majority in England. Its 1967 report, drafted by journalist Katharine Whitehorn, makes enlightening reading on attitudes to the status of young people, and social change.[62] The committee voiced popular misgivings about early marriage: that all too frequently, such liaisons constituted 'a brake on a young man's career and an end to a young girl's dream'.[63] Though they recognized that early marriages were 'especially vulnerable and not to be encouraged', they admitted that the requirement of parental consent was about as effective as Canute in holding back the tide of young love.[64] Some witnesses advocated the raising of the minimum legal age for marriage from sixteen to eighteen, on the grounds that 'a young girl would less readily agree to follow a boy behind the bicycle sheds if her fears of pregnancy could not be soothed by a promise to marry her "if anything goes wrong"'.[65] But the Committee rejected this, noting that young people were reaching puberty earlier and presumably, as a consequence, were earlier bent on seeking 'love' (they didn't differentiate here between sex and love). Raising the age at which one could legally marry would thus constitute 'a hopeless attempt to swim against the tide'. They calculated that 'since in 1964, some 10,000 brides aged 16 and 17 were pregnant on their wedding day, such a raising [of the minimum age for marriage] would almost certainly land the community with a further 10,000 or so illegitimate children'.[66] It would also leave an impossible situation in respect of the age of consent to sexual intercourse. If that were not to be raised at the same time, society would be sanctioning sex *outside* marriage but not *within* it, at that particular age. Alternatively, if the age of consent to sexual intercourse were to be raised,

> Some thousands of young men could be convicted as criminals for making love to their girlfriends, in many cases girls whom they actually wished to marry. Convicted—and what? Sent to prison? Fined? Told not to do it again?

If the law wasn't to look like an ass, the Latey Committee concluded rather lamely, 'we must plainly avoid trying to put a padlock on young emotions to quite this extent'.[67]

The Committee gave some thought to the question of whether the minimum age for marriage should be raised to eighteen for boys, leaving girls free to marry two years earlier. Differentiating between the sexes might be justified on the grounds of girls maturing earlier than boys, they suggested, but more importantly because the burden of marriage fell heavier on the male sex: 'there is no doubt that a man on marrying takes on a heavier commitment in undertaking to provide for a family than does a girl.' But what worried them was that any attempt 'to save a young man from the premature responsibilities of being a paterfamilias' would only succeed at the cost of leaving more young women stranded as unmarried mothers.[68] With this in mind, they recommended that the minimum ages of consent to sexual intercourse and for marriage stay the same for both sexes, while the age of majority should come down as soon as possible, to eighteen from twenty-one.

How did girls' intense desire to wed as soon as possible impact upon young men in the 1950s? The language of 'hunting' and 'trapping' someone who would pay to take you out, and marry and provide for you, certainly suggested a potential conflict of interests, and the possibility of tension, particularly over sex. Philip Larkin's poem *Annus Mirabilis* expressed distaste for the ways in which, before the 1960s, women might barter sex in exchange for commitment to marriage, 'a sort of bargaining', 'a wrangle for the ring'.[69] There was a fund of bitterness and resentment in Larkin's letters to his friend and fellow writer Kingsley Amis: 'Don't you think it's ABSOLUTELY SHAMEFUL that men have to pay for women', he complained, 'without BEING ALLOWED TO SHAG the women afterwards AS A MATTER OF COURSE?'—adding that he found the situation disgusting, and that like everything about 'the ree-lay-shun-ship between men and women', it made

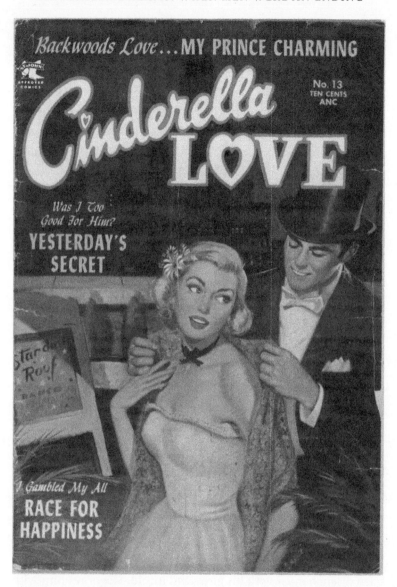

7. *Cinderella Love* included regular advice on how to secure a Prince Charming

him angry.[70] Larkin's misogyny could be extreme, especially when he was trying to impress Amis by posing as tough and worldly, but he wasn't alone in feeling that shouldering the cost of taking a girl out should 'pay off' in some way, generally by conferring sexual favours. In David Lodge's novel about National Service in Britain, *Ginger, You're Barmy* (1962), central character Jonathan puts a lot of effort into plotting how to wheedle his girlfriend Pauline into allowing him to take physical liberties with her person.[71] Sexual exploration between the two proceeds by increments and far too slowly for his liking. So without any desire or intention of marrying her, he plans to present her with an engagement ring to hurry things along. This works, but, half-hearted about contraception, Jonathan bungles things and gets Pauline pregnant. They marry, and we leave him not long after feeling 'shackled' by a wife and family 'I do not greatly love'.[72]

This kind of predicament wasn't uncommon in the novels of those British writers of the 1950s and early 1960s generally known as the 'Angry Young Men'. The anger of the male characters in these texts derived from a number of sources but was often vented on women. Arthur Seaton, in Alan Sillitoe's *Saturday Night and Sunday Morning* (1958), refers to women as 'tarts' and 'whores' and he juggles three female lovers, exploitatively. He's keen to hold off marriage for as long as possible, envisaging it as a state where he has to drop his wages into his wife's lap and put up with her nagging him about there not being enough to live on.[73] Vic Brown, the central character in Stan Barstow's *A Kind of Loving* (1960), is soon disenchanted with his girlfriend Ingrid. She bores him with her small talk, but he stays with her because she continues to provide him with sex. Ingrid gets pregnant and Vic is driven into a shotgun marriage by family pressure on both sides. His behaviour degenerates as he stews in self-pity: 'How can I tell her I've been taken in', he laments, 'because sex and a dream have got all mixed up inside me?'[74]

More than two million men were conscripted into peacetime National Service in Britain between 1945 and 1960. This had a major impact on society and culture in the 1950s, not least in shaping ideas about masculinity and femininity. Historian Richard Vinen has described how prescriptions about manly behaviour among servicemen might involve the denigration of domesticity and feminine influence.[75] Experience in the army also conveyed tangled views about women and sexuality. Warnings about venereal disease and foreign prostitutes, ubiquitous use of foul language, and crude talk about sex were common, Vinen found, even among younger recruits who were most probably still virgins and deeply attached to their mothers. Stanley Price, who did his two years of National Service before going up to Cambridge, remembered how many of his peer recruits had been brought up 'to see sex as the culmination of romance', but they now suddenly found themselves 'faced with it merely as a component in a vast litany of filth'.[76] David Lodge, revisiting the text of *Ginger, You're Barmy* for a new edition in the 1980s, was ruefully aware of how sexist its attitudes seemed, twenty years after it had been written. He wasn't really surprised, reflecting that 'conscription, being sexually discriminating, encouraged sexist attitudes'.[77]

Expectations about the education and training of young men in the 1950s often meant that these youths went for a long time without female company. This was particularly the case for middle-class boys, who were more likely to attend single sex grammar schools and then to go on to all-male colleges in Oxford, Cambridge, or London. Professional education—preparation for the law, medicine, or civil service—required parental investment and backing which could entail families making considerable sacrifices. National Service had to be fitted in before or after all this, and the reality of having to live away from home in training camps, or being sent abroad, put strain on many marriages and often disrupted love affairs. An early marriage, if a young man was unwise enough 'to get a girl into trouble', could derail career ambitions catastrophically. Cyril Connolly's well-known essay on the 'Enemies of Promise' referred to 'the pram in the hall' as an obstacle in the way of a creative artist (assumed to be a young man, of course) achieving his potential, but it was widely understood to apply to career aspirations more generally.[78] An attentive but self-sacrificing wife might just about prove an asset, but a baby would scupper things completely.

The phrase 'enemies of promise' stuck in the popular imagination. Writer and academic Lorna Sage, who became pregnant while still at school in the 1950s and who married her sixteen-year-old boyfriend, remembered that, at the time, girls were seen as 'the enemies of promise; a trap for boys', although she reflected with hindsight that the opposite had been the case.[79] The question so often evoked Adam and Eve, the serpent and the apple: who tempted whom to stray? The concern to save young men from 'the premature responsibilities' of fatherhood which was voiced in the Latey Report was grounded in a very clear set of social assumptions about the sexual division of labour: assumptions which were built into everything from welfare provision to the way families were represented in children's books. Daddy goes to work,

Mummy stays at home: women were going to become mothers, and men's job was to provide for them.

So a young girl dreaming of Prince Charming was dreaming about someone who would protect her, and who would provide for her. This was what love meant, and as in the words of the popular song of the 1950s, love and marriage went together like a horse and carriage.[80] You couldn't have one without the other. Such assumptions appalled the very un-princely and by no means altogether charming Philip Larkin, who confessed that his relationships with women were governed by 'a shrinking sensitivity, a morbid sense of sin, a furtive lechery' and complained:

> women don't just sit still and back you up. They want children: they like scenes: they want a chance of parading all the emotional haberdashery they are stocked with. Above all, they like feeling they 'own' you—or that you 'own' them—a thing I hate.[81]

Larkin's love life was unorthodox, and his closest long-term partner, Monica Jones, suffered a great deal over his hesitancies and dallying.[82] But he does put into words just how scary the burdens and responsibilities of marriage might appear to some unmarried men in the 1950s. Larkin weighed himself up and recognized that he was definitely not 'husband material', given the expectations and assumptions of the time.

Were these expectations too high? In recent years historians such as Claire Langhamer have argued that attitudes to marriage, and ideals of married love, had undergone something of a revolution in the early years of the twentieth century. Marriage had become less an institution governed by pragmatism and necessity and had come instead to represent the highest point of emotional experience for individuals, who hoped to find in it romance, love, sex, partnership, commitment for life, and personal fulfilment.[83] By the 1950s it was also burdened by highly prescriptive notions of gender; rigidly defined ideas about how men and women should behave and what they should do. Moreover, young people were blithely rushing into marriage just after leaving school.

The wobbliness of this situation didn't escape contemporaries. Eliot Slater and Moya Woodside, for instance, who made a study of two hundred working-class marriages in Britain after the War, lamented that for 'the ordinary, unthinking man and woman, marriage is surrounded by the rosy haze of the fairy tale in which "they lived happily ever after".'[84] They pointed out that 'novelettes, magazines, dance melodies and the technicoloured sunsets of the cinema' all told the same story. People imagined that the ceremony would 'put a magical stamp on their life thereafter'. Most disturbingly, for the unmarried, 'marriage becomes a mental full stop'.[85]

There were hazards for both sexes in all this. For men, there was the risk that if love failed, at any point, your responsibilities for supporting a wife—quite apart from any children—remained. You had effectively become a lifelong meal ticket. For women, marriage might be seen as even more of an ending: 'You meet 'em and that's it', commented one respondent, bluntly, to historian Judy Giles in the course of the latter's investigation into working-class women's attitudes to romance, just before the war.[86] Marriage often put a stop to any ambitions for self-fulfilment in a woman, and a home of her own might turn easily into a prison.

8. Family Planning Association warning against unwanted teenage pregnancy, 1970s

9. Single motherhood in an institutional setting, *Picture Post*, 1954

10. Young couple at Hammersmith Palais, 1947

Notes

1. Adams, James Truslow, *The Epic of America* (Boston: Little, Brown and Company, 1931); Clark, Jonas, 'In Search of the American Dream', *The Atlantic*, June 2007, https://www.theatlantic.com/magazine/archive/2007/06/in-search-of-the-american-dream/305921/, accessed 14/07/2019.

2. See, *inter alia*, Vagianos, Alanna, '23 Ways Gloria Steinem Taught Us to Be Better Women', *Huffington Post*, 25 March 2014, https://www.huffingtonpost.co.uk/entry/ways-gloria-steinem-taught-us-to-be-better-women_n_5022031, accessed 30/07/2018. However, it isn't easy to track down the exact sources for so many of the quotations widely attributed to Gloria Steinem on the internet. See Graham, Ruth, 'Why the Internet Is Full of Feminist Quotes Falsely Attributed to Gloria Steinem', *Slate*, 5 October 2017, http://www.slate.com/blogs/xx_factor/2017/10/05/the_internet_is_full_of_feminist_quotes_falsely_attributed_to_gloria_steinem.html, accessed 30/07/2018.

3. A rough count shows well over thirty new versions.

4. See, *inter alia*, Ladybird series 413 version of *Cinderella* (Loughborough: Wills and Hepworth, 1944), with text by Muriel Levy, illustrated by Evelyn Bowmar. This cost 2/6 in the UK and had gone through seventeen editions by 1957. *Cinderella* (New York: Grosset and Dunlap, Wonder Books, 1954), with text by Evelyn Andreas and illustrated by Ruth Ives, appeared with a slightly different cover illustration in 1956. Another Ladybird version (by Vera Southgate, illustrated by Eric Winter) appeared in 1964. There was also a 'Walt Disney's Cinderella' Ladybird Books version.

5. British Universities Film and Video Council, http://bufvc.ac.uk/screenplays/index.php/prog/1689, accessed 21/01/2019.

6. For a recent history of domestic service in the UK, see Delap, Lucy, *Knowing Their Place: Domestic Service in Twentieth Century Britain* (Oxford: Oxford University Press, 2011); for the US, see Sutherland, Daniel E., *Americans and Their Servants: Domestic Service in the United States from 1880 to 1920* (Baton Rouge: Louisiana State University Press, 1981).

7. For the vexed question of whether to use soap in washing potatoes, see Peck, Winifred, *House-Bound* (first published 1942. This edition London: Persephone Press, 2007), 72.

8. Strasser, Susan, *Never Done; A History of American Housework* (New York: Henry Holt, 1982); Davidson, Caroline, *A Woman's Work Is Never Done: A*

History of Housework in the British Isles 1650–1950 (London: Chatto and Windus, 1984).

9. Cinderella Show History, https://www.rnh.com/show/22/Cinderella# shows-history, accessed 31/07/2018.

10. Berman, Eliza, 'See the Cinderella Whose Performance Reached 100 Million Viewers in 1957', *Time*, 12 March 2015, http://time.com/3732139/ cinderella-1957/, accessed 31/07/2018.

11. There are insights in Cantu, Maya, *American Cinderellas on the Broadway Musical Stage: Imagining the Working Girl from Irene to Gypsy* (Palgrave Studies in Theatre and Performance History) (Basingstoke: Palgrave Macmillan, 2015).

12. Dyhouse, C., *Heartthrobs: A History of Women and Desire* (Oxford: Oxford University Press, 2017), 85–7; Revlon's 'Cinderella's Pumpkin' Once Upon a Lifetime's Colour advertisement, reproduced at https://www.cosmeticsandskin.com/companies/revlon.php, accessed 31/07/2018; advertisement for Shell Petroleum from Life Magazine, 2 December 1946, reproduced by Sally Edelstein at https://envisioningtheamericandream.com/2012/06/01/queen-for-a-day/, accessed 31/07/2018.

13. Steedman, Carolyn, *Landscape for a Good Woman: A Story of Two Lives* (London: Virago, 1986), 11, 16.

14. Bailey, Beth L., *From Front Porch to Back Seat: Courtship in Twentieth-Century America* (Baltimore: Johns Hopkins University Press, 1989).

15. Langhamer, Claire, *Women's Leisure in England, 1920–1960* (Manchester: Manchester University Press, 2000), 58.

16. On dancing in the UK see Nott, James, *Going to the Palais: A Social and Cultural History of Dancing and Dance Halls in Britain, 1918–1960* (Oxford: Oxford University Press, 2015). There is an extensive literature on cinema-going. For Britain, Kuhn, Annette, *An Everyday Magic: Cinema and Cultural Memory* (London: I. B. Tauris, 1998) is still useful. A brief introduction to cinema-going in North America is Stokes, Melvyn and Maltby, Richard (eds), *American Movie Audiences: From the Turn of the Century to the Early Sound Era* (London: BFI Publishing, 1999).

17. For an idea of earlier restrictions on women students socializing with their male peers in British universities, see Dyhouse, Carol, *No Distinction of Sex? Women in British Universities 1870–1939* (London: UCL Press, 1995), especially chapter 2.

18. Groves, Dulcie, 'Dear Mum and Dad: Letters Home from a Women's Hall of Residence at the University of Nottingham, 1952–1955', *History of Education*, vol. 22, no. 3, 1993, 289–301.

19. Ibid. 299.
20. Stevens, Malcolm, 'Cometh the 60s', University of Nottingham Blogpost, 18 August 2014, http://blogs.nottingham.ac.uk/pharmacy/2014/08/18/blog-3-cometh-the-60s/, accessed 31/07/2018.
21. Ibid.
22. Groves, 295.
23. Quoted in Kynaston, David, *Family Britain, 1951–1957* (London: Bloomsbury, 2010), 198.
24. Ibid and Berkoff, S., *Free Association* (London: Faber & Faber, 1996), 34–41.
25. Jephcott, A. Pearl, *Rising Twenty: Notes on Some Ordinary Girls* (London: Faber & Faber, 1945), 68.
26. There is an extended discussion of representations of 'the good-time girl' as a kind of folk-devil in Dyhouse, C., *Girl Trouble: Panic and Progress in the History of Young Women* (London: Zed Books, 2013), chapter 4.
27. For an insightful discussion of early twentieth-century attitudes to 'true love' see Langhamer, C., *The English in Love: The Intimate Story of an Emotional Revolution* (Oxford: Oxford University Press, 2013), especially chapter 1.
28. Nolan, Michelle, *Love on the Racks: A History of American Romance Comics* (Jefferson, NC: McFarland, 2008); Gibson, Mel, *Remembered Reading: Memory, Comics and Post-War Constructions of British Girlhood* (Leuven: Leuven University Press, 2015).
29. http://comicbookplus.com/?cid=1875, accessed 31/07/2018.
30. Alice Hooper, Beck, 'How to Get Married', *Housewife*, August 1954, 28–9.
31. *Date*, incorporating *Picturegoer*, 30 April 1960, 22; 3 September 1960, 9; Adam Faith, 'The Girl I Shall Marry', 16 July 1960, 12.
32. *Mirabelle and Glamour*, May 1959.
33. 'Is 17 Too Young to Marry?' *Date*, 14 January 1961.
34. '29—and Desperate!' *Mirabelle*, 10 September 1956, 13.
35. Gibson, *Remembered Reading*, 50.
36. Ollerenshaw, K., *Education for Girls* (London: Faber & Faber, 1961), 38.
37. Grebenik, E. and Rowntree, G., 'Factors Associated with the Age at Marriage in Britain', *Proceedings of the Royal Society 1963–4, Series B, Biological Sciences*, vol. 159, 1963–4, 178–202.
38. Kurtzleben, Danielle, 'Think We're All Getting Married Too Late? Think Again', *US News*, 14 February 2014, https://www.usnews.com/news/blogs/data-mine/2014/02/14/think-were-all-getting-married-super-late-think-again, accessed 31/07/2018.

39. For the UK, see 'The Trend to Early Marriage' and tables in Dyhouse, *Students: A Gendered History* (Abingdon: Routledge, 2006), 92–4.

40. Schofield, M., in collaboration with Bynner, John, Lewis, Patricia, and Massie, Peter, *The Sexual Behaviour of Young People* (London: Longmans, 1965), 107, 124.

41. The Family Law Reform Act of 1969 brought the age of majority down from twenty-one to eighteen in England and Wales, effective from the beginning of 1970.

42. Rowntree, Griselda, 'New Facts on Teenage Marriage', *New Society*, 4 October 1962, 12–15.

43. Schofield, 124.

44. Fisher, Kate, *Birth Control, Sex and Marriage in Britain, 1918–1960* (Oxford: Oxford University Press, 2006), 5–6, 66.

45. Ibid.

46. Cohen, Deborah, *Family Secrets; Living with Shame from the Victorians to the Present Day* (London: Viking, 2013), 124.

47. Among the most authoritative accounts for the UK is Thane, Pat and Evans, Tanya, *Sinners? Scroungers? Saints? Unmarried Motherhood in 20th-Century England* (Oxford: Oxford University Press, 2012); Mazie Hough has explored the history of white unmarried mothers in rural America: *Rural Unwed Mothers: An American Experience, 1870–1950* (London: Pickering and Chatto, 2010).

48. Dyhouse, *Students: A Gendered History*; see especially 'The Sexual Revolution and the Woman Student', 103–7. There are several treatments of unwanted pregnancy and abortion among students in the novels of the period. See, for instance, Newman, A., *A Share of the World* (London: Bodley Head, 1964); Drabble, Margaret, *The Millstone* (London: Weidenfeld and Nicolson, 1965); Grossman, Judith, *Her Own Terms* (London: Grafton, 1988).

49. See, for instance, Kandiah, Michael D. and Staerck, Gillian (eds), *The Abortion Act of 1967* (Institute of Contemporary British History Witness Seminar, 2002).

50. Ollerenshaw, Kathleen, *Education for Girls* (London: Faber & Faber, 1961), 107.

51. See Dyhouse, *Students: A Gendered History*, especially 'Sinks, Waste and Drains', 79–81.

52. Newsom, J., *The Education of Girls* (London: Faber, 1948).

53. See for instance Dyhouse, *Girl Trouble*, 126–9.

54. Ministry of Education, *Half Our Future* (Newsom Report) (London: HMSO, 1963); Ministry of Education, *Fifteen to Eighteen*, A Report of the Central Advisory Council for Education (England) (Crowther Report) (London: HMSO, 1959); Ministry of Education, *The Youth Service in England and Wales* (Albemarle Report) (London: HMSO, 1960).
55. Crowther Report, 33–4.
56. Ibid.
57. Spencer, Stephanie, *Gender, Work and Education in Britain in the 1950s* (Basingstoke: Palgrave Macmillan, 2005), especially chapter on 'The Career Novels', 104–28.
58. Barber, Lynn, *An Education* (London: Penguin, 2009).
59. See Report of the Committee on the Age of Majority (Latey Report), Cmnd 3342, London: HMSO, 1967, 'Historical background', especially paragraphs 107–11; Dyhouse, *Girl Trouble*, 169 ff.
60. See, for instance, 'Three "Brides" Visit Gaol', *Daily Mirror*, 8 September 1959; 'Gretna Grief', *Daily Mirror*, 30 November 1961, 8–9.
61. Latey Report, see comments by Sir Jocelyn Simon, paragraph 79.
62. Note 52, *supra*.
63. Latey Report, paragraph 63.F.
64. Latey Report, paragraph 66.
65. Ibid. Paragraph 102.
66. Ibid. Paragraph 103.
67. Ibid.
68. Ibid. Paragraph 172.
69. https://allpoetry.com/Annus-Mirabilis.
70. Larkin's letter to Kingsley Amis quoted in Motion, Andrew, *Philip Larkin: A Writer's Life* (London: Faber, 1993), 143.
71. Lodge, David, *Ginger, You're Barmy* (first published London: MacGibbon & Kee, 1962; this edition London: Vintage, 1982).
72. Ibid. 211, 214.
73. Sillitoe, Alan, *Saturday Night and Sunday Morning* (London: W. H. Allan, 1958), 164.
74. Barstow, S., *A Kind of Loving* (London: Michael Joseph, 1960), 142.
75. Vinen, Richard, *National Service: Conscription in Britain 1945–1963*, (London: Allen Lane, 2014), chapter 8.
76. Ibid. Stanley Price quoted, 181.
77. Lodge, David, 'Afterword' reflecting on first edition of *Ginger, You're Barmy*, new edition (London: Vintage, 1982).

78. Connolly, Cyril, *Enemies of Promise* (London: Routledge, 1938), 116.
79. Sage, Lorna, *Bad Blood* (London: Fourth Estate, 2000), 234.
80. Frank Sinatra's first recording of the song 'Love and Marriage' was in 1955. Music by Jimmy van Heusen, lyrics by Sammy Cahn.
81. In letter from Larkin to James Sutton, 26 January 1950, reproduced in Thwaite, Anthony, *Selected Letters of Philip Larkin, 1940–1985* (London: Faber and Faber, 1992), 157–8.
82. See (inter alia) Hitchens, Christopher, 'Philip Larkin, The Impossible Man', *The Atlantic*, May 2011, https://www.theatlantic.com/magazine/archive/2011/05/philip-larkin-the-impossible-man/308439/, accessed 1 August 2018 and Mars-Jones, A., 'Letters to Monica by Philip Larkin, Edited by Anthony Thwaite', *The Observer*, 17 October 2010, https://www.theguardian.com/books/2010/oct/17/philip-larkin-letters-monica-jones-review, accessed 1 August 2018.
83. Langhamer, Claire, *The English in Love: The Intimate Story of an Emotional Revolution* (Oxford: Oxford University Press, 2013).
84. Slater, Eliot and Woodside, Moya, *Patterns of Marriage: A Study of Marriage Relationships in the Urban Working Classes* (London: Cassell, 1951), 116.
85. Ibid.
86. Giles, Judy, '"You Meet 'em and That's It": Working Class Women's Refusal of Romance Between the Wars in Britain', in Pearce, L. and Stacey, J. (eds), *Romance Revisited* (London: Lawrence and Wishart, 1995), 279–92.

3

MARRIED LOVE

Domesticity and Its Discontents

If many women in the 1950s saw getting married as a goal, the successful outcome of a quest, or a happy ending, others saw things in a much less rosy light. A female respondent to Britain's Mass Observation's research into 'Close Relationships' in 1990 looked back and confessed that marriage had never appealed to her: 'Fairy stories I read as a young child which ended "And then they got married and lived happily ever after" always filled me with a sense of horror and doom', she wrote. 'No more adventures. Settled. Awful.'[1] This particular woman identified herself as lesbian, and heterosexual romance narratives had little appeal for her, but it is interesting that what she found disturbing about long-term commitment, early in life, was the notion of settling down as a form of *closure*.

Why did women want so much to 'settle down' so early in their lives? We have seen that in part this reflected an absence of other choices. The job market in the 1950s was highly gendered, and promotion prospects for women were extremely limited. Girls' educational ambitions, in the main, were curbed by a realistic estimation of their opportunities; more accurately, the lack of them. Most girls left school as soon as the law allowed.[2] Even the tiny minority who did continue their education to university level were more likely to improve their life chances by marrying male graduates with good career prospects than by relying on their own.[3] But this begs the question of whether bagging Prince Charming, or marrying Mr Right, was envisaged as a settling and an ending mainly because the man was a *means* to an end, a way of improving one's life. Many women wanted children: they wanted to rear them in comfort in their own home, and to enjoy a reasonable family lifestyle. Given the social conditions of the 1950s this was well-nigh impossible outside marriage.

On the eve of the Second World War, the Pilgrim Trust, which was investigating unemployment in Britain, expressed unease about young women's ambitions. The girls that they interviewed weren't realistic about their futures, they judged.[4] Most had no real interest in work: they just wanted to marry somebody rich 'so that they could own a motor car or travel or enjoy other forms of luxurious living'.[5] Or they entertained some unrealistic 'phantasy' of escape from their bleak and impoverished communities and the 'Junior Instruction Centres' (government-backed training centres for the young unemployed) in which they currently passed their days.[6] It is hard not to sympathize with these girls today: those Junior Instruction Centres must have been dispiriting places. The Pilgrim Trust researchers found many of the girls attending them 'of a rough type', and often 'defiant and suspicious'.[7] They worried about the kind of marriages these girls might rush into, and whether they would be likely to 'settle' in them. Similar concerns were voiced by researchers Eliot Slater and Moya Woodside just after the war. When these investigators questioned working-class couples about why they had chosen to marry when they did, by far the most common reason they were given was not falling in love, or even planning for a family, but 'wanting a home'.[8]

A home of one's own was an ambitious dream in post-war Britain. Cities were still disfigured by heaps of rubble from bombing raids. There was an acute shortage of housing, and in spite of efforts to ease the problem by building 'prefabs' (factory-built single-story bungalows, originally intended as temporary accommodation) and inexpensive pre-cast concrete 'council housing', many newlywed couples had to start their married lives by living with parents, often in cramped and difficult conditions. An estimated 1,300,000 people visited the *Daily Mail*'s Ideal Home Exhibition at Olympia in 1958, marvelling at the clean modern design, 'show house' bathrooms and kitchens, and easy-wipe 'Formica' worktops on offer.[9] Such wonders were becoming more widely available. For working-class families living in cramped urban terraces, though, they generally remained an impossible dream.

Few women were in any position to set up house independently, although some of the more adventurous young women of the 1950s might leave parental homes for bedsits or shared flats in a city. This was still regarded as a bit daring, requiring courage: *Picture Post* published an article headed 'Lonely in London' in 1956, illustrated by Bert Hardy's photographs of a young Katharine Whitehorn crouching pensively in front of a gas fire.[10] The implied sense of pathos was accentuated by a milk bottle on the table and a tangle of underwear drying over the clothes horse beside her. In reality, Whitehorn, expensively educated at Roedean and Newnham College Cambridge, didn't need to penny-pinch and certainly wasn't as lonely as she looked. She later remembered the

1950s as a decade of excitement and promise.[11] Living in a bedsit had begun to acquire a certain risqué glamour. There was fun in contrivance, and in making-do, creatively, with a gas ring: Whitehorn's book *Cooking in a Bedsitter* first appeared in 1961 and proved lastingly popular.[12] But single women, unless they happened to be exceptionally rich, couldn't aspire to owning property in the 1950s: banks and mortgage companies wouldn't contemplate lending to them. For most women, then, a husband was a necessary first step to acquiring a home of one's own.

This brings us back to the question of marriage as a means to an end. In 1956 Joyce Joseph and Thelma Veness, two women academics at Birkbeck College, London, set out to study adolescents' hopes for their lives after leaving school. They focused on the attitudes of some 1300 boys and girls who were then attending schools in the Home Counties and the West of England.[13] Joseph and Veness were disconcerted to hear the stories many of the girls imagined shaping their future lives. Most planned to marry as soon as possible: they had dreamt a lot about the details of the wedding and particularly the wedding dresses they would wear. They also planned to have children. But what was unexpected was that well over a third of them reported fantasies about the early death of their husbands. They imagined their middle-aged husbands meeting violent deaths, through road accidents and the like. For these girls, the researchers concluded with some horror, 'bereavement seemed almost an ambition'. There was a great deal of 'romanticism about widowhood', a state which seemed to offer some restoration of autonomy to middle-aged wives.[14] Joseph and Veness surmised that, once a husband had fulfilled his biological and economic functions as father and provider, the girls could imagine little use for him: they rarely imagined him as a person in his own right, who might become a cherished companion or partner in old age.[15]

This study and its findings were published at the beginning of the 1960s. Lives were changing fast, and social expectations might adapt unevenly. The prescriptiveness of advice columns and manuals setting out formulae for happy marriages in the 1950s can serve to obscure the profound changes that were taking place in that decade. Social historian Stephen Brooke has pointed to the ways in which lived experience was beginning to challenge convention and to undermine prejudices about male and female roles. Some of the most potent pressures for change were connected with women's working lives.[16] Contemporaries were becoming acutely aware of this: the subject aroused a great deal of public controversy and generated a large body of research and literature in the twenty years following the end of the Second World War.[17] At root was the question of whether women's paid work outside the home was a threat to domestic harmony. Did a working wife undermine her husband's status as breadwinner and provider, hence his masculinity? Did working outside the home mean that she was likely to be a bad or neglectful mother? Would her babies starve through want of motherly love, as some readings of psychologist John Bowlby seemed to suggest, if she left them in the care of others, while she pursued employment and interests outside the home?[18]

In 1958 Richard Titmuss, then Professor of Social Administration at the London School of Economics, included an article entitled *The Position of Women: Some Vital Statistics* in his classic collection of essays on the British welfare state.[19] Titmuss's argument was that demographic changes had completely reshaped women's experiences since the beginning of the century, and that their social position, in respect of work and family life, was now becoming something of a problem. Women were marrying young, and having far fewer children than in Victorian times. They were also living longer. In the past, most of a married woman's life had been given over to child-bearing and child-rearing. But the new pattern meant that a woman would be likely to complete the business of family-building by early middle age and still had some thirty-five to forty years of active life ahead of her.[20] What was she to do with these years, especially if her horizons had been altogether limited to the home and domesticity?

This whole question of what contemporaries came to call 'sex roles' or 'the sexual division of labour' was not new, but it was becoming increasingly vexed. In Britain, a passage in the Pilgrim Trust's report on *Men without Work*, published just before the war, had very clearly expressed what was at stake in visions of women devoting themselves wholly to domesticity:

> Do we consider that by making it possible for a woman to devote herself to her home, society is securing for itself a paramount advantage in the maintenance of a high standard of home life? Or do we believe that this view is out of date; that the modern woman can both work and keep house, and that by doing so, she gains a status of which her predecessors have been unjustly deprived?[21]

It wasn't just women who might suffer from overly rigid role-prescriptions. Around the same time that the Pilgrim Trust was investigating the effects of male unemployment in Britain, Mirra Komarovsky was interviewing families in New York for a study which was later published as *The Unemployed Man and His Family* (1940). It was a pioneering piece of social research which showed how men who thought of themselves exclusively as providers suffered disproportionately from unemployment.[22] Could it be that families where husbands and wives had a more flexible attitude to their roles and responsibilities were better equipped to survive in modern conditions?

Most observers, academic social scientists, and journalists agreed that when wives went out to work the relationships between them and their husbands changed. What was much more contentious was whether these changes were for the better. Two studies of women's work in Britain were optimistic: one by Ferdynand Zweig, published as *Women's Life and Labour* in 1952; the second by Pearl Jephcott, *Married Women Working* (1962).[23] Zweig was impressed by the independence and dignity of the working wives he met. Most of them were conspicuously good managers, their sense of pleasure and self-worth derived not least from knowing that their wage enabled them to buy 'extras': small comforts and luxuries that benefited both their families and their homes. He deemed this sense of having one's own money extremely important: 'Many women staying at home confessed the humiliation they feel if they have to ask their husband for a shilling or two for a ticket to a cinema', he wrote, while a sense of economic independence was for many 'a great joy'.[24]

Jephcott's study of wives who worked in the Peek Freans biscuit factory in Bermondsey reported similar findings. She found that women workers delighted in being able to use their pay-packets to buy things for their homes. They hankered after modern equipment, including cooking stoves, sink units, washing machines, refrigerators, kitchen cabinets, and electric dryers. They wanted carpets to replace old fashioned lino, and 'To the essentials were added fancy cushions, satin bedspreads, ivy-leaved mirrors, smoker stands, wall plaques, "jardinaire boats" [sic], trinket sets, ding-dong bells, and occasionally a framed picture'.[25]

Jephcott recorded a new and passionate concern among working people for 'a lovely home'. Husbands, she noted, often shared this ambition and were willing to help out domestically. Even more importantly, a wife's wages allowed the husband 'more money for his personal pleasures', and was 'a definite sweetener of relationships' in the marriage.[26]

Zweig also found that working wives expected—and often received—more help from husbands in the home, although he was ruefully aware that this wasn't always the case. Many women had insisted that going out to work without support from their husbands was 'hell'. It led to constant 'squabble and bickering', and in some cases to the breakdown of a woman's health.[27] Zweig argued the need for 'a fairer balance' between the rights and duties of the sexes within and outside the home, but he felt confident that things were moving in the right direction: 'It looks as if a new balance will be struck between the sexes, and the traditional sex barriers and fences brought down', he wrote, somewhat optimistically.[28] Jephcott similarly rejected any notion that women workers endangered the stability of family life. The rise in married women's work, she suggested, was now an established trend. Before the war, many employers had avoided employing married women. Now things were very different:

> Married women's employment can be seen as one of the social changes resulting from smaller families, better health, improved services and lighter domestic duties. These Bermondsey wives had developed an attitude in which they viewed going out to work not as neglect of their family, but as a sign of their concern for it.[29]

A sympathetic attitude to women's work and the benefits it might confer on family life was usually qualified by acceptance of the belief that the mothers of very young children were best employed by staying at home to look after them. Recognition of new demographic patterns meant that these stay-at-home years were increasingly being seen as an interval, constituting a brief period in a woman's life. Hence researchers such as the Swedish social scientist Alva Myrdal, and her colleague Viola Klein, popularized the idea of modern women as having 'two roles'—or a 'dual role' model, whereby mothers might increasingly expect to return to the labour force after bringing up their children.[30]

All the researchers mentioned so far shared a belief that confinement to domesticity could have a belittling effect on an adult woman, narrowing her horizons and shrivelling her spirit. Zweig commented that in the home, a woman might find 'her spirit crushed and her self-confidence broken'. The husband was often to blame, he thought:

> A woman regards herself primarily as a helpmate to man, but that conception may in practice be carried too far, and her status of a helpmate deteriorates to that of a servant or a little slave. And how many examples have I seen of that? Having the worst jobs in industry, woman also has the worst jobs at home, the job of fighting constantly with dirt, filth and dust, the job of carrying excessive loads in her shopping, of pinching and scraping. The most menial jobs are again allotted to her.[31]

'Is it to be wondered', he asked, 'that her mind becomes a rubbish heap full of bits and pieces here and there, unable to concentrate and think consecutively?'[32]

The psychological costs of staying at home were mulled over more fully in Britain by Hannah Gavron, who studied young wives and housebound mothers of small children in the 1960s.[33] She found worrying levels of social and personal isolation. Many of her respondents confessed that they regretted marrying so young and missing out on opportunities for education and travel. Working-class women in Gavron's sample were particularly prone to regret that 'they had not really got the most out of their youth before settling down'.[34]

An earlier study which had offered insights into the predicaments of middle-class wives was Judith Hubback's *Wives Who Went to College*, published in book form in 1957.[35] Starting from the assumption that 'an entirely domestic existence is too limited for a highly educated woman', Hubback framed her enquiry in terms of whether society was making the best use of these women's talents. Her answer was clearly that it wasn't. Hubback argued that there was a pent-up demand for more attractive, part-time professional work. What about the women themselves? Were their brains going to rot? More than one respondent admitted to fears of 'mental decay'. Had they lost the ability to make intelligent conversation? Hubback herself opined that 'the mother who can only talk about her little darlings' brilliant and precocious exploits' was 'a well-known type of bore'.[36] Her study uncovered a seething mass of frustration, polite discontent, and sheer exhaustion. Hubback described this last problem as 'overtiredness', and devoted a whole chapter to it. Some of her (male) colleagues were sceptical about this, querying the concept of 'overtiredness' as 'too subjective, too human, too *feminine* in fact' (my italics).[37] She insisted that this was male bias, and that the women she had talked to understood the subject all too well. Lack of leisure, lack of domestic help, the strain of looking after young children, health problems, frustration, and too little sleep were all factors which accounted for it.[38]

Hubback, like Zweig, emphasized the importance of a husband's support, if a wife was to find personal fulfilment in work outside the home. However, the kind of support she had in mind here seems to have been more psychological and sympathetic than practical. She ends her book with what sounds like a slightly rhetorical bit of wish-fulfilment. Women needed to 'combine some at least of the attitudes which were once believed to be found only in men', she thought, with 'feminine values'. They needed to avoid 'aggressive insistence' on their status, but also to step around 'the mud-flats of self-deprecation'.[39] They shouldn't be too pushy, in other words, but nor should they allow themselves to become doormats. Hubback stopped well short of any challenge to male authority. It was still a man's world, she conceded, and new arrangements in the family would be very difficult to achieve without co-operation from men. But a wife might be lucky in her husband, in which case 'With his love, his trust and his help she will do great things'.[40]

That Hubback didn't envisage much masculine support with housework was at least in part a reflection of social class. The questionnaire which she devised for her survey is a give-away here: question number seven asked '(a) Have you a resident domestic? (b) Is she a foreigner, here for one year or less? (c) If you have non-resident domestic help, for how many hours per week?' Many middle-class wives still benefited from domestic help, though this tended to be in the form of a cleaner or 'charlady', often just called 'the help': a woman who came to the house daily, rather than the live-in maid of the past. 'Au pairs', young women from abroad wanting to learn English who were willing to do light domestic work in exchange for board and lodging, were also becoming a common feature in English middle-class households of the 1950s and 1960s. Almost three quarters of the women in Hubback's survey had domestic help of some kind.[41]

Novels of the period focusing on middle-class family life suggest that at least some degree of domestic support was taken for granted. The middle-class households depicted by British women writers such as Elizabeth Jenkins and Penelope Mortimer are often dysfunctional in terms of the relationships between husband and wife. But these households are well-appointed, and run smoothly—at least on the surface—because of some wage-earning, reliable 'treasure' of a middle-aged woman who 'does' for them. These women hover in the background, but are still capable of complicating the relationship between husband and wife, subtly undermining the confidence of one or the other of the partners when there's conflict in the air. Elizabeth Jenkins's *The Tortoise and the Hare* (1954), for instance, depicts the highly privileged existence of barrister Evelyn Gresham and his wife Imogen in their elegant riverside home in Berkshire. Meals are thoughtfully contrived, picnics packed, and beds made up at a moment's notice by a daily housekeeper, 'the estimable Malpas'.[42] Miss Malpas gets on with the young son of the household rather better than his mother does. Evelyn, bored by his wife's dependency, passes on his contempt for her to their son, who thus learns to despise his mother. A similar pattern occurs in Penelope Mortimer's *Daddy's Gone A-Hunting* (1958).[43] Here the husband appoints a housekeeper, Miss de Beer, who is entrusted, in addition to her domestic duties, with keeping an eye on his unhappy, neurotic wife. Ruth, the wife, resents this surveillance and finds Miss de Beer ghastly. But when Ruth's sons come home from public school for the holidays she finds that the housekeeper's ability to conjure up large quantities of rock cakes and apple pie goes down very well with the boys. Middle-class families in houses with large gardens sometimes employed gardeners as well as female domestic help. In *Daddy's Gone A-Hunting*, Ruth trips over a pair of gumboots in the kitchen passageway, observing with some acidity that it was her husband Rex's habit to put his gumboots on when talking to the gardener.[44]

These novels of middle-class life in the 1950s begin to probe the dissatisfactions of wives whose lives revolve round house and home, however well-appointed and materially secure. Husbands are absent during the day; wives left stranded in suburban or semi-rural commuter belts. The children are quite often away at public school or university. In *The Tortoise and the Hare*, Imogen is undermined by an increasing awareness of her husband's lack of respect for her intelligence and capacities. As their marriage stales, she frets at her own ineffectuality. In *Daddy's Gone A-Hunting*, Ruth is ill with despair at the pointlessness of her life; Rex is bored and uncomprehending, ripe for affairs with younger and more admiring female acquaintances. It is well known that Penelope Mortimer drew heavily on personal experience in her writing, and that the depiction of Rex owed more than a passing resemblance to her then husband, prominent British barrister John Mortimer. In her best-known novel, *The Pumpkin Eater* (1961), which was turned into a very successful film in 1964, the echoes of the Mortimers' disintegrating marriage are perhaps even stronger.[45] In both titles we hear reference to nursery rhymes, although the comfort that might be suggested by softly hypnotic bed-time lullabies and gentle rocking (Bye, Baby Bunting) is menaced by narrative content. In *Daddy's Gone A-Hunting*, Rex is far from a benign provider of rabbit skins to wrap babies in. He is self-centred, insensitive, duplicitous, and unfaithful. Frustrated by what he sees as his wife's listlessness and despair, he gives her money to go away and convalesce. He wants her out of the way so as not to be bothered, and also so that he can continue to explore his affair with a younger woman. Instead, his wife uses the money surreptitiously to pay for their daughter to have an abortion. Neither of the women, mother or daughter, trust Rex enough emotionally to tell him the truth. Ruth's sense of competence is restored only when she finds herself driven to protect her daughter in a world where male power stacks the odds against women's wellbeing.

The Pumpkin Eater similarly probes the sore spots in nursery rhyme and fairy tale. The rhyme itself is unsettling ('Peter, Peter, pumpkin eater/had a wife but couldn't keep her/He put her in a pumpkin shell/and there he kept her very well'). The reference to confinement in a home is obvious enough, but it is more than this: in the novel, Mrs Armitage has tried more than one marriage, has a whole brood of children, and is on the brink of total despair and breakdown. There is no fairy-tale marriage; maybe no happiness whatsoever in marriage. Mr Armitage is distant and self-centred. If she is imprisoned by her husband, though, Mrs Armitage is also a prisoner of her own fertility. The pumpkin—once the shell of Cinderella's golden, fairy-tale coach—has morphed into something more threatening. Fleshy, soft inside, and packed with seeds, it comes to stand for female fertility, the body as pregnable, and femininity as something close to biological destiny—therefore inescapable.

These and similar novels have been seen as 'proto-feminist' rather than overtly feminist, both because their writers didn't identify themselves as feminists and also because they were published before the rise of the women's liberation movement, or 'second-wave' feminism, in the 1960s and 1970s.[46] Even so, they are feminist in the sense that they explore and question sex roles, domesticity, and the social arrangements between men and women. Mortimer explained to a television audience in 1963 that she had put practically everything she could say 'about men and women, and their relationship to one another' into *The Pumpkin Eater*.[47] Today we read the work as encapsulating something of the lifestyles and relationships of a particular social class, at a particular historical moment. At the end of this novel the narrator confesses to the reader that 'Some of these things happened, and some were dreams. They are all true as I understood truth. They are all real, as I understood reality.' For the historian, novels are less a reflection of literal or autobiographical 'truth' than a distillation of attitudes or emotional insights which can be read alongside the social scientific investigations of the time. The female characters in Penelope Mortimer's novels are well off, but their sense of helplessness, their listless enervation, and their lassitude about their domestic affairs resonates with the 'overtiredness' of so many of Judith Hubback's respondents.

The stereotypical image of the 1950s housewife is a happy-looking woman, apron-clad, content in her kitchen. The images easily slip into parody or pastiche: the woman begins to look demented as she beams ecstatically over kitchen devices, spongy cupcakes, and the whiter-than-white washing piled high in her laundry basket. Surely nobody in sane mind could be expected to go beatific over corned beef loaf or detergent? A Google image search for '1950s housewives' yields many images of uncertain date and provenance—have they been taken from adverts of the period or are they products of modern nostalgia, or even satire? To what extent were all these stay-at-home mums, obsessed with the potential of Omo (washing powder) or Oxo (gravy cubes) or Bird's custard, figments of the adman's—and hence commercial—imagination? They don't look like Zweig or Jephcott's working mothers, nor Hubback's graduate wives, and certainly not like the ladies of the house portrayed in the novels written by Mortimer, Jenkins, or Elizabeth Taylor. Perhaps they're not really British at all, but more an excrescence of the American Dream?

But we know that many wives—around 74 per cent of them in Britain in 1951, falling to around 65 per cent in 1961—did stay at home in the 1950s, and that they bought magazines such as *Woman* and *Woman's Own*, the pages of which were full of advertisements depicting happy housewives.[48] They followed the recipes for corned beef loaves and stirred Bisto gravy and assembled trifles from Bird's custard, stale sponge-cake, and tinned peaches. They imbibed advice from columnists and 'agony aunts' like 'Evelyn Home' (a pseudonym for Peggy Makins), who advised them to pamper their husbands with home-cooked meals, ready on the table when the menfolk came back from work, and a gentle for-givingness whenever these exhausted men became insufferable.[49] Their children were taught to read with books that described a world where Daddy went to work and Mummy stayed at home. The stay-at-home British housewife of the 1950s wasn't just an illusion. She existed, in large numbers. Some years ago, architectural historian Alison Ravetz observed that there is a sense in which the 1950s 'invented' the housewife.[50] Historically, the decade was a watershed because, as Ravetz pointed out,

> By then, two things of fundamental significance had occurred: the middle-class wife had finally and irrevocably lost her servants, and the working class wife had acquired, or was in the process of acquiring, a house to look after. Thus the two stereotypes that had dominated the nineteenth-century domestic scene, the mistress of servants and the poor woman, had finally bowed out, leaving the stage to a new housewife, who had no doubt been present for a considerable time, but invisible.[51]

As the image of the happy housewife proliferated in the pages of magazines and in on-screen advertising in the 1950s and 1960s, social investigators and critics were becoming more audible in their critique and more insistent in their warnings about the personal, psychological, and social costs of boxing up women in the home. A darker, more sinister set of images of housewives began to appear in the medical and pharmaceutical journals of the time. Here we see housewives bowed over kitchen sinks full of unwashed dishes, retreating into bedrooms, their features contorted in despair. They rub their temples, shield their eyes from the light, weep impotently, and look like all they want is for the world to stop so that they can get off it and die. Adverts for mood-changing drugs—tranquillizers, soporifics, nerve tonics, uppers and downers—multiplied in these journals, which were targeted at doctors who had to deal with what was represented in these adverts as an increasingly recognizable type of patient: the housewife who couldn't cope.[52]

Amid the many journalists and social critics picking up on this 'new' phenomenon, American feminist Betty Friedan stands out as having written a book which, in the words of Alvin Toffler, 'pulled the trigger on history'.[53] This was of course *The Feminine Mystique*, first published in 1963. The book fired a salvo straight into the heart of the American Dream. It is no coincidence that the text of *The Feminine Mystique* keeps returning to women's dreams—and how they have faded, been betrayed, warped, or turned sour. The suburban housewife was 'the dream image of the young American women and the envy, it was said, of women all over the world',[54] Friedan wrote; she was widely assumed to have everything. So what had gone wrong? Why did so many housewives express misery and frustration, feel tired all the time, or break out in blisters? A number of women had reported unexplained skin diseases, Friedan claimed, 'great bleeding blisters that break out on their hands and arms'.[55] A family doctor in Pennsylvania had explained that he called this 'the housewife's blight', and told her that he had often come across it in women with a number of small children 'who bury themselves in their dishpans', adding but 'it isn't caused by detergent and it isn't cured by cortisone'.[56]

Swallowing tranquillizers 'like cough drops' had become common among suburban wives, Betty Friedan observed. One woman confessed that 'You wake in the morning and you feel as if there's no point in going on another day like this. So you take a tranquillizer because it makes you not care so much that it's pointless.'[57] Friedan scrutinized the magazine images of happy housewives for clues to what she called 'the problem that has no name'. An image might hint at a problem, she suggested, 'as a dream gives a clue to a wish unnamed by the dreamer'.[58] These housewives, she surmised, were completely cut away from 'the world of thought and ideas, the life of the mind and spirit'. What had happened to their dreams of careers, of creation of the future? At root this was a problem of identity: the stifling of passion and purpose.

Friedan's analysis of 'the problem that has no name', which she named 'the feminine mystique', struck a chord with women on both sides of the Atlantic—though it had decidedly more relevance to the lives of white, middle-class wives than to women of colour or to women of the working class.[59] Friedan was besieged with letters from readers who found her book a revelation and a solace, women who confessed that they had not known what was

11. Advert for Serax, 1967. Might drugs lessen the misery of endless housework?

wrong with them and feared they were going mad until they learned that so many others felt the same way. Friedan's contention that 1950s prescriptions for happy marriages often infantilized and diminished women as human beings still convinces. Though the book was not always as radical as she herself would have had it, her insights were conveyed with verve and style. Her analysis of the ways in which commerce and advertising both shaped and exploited the representation of happy housewives was sharp.[60] More questionable were her views on sexuality: not only prejudice against homosexuality, but also her belief that suburban domesticity had turned women into aggressive sex monsters who were draining and emasculating their husbands with insatiable demands. Friedan read the cultural trend towards more explicit sexuality in literature and on the cinema screen as evidence of bored women hungry for sexual fantasy because they had so little else in their lives.[61]

This image of suburban wives as voracious sex addicts is hard to square with information from other sources.[62] Many of the historians who have investigated sexuality in Britain in the 1950s have concluded that women's experiences of sex were often clouded by ignorance and inhibition and fundamentally unfulfilling: sex was commonly seen as a duty rather than as a pleasure, and a husband's needs were almost always accorded priority over the wife's.[63] Agony aunts in women's magazines of the period advised women to pamper their husbands, to be forgiving, self-sacrificing, and submissive. Women who sought their own pleasure were likely to be viewed as selfish, unfeminine, and immature. This notion of feminine self-seeking as 'immature' was noticeable in the ideas of marriage guidance therapists in post-war Britain.[64] Psychology historian Teri Chettiar has shown how there was a shift away from the kind of advice on marital harmony offered to couples earlier in the century—which sought primarily to dispel ignorance about sexual matters—and a new emphasis on 'emotional maturity'. Notions of emotional maturity, she points out, were closely tied up with contemporary ideas about gender roles. Men were judged 'mature' if they were masterful and competent providers; women if they successfully adapted to subordinate status, motherhood, and domesticity.[65]

Helena Wright, whose pioneering work in birth control and sex therapy spanned both the inter- and post-war years in Britain, was the author of several widely read advice books on sexual issues, including *The Sex Factor in Marriage* (1930) and *More About the Sex Factor in Marriage* (1947).[66] She suggested that at least half of all married women in Britain missed out on sexual pleasure, not even recognizing 'that physical satisfaction can, and should, be as real and vivid for them as it is for their husbands'.[67] Before the Second World War, women's attitudes to sex were greatly affected by the fear—often amounting to a visceral terror—of unwanted pregnancy. *The Sex Factor in Marriage* appeared only a year after Marie Stopes had published *Mother England*, a devastating series of letters from married individuals completely desperate over their inability to secure birth control.[68] Several of the women who wrote to Stopes were in very poor health, and admitted that they had even contemplated suicide as an alternative to enduring the prospect of giving birth again. 'I am frighten [sic] to Death', wrote one poor woman, beside herself at the thought of another child. She was sick and frail and already had three small children in tow: 'My life is only a living Hell.'[69] Fear and dread were hardly conducive to happy sex lives, and fear and dread were widespread. Warned by her doctor to avoid pregnancy, but without any advice on birth control, 'Mrs J. H.' pleaded: 'I cannot always refuse my husband as it only means living a cat and dog life for both of us. Would you please try and help me?'[70] Stopes received many, many letters like this.

Researchers Slater and Woodside found that many of the working-class wives that they studied just after the war saw sex as a duty, and didn't expect to find it pleasurable.[71] Husbands tended to be valued in an inverse attitude to sexuality: 'He's very good, he doesn't bother me much', and the women's attitude was often one of passive endurance, shading into 'barely veiled sex antagonism', with the word 'they' being commonly used as a generic term for demanding males.[72] Birth control and contraceptive advice was easier to obtain by the 1950s, but services were patchy, and attitudes took time to change.[73] Eustace Chesser, whose investigation

The Sexual, Marital and Family Relationships of the English Woman was published in 1956, found many of the women who completed questionnaires for his study vague about their experience of sexual pleasure, and imprecise about describing the pleasure itself.[74] The language available presented difficulties. When anthropologist Geoffrey Gorer conducted the first of his two major enquiries into sexual attitudes as part of the study *Exploring English Character*, in 1950, he alleged that he was not allowed to ask concrete questions about the female orgasm lest he cause offence or embarrassment—particularly to the young women who would have to code his questionnaires.[75] In his follow-up study, twenty years later, it was thought prudent to use the term 'physical climax' rather than 'orgasm'. One of the interesting findings of this later study, published in 1971 as *Sex and Marriage in England Today*, was that more men (over three quarters of the sample) than women (just over half) thought that women experienced a physical climax and sense of release in sex that was comparable to that commonly experienced by a man.[76]

Modern historians have questioned many of the assumptions made in earlier studies of sexual behaviour and experience. Kate Fisher has reminded us that dutiful sex didn't necessarily imply an absence of pleasure, especially at a time when it might be thought unfeminine to be too explicit or demanding.[77] Fisher and Simon Szreter's larger study of sex 'before the sexual revolution' suggests that modern ideas about sexual pleasure may blind us to the caring, private, often affectionate accommodations of married love in the past.[78] Even so, these surveys from the 1950s contain much evidence of despair. There are many sad stories, for instance, in Mass Observation's 'Little Kinsey' study of sexual attitudes and behaviour in 1949. 'Sex isn't very nice', confided one female voice in the survey, adding: 'Yes, it can be harmful, it can ruin a woman's inside as easy as pie, ruin any girl's innards, intercourse can.'[79] 'My husband accused me of being "cold", but little knew the passionate longing I experienced', confessed another woman. 'If only he had made love to me, instead of using me like a chamber pot.'[80]

Working-class women were by no means all passive or powerless about sex. In Nell Dunn's conversations with working-class women in South London in the early 1960s, for instance, and in her fiction, young women come across as independent and resourceful: not remotely deferential towards men.[81] But their accounts of sexuality, of love lives, and pregnancies are still tinged by a certain fatalism. They may have few illusions about men as rescuers or princes, but their power—and their options—are limited. In Shelagh Delaney's *A Taste of Honey*, first staged in 1958 and adapted into a highly successful film in 1961, the young white working-class protagonist Jo becomes pregnant after a brief affair with a black sailor. She has next to no resources.[82] Help comes from a young homosexual man, Geoff, whose care and attention serve to into throw into sharp relief what might be seen as the cruelties and conventions of 'respectable' society, or indeed patriarchy. In Margaret Forster's *Georgy Girl* (1965) the heroine marries a rich older man who she feels little or no attraction for because he will provide for her and the baby that she has decided to bring up as her own.[83] The popularity of novels and films drawing attention to women's vulnerabilities as unsupported young mothers in the late 1950s and early 1960s might be read as showing an increasing public understanding and even a critique of convention. Equally, these texts could still provoke outrage. Edna O'Brien's early writing about women's sexual desire in *The Country Girls* (1960) was ritually burned in Catholic Ireland.[84]

The spatial arrangements of middle-class homes might allow these wives to more effectively distance themselves from a husband's unwanted sexual demands than their working-class equivalents could. A wife described in contemporary discourse as 'frigid' might suggest that the housekeeper make up a single bed in her husband's dressing room—that is, if he hadn't sulkily taken himself off to sleep there anyway. The novels of the period are full of such references, with sleeping arrangements an oblique way of signifying sexual happiness and marital harmony. In Elizabeth Jenkins' *The Tortoise and the Hare*, Imogen's husband retreats to his single bed in the dressing room once he embarks on an adulterous affair. His wife's response is an uneasy combination of regret and relief. In Penelope Mortimer's fiction, unsatisfactory husbands maintain small apartments in town during the week, allowing dalliances or even long-term relationships with other women. Billy Wilder's brilliant black comedy film *The Apartment* (1960) satirized similar patterns of middle-class infidelity among businessmen in North America.[85] Lower down the social scale in Britain, women living in small houses might delay going to bed until husbands came back from the pub, hoping that the evening's beer ration would soon send him off to sleep.

Returning to the social survey, in *Wives Who Went to College*, Judith Hubback reported that many of her middle-class female respondents who described themselves as suffering from 'overtiredness' found themselves too exhausted for sex.[86] Incessant day-time demands from children and wearisome domestic routines drained them of vitality and made them feel 'stale and uninspired': by the evening they were worn out. She also suggested that once women had become mothers, their attitude to sex changed.[87] It was not possible for a woman to be as emotionally detached in sexual activity as a man, Hubback asserted confidently, and, once the couple decided they wanted no further children and resorted to contraception, sex could lose its creative and emotional edge. She advised a woman faced with this problem to 'direct her remaining creativeness into other channels'. A wise woman might choose 'from minor activities such as cake- or jam-making, through knitting and house-decorating to the more permanent types of craft and art'.[88]

Post-war dreams of happy families living in spacious suburban settings held strong in Britain and North America in the 1950s, and well beyond. Many were excluded from achieving anything like this vision of affluence, of course. But by the 1960s and 1970s the vision itself had its sceptics and detractors. Did such arrangements isolate women? Did they demand compliance from men, turning them into mechanistic commuters, wage earners, and providers? Questions like this were hinted at, or threaded through, much of the literature of the period. Sloan Wilson's *The Man in the Grey Flannel Suit*, a best-seller in 1955, showed men as well as women uneasy with materialistic domesticity.[89] In John Updike's *Couples* (1968), both men and women are bored by their lives in comfortable suburbia and turn to promiscuity to try to improve matters.[90] Mira, in Marilyn French's *The Women's Room* (1977), is driven nuts by her life of floor-scrubbing, dinner parties, and small-town sexual politics in the town of Beau Reve—'Sweet Dream'.[91] Fleeing to a rented apartment and returning to higher education saves her sanity. One of the most powerful critiques of the kind of gender arrangements underpinning the suburban lifestyle came from Ira Levin. His chilling horror story *The Stepford Wives* (1972) depicted suburban wives 'cured' of any restlessness or discontent by being brainwashed into groomed and glossy fembots.[92] *The Stepford*

Wives was filmed twice, and the term entered the culture: a ghoulish warning of what extreme domesticity might do to women.[93] It was all too easy for women's dreams to turn into nightmares.

Notes

1. Mass Observation Archive (MOA), Close Relationships Directive, 1990, G2377.
2. Ollerenshaw, K., *Education for Girls* (London: Faber and Faber, 1961), 38, 107.
3. See Dyhouse, Carol, 'Graduates, Mothers and Graduate Mothers: Family Investment in Higher Education in Twentieth-Century England', *Gender and Education*, vol. 14, no. 4, 2002, 325–36 and especially 332.
4. Trust, Pilgrim, *Men without Work* (Cambridge: Cambridge University Press, 1938), 254.
5. Ibid.
6. Ibid. The 'phantasies' of escape instanced were 'professions outside their reach'. For instance, 'One would have liked to be a kindergarten teacher or dancer, another a trained children's nurse, another a stewardess as a means of seeing the world'.
7. *Men without Work*, 259.
8. Slater, E. and Woodside, M., *Patterns of Marriage: A Study of Marriage Relationships in the Urban Working Class* (London: Cassell, 1951), 117.
9. See Daily Mail Ideal Home Exhibition Archive, V&A Archive of Art and Design, https://archiveshub.jisc.ac.uk/data/gb73-aad/1990/.
10. Anant, V., 'Big City Loneliness', *Picture Post*, 3 March 1956, 12–13.
11. Whitehorn, K., *Selective Memory: An Autobiography* (London: Virago, 2007).
12. Whitehorn, K., *Cooking In a Bedsitter* (Harmondsworth: Penguin, 1961).
13. Joseph, Joyce, 'A Research Note on Attitudes to Work and Marriage of Six Hundred Adolescent Girls', *The British Journal of Sociology*, vol. 12, no. 2, June 1961, 176–83.
14. Ibid. 182–3.
15. Ibid. 182.
16. Brooke, Stephen, 'Gender and Working Class Identity in Britain During the 1950s', *Journal of Social History*, vol. 34, no. 4, Summer 2001, 773–95.

17. Two articles by Helen McCarthy bring together and usefully illuminate some of the controversy: McCarthy, H., 'Women, Marriage and Paid Work in Post-War Britain', *Women's History Review*, vol. 26, no. 1, February 2017, 46–61, and 'Social Science and Married Women's Employment in Post-War Britain', *Past and Present*, vol. 233, no. 1, November 2016, 269–305.
18. Bowlby, J., *Child Care and the Growth of Love* (London: Penguin, 1953).
19. Titmuss, R., 'The Position of Women: Some Vital Statistics', in *Essays on 'The Welfare State'* (London: Allen and Unwin, 1958), 54–64.
20. Ibid. 91, 96.
21. Pilgrim Trust, *Men without Work*, 233.
22. Komarovsky, Mirra, *The Unemployed Man and His Family* (New York: Dryden Press, 1940)
23. Zweig, Ferdynand, *Women's Life and Labour* (London: Gollancz, 1952); Jephcott, A. P., *Married Women Working* (London: George Allen and Unwin, 1962).
24. Zweig, *Women's Life and Labour*, 21, 155.
25. Jephcott, *Married Women Working*, 153.
26. Ibid. 122.
27. Zweig, *Women's Life and Labour*, 154.
28. Zweig, *Women's Life and Labour*, 153.
29. Jephcott, *Married Women Working*, 135.
30. Myrdal, A. and Klein, V., *Women's Two Roles: Home and Work* (London: Routledge and Kegan Paul, 1956). See the interesting review of this book by Olive Banks in *British Journal of Sociology*, vol. 8, no. 1, March 1957, 75–80.
31. Zweig, *Women's Life and Labour*, 154.
32. Ibid.
33. Gavron, Hannah, *The Captive Wife: Conflicts of Housebound Mothers* (London: Routledge and Kegan Paul, 1966).
34. Ibid. 56 and *passim*.
35. Hubback, Judith, *Wives Who Went to College* (London: Heinemann, 1957).
36. Ibid. 40.
37. Ibid. 70.
38. See Hubback's chapter 5, 'The Answers: III "Overtiredness"'.
39. Hubback, *Wives Who Went to College*, 159.
40. Ibid.
41. Ibid. 36–7 and Appendix.
42. Jenkins, Elizabeth, *The Tortoise and The Hare* (London: Gollancz, 1954).

43. Mortimer, Penelope, *Daddy's Gone A-Hunting* (London: Michael Joseph, 1958).

44. Ibid. 118.

45. Mortimer, Penelope, *The Pumpkin Eater* (Harmondsworth: Penguin, 1964); film version directed by Jack Clayton, with screenplay by Harold Pinter, 1964.

46. See, for instance, the New York Review of Books Reading Group Guide to Mortimer's *The Pumpkin Eater*, http://www.nybooks.com/media/doc/2011/02/08/pumpkin-eater-rgg.pdf, accessed 3/08/2018.

47. Merkin, Daphne, 'Revisiting Penelope Mortimer's *The Pumpkin Eater* and its Devastating Portrait of a Marriage', *Slate* Magazine, April 2011, http://www.slate.com/articles/double_x/doublex/2011/04/home_dis-comforts.html, accessed 3/08/2018.

48. Figures from census data taken from Lewis, Jane, *Women in Britain since 1945* (Oxford: Blackwell, 1992), 65.These figures probably underestimate women's labour market participation but are cited as a rough guide.

49. Makins, Peggy, *The Evelyn Home Story* (London: HarperCollins, 1975).

50. Ravetz, Alison, 'The Home of Woman: A View from the Interior', *Built Environment*, vol. 10, no. 1, 1984, 8–17.

51. Ibid. 10.

52. See advert for 'Equanil', for instance, 'For Ladies in Distress', in *British Medical Journal*, vol. 1, no. 5190, 25 June 1960; or for 'Strimplete', 'for overwrought, miserable patients who cannot cope calmly', *BMJ*, vol. 2, no. 5216, 24 December 1960. On the whole subject of medicating depressed housewives in North America see Metzl, Jonathan, '"Mother's Little Helper": The Crisis of Psychoanalysis and the Miltown Resolution', *Gender and History*, vol. 15, no. 2, August 2003, 240–67.

53. Quoted in McCrum, Robert, 'The 100 Best Non-Fiction Books of All Time', Number 18, *The Feminine Mystique* by Betty Friedan, in *The Guardian*, 30 May 2016, https://www.theguardian.com/books/2016/may/30/feminine-mystique-100-best-nonfiction-books-robert-mccrum, accessed 3/08/2018.

54. Friedan, Betty, *The Feminine Mystique* (Harmondsworth: Penguin, 1965), 18.

55. Ibid. 18.

56. Ibid.

57. Ibid. 28.

58. Ibid. 30.

59. Coontz, Stephanie, *A Strange Stirring: The Feminine Mystique and American Women at the Dawn of the 1960s* (New York: Basic Books, 2011) provides an insightful and balanced assessment.

60. Ibid.

61. Friedan, *The Feminine Mystique*, chapter 11.

62. On this see Germaine Greer's obituary of Betty Friedan in *The Guardian*, 'The Betty I Knew', 7 February 2006, https://www.theguardian.com/world/2006/feb/07/gender.bookscomment, accessed 3/08/2018.

63. This is a huge and complex subject. There is abundant material in letters written to Marie Stopes in the early twentieth century to suggest ignorance, fear of pregnancy and a lack of communication between men and women over sexual experience. See, for instance, Hall, Ruth (ed.), *Dear Dr Stopes: Sex in the 1920s* (Harmondsworth: Penguin, 1981). Szreter, Simon and Fisher's Careful, Kate, *Sex before the Sexual Revolution: Intimate Life in England, 1918–1963* (Cambridge: Cambridge University Press, 2010) challenges easy generalizations. See also Fisher, Kate, '"Lay back, enjoy it and shout happy England': Sexual Pleasure and Marital Duty in Britain, 1918–60' in Fisher, Kate and Toulalan, Sarah (eds), *Bodies, Sex and Desire from the Renaissance to the Present* (Basingstoke: Palgrave Macmillan, 2011). Insightful on class and assumptions about the 'modernization' of sexual experience is Brooke, Stephen, 'Bodies, Sexuality and the " Modernization" of the British Working Classes, 1920s to 1960s', *International Labour and Working Class History*, Working Class Subjectivities and Sexualities, no. 69, Spring 2006, 104–22. Stanley's, Liz, *Sex Surveyed, 1949–1994: From Mass Observation's 'Little Kinsey' to the National Survey and the Hite Reports* (London: Taylor and Francis, 1995) looks at research on sexuality.

64. Chettiar, Teri, '"More than a Contract": The Emergence of a State Supported Marriage Welfare Service and the Politics of Emotional Life in Post 1945 Britain', *Journal of British Studies*, vol. 55, no. 3, July 2016, 566–91.

65. Ibid.

66. Wright, Helena, *The Sex Factor in Marriage: A Book for Those Who Are, or Are about to Be Married* (London: Williams and Norgate, 1937) and *More about the Sex Factor in Marriage* (London: Williams and Norgate, 1954). Both books went through several editions. See also Wright, Helena, *Sex and Society* (London: George Allen and Unwin, 1968).

67. Wright, Helena, *More about the Sex Factor*, 11. But see also Fisher, '"Lay back, enjoy it and shout happy England"'.

68. Stopes, M., *Mother England: A Contemporary History*, 'Self Written by those Who Have Had No Historian' (London: John Bale, Sons and Danielsson, 1929).
69. Ibid. 123.
70. Ibid. 83.
71. Slater, E. and Woodside, M., *Patterns of Marriage*, 168–75.
72. Ibid. 167–8.
73. In England the Ministry of Health first allowed local health authorities to provide birth control advice to married women for whom a future pregnancy would be detrimental to health in 1930. The Family Planning Association (an amalgam of earlier voluntary associations and clinics) dates from 1939. Family planning services were not covered by the National Health Services Act. Family Planning Association clinics first started to give advice to women who were about to get married in 1952. This information from FPA website, https://www.fpa.org.uk/factsheets/history-family-planning-services, accessed 5/08/2018.
74. Chesser, Eustace, *The Sexual, Marital and Family Relationships of the English Woman* (London: Hutchinson's Medical Publications, 1956), 422. For a full discussion of Chesser's research see Stanley, *Sex Surveyed*, 40–4.
75. Gorer, G., *Sex and Marriage in England Today: A Study of the Views and Experience of the under 45s* (London: Nelson, 1971), 124; *Exploring English Character* (London: Cresset Press, 1955).
76. Gorer, *Sex and Marriage*, 125.
77. Fisher, Kate, *Birth Control, Sex and Marriage in Britain 1918–1960* (Oxford: Oxford University Press, 2006), 210 and *passim*.
78. Fisher and Szreter, *Sex before the Sexual Revolution, passim*.
79. Quoted in Stanley, *Sex Surveyed*, 97.
80. Ibid.
81. Dunn, Nell, *Talking to Women* (London: Silver Press, 2018). See also Dunn, Nell, *Up the Junction* (London: MacGibbon and Kee, 1963).
82. Delaney, S., *A Taste of Honey* (London: Eyre Methuen, 1959).
83. Forster, M., *Georgy Girl* (London: Secker and Warburg, 1965).
84. Cooke, Rachel, Interview with Edna O'Brien, *The Observer*, 6 February 2011, https://www.theguardian.com/books/2011/feb/06/edna-obrien-ireland-interview?INTCMP=SRCH, accessed 7/11/2018. O'Brien, Edna, *The Country Girls* (London: Hutchinson, 1960).
85. *The Apartment*, 1960, directed by Billy Wilder and starring Jack Lemmon and Shirley MacLaine.
86. Hubback, *Wives Who Went to College*, Chapter 5, and 148.
87. Ibid. 149–50.

88. Ibid. 150.
89. Wilson, Sloan, *The Man in the Gray Flannel Suit* (London: Cassell, 1956). Sloan Wilson's novel was filmed in 1956, with the same title as the book, directed by Nunnelly Johnson, starring Gregory Peck.
90. Updike, John, *Couples* (New York: Alfred A. Knopf, 1968).
91. French, Marilyn, *The Women's Room* (New York: Simon and Schuster, 1977).
92. Levin, Ira, *The Stepford Wives* (New York: Random House, 1972).
93. *The Stepford Wives* was first filmed in 1975, directed by Bryan Forbes, and was filmed again in 2004, directed by Frank Oz.

4

UNCOUPLINGS

Transitions and Turning Points

At the turn of the millennium, British socialist and feminist historian Sheila Rowbotham published an autobiographical account of her life as a young woman in the 1960s called *Promise of a Dream*.[1] Writer Jenny Diski, in a less than enthusiastic review in the *London Review of Books*, sneered at what she called the book's 'drippy title', which, she declared, whirled her back 'to a Disney world of Snow Whites and Sleeping Beauties', and soppy love songs such as 'A Dream Is a Wish Your Heart Makes' warbled by Disney princesses.[2] Rowbotham's memoir, she judged, was 'an attempt to redeem the dream from a scornful world that has, according to her, lost its dreaming capacity'. Diski's tone is dismissive, implying that the dreams—and the political idealism— of an ageing generation are inevitably outdated, contaminated with nostalgia, and cannot be of much interest to the young.

The 'flower children' and visionaries of the 1960s are now pensioners. For radical thinkers and idealists who dreamed back then of a wholly new, fair, and peaceful society, the late 1960s and early 1970s may indeed seem to have promised more than they delivered. Even so, these years were a watershed. Often associated with sexual revolution, they coincided with a set of deep-rooted changes in expectations and culture which completely transformed many women's lives. And Rowbotham's memoir, for many readers other than Jenny Diski, does manage to convey the way these changes gave contemporaries in Britain and North America 'the exhilarating sense of being history in the making', what another reviewer, Nicci Gerrard, described as 'a grass-roots, present tense and emotionally charged revolution, a world turned upside down and flooded with new freedom'.[3]

What happened in the late 1960s and early 1970s certainly had roots which went back earlier in time, but the cumulative impact of change was unforeseen. When Richard Titmuss analysed the social position of women in the 1950s, he, like most of his contemporaries, saw the evolving pattern of early marriage and parenthood as an established and permanent trend.[4] Policy implications followed. We have seen, for instance, that the lowering of the age of majority in England at the end of the 1960s was in part an attempt to adjust to this trend. Few could have predicted what actually happened, which was that after 1970 the trend to early marriage went suddenly and dramatically into reverse, and young people began postponing marriage into their more mature years, or even eschewing marriage altogether, in favour of cohabitation.[5] Indeed, as time went on, the youthful marriages of the post-war years in both Britain and North America began to look less like a trend than a historical discontinuity, calling for historically specific explanation.[6] The more general explanations sometimes offered at the time (such as young people reaching physical and biological maturity earlier, or increasing affluence) were no longer convincing.

We can best envisage what happened in the late 1960s and early 1970s as a process of *uncoupling*. Things which had previously been assumed to go together were beginning to come apart—the popular song's horse-and-carriage association of love and marriage, for instance.[7] Social attempts to discourage sex outside marriage were failing, as pre-marital sexual experience became first common-place then normative among young people. Sex was increasingly recognized as a source of pleasure, not necessarily (even if still ideally) connected with commitment or love. Women's pleasure in sex was increasingly recognized as a possibility and uncoupled from marital duty. Sex and reproduction were uncoupled by better contraception and legalized, safer abortion. Divorce became easier in the UK after the Divorce Reform Act of 1969, and the number of couples opting for separation and divorce rose. The ties between marriage and parenting loosened as young people began having children outside marriage and the terrible stigma associated with illegitimacy faded. Most profoundly, perhaps, sex was becoming uncoupled from gender and its role expectations, and all of these categories were becoming more separate from the desire and capacity for parenting.

Historians will probably continue to quibble about the appropriateness of the term 'sexual revolution' and its timing—whether change is best seen as having happened suddenly, or as the result of a set of interacting, longer term trends.[8] A case can be made either way, and it is possible to accept that both perspectives have some truth to them. Feminist historians have long argued about whether 'the sexual revolution' was altogether good news for women.[9] It certainly didn't eradicate sexual inequalities, or patriarchy, and the 'permissiveness' associated with the sexual revolution can be seen to have made life more difficult, at times, for some young women. But the relationship between what came to be called the women's liberation movement or 'second-wave' feminism and the sexual revolution in the 1960s and 1970s was very close; they were rooted together even if the branches, as they matured, sometimes diverged.

What were the roots of such movements and changes? It has often been maintained that second-wave feminism grew out of the civil rights movement in North America.[10] Both in America and Britain, feminism was fuelled by women's reaction against domesticity in the post-war years. In both countries, two trends were fundamental to the ways in which women's lives were transformed in this period: the better education of girls and women, and the technologies which permitted control of reproduction, thus allowing for the separation of sexual activity from child-bearing. Education and contraception were not the stuff of dreams or fairy tales: they were practical, solid changes which materially affected women's lives. Yet they allowed women's aspirations in the 1960s, 1970s, and beyond to grow much more freely than those of their mothers.

America was ahead of Europe in its provision for education through the high school system. Britain planned for secondary education for all only after the Butler Education Act of 1944, which extended free secondary schooling to children up to the age of fifteen, with the intent of raising this to sixteen as early as possible (this was effected, eventually, in 1972). Although in both countries white middle-class children benefited the most from improvements in schooling after the war, girls in these categories gained substantially. Even when held back by an emphasis on housewifery and domestic skills in the curriculum (both at secondary and even at college level), girls were quick to prove themselves competent scholars. In England, where entrants to secondary education were subject to the 'eleven plus' examination which was supposed to sift out children with more academic potential (who would go to grammar schools) from the rest (consigned to 'secondary modern' or technical schools), local authorities were soon effectively discriminating *against* girls, who did so well in tests that they threatened to occupy too many places in the grammar schools.[11] A significant minority of girls performed very well indeed in grammar schools, and began to set their sights on higher education. The expanding university system in Britain, particularly the 'new universities' of the 1960s and a newly introduced and generous system of provision for student grants, made this possible.[12]

The advent of the contraceptive pill had a dramatic—even seismic—impact on women's experiences in the late 1960s and early 1970s. Historian Elaine Tyler May has succinctly dissected many of its far-ranging consequences. Licensed for use in the United States by the Food and Drug Administration (FDA) in 1960, by 1964 some 6.5 million married and an uncertain number of unmarried American women were taking oral contraceptives.[13] In Britain, the National Health Service licensed prescriptions for the pill for married women from 1961; from 1967, single women could also obtain prescriptions.[14] The pill was no panacea and not all women welcomed it: health scares and concerns over the safety of long-term use have never entirely disappeared. Even so, it was a milestone in the separation of sexuality from reproduction, allowing women to imagine and to achieve more control over their bodies than ever before in history.

The decriminalization of abortion in both countries also had the effect of allowing women more control over their bodies: some would argue that this restored earlier rights which legal changes, through defining abortion as a crime, had previously eroded.[15] Here the milestones were the Abortion Law Reform Act in Britain, in 1967, and the *Roe v Wade* decision in the US.[16] Kate Fisher's research has suggested that in Britain, decisions over contraceptive practice in the first half of the twentieth century had tended to be made by men. Women were highly invested in seeming innocent, even if not totally ignorant about such matters, and Fisher observed that they often affected passivity or a kind of fatalism.[17] Even so, we know from a range of other sources how common it was for women to seek ways of ending unwanted pregnancies. Desperate attempts at self-help involving gin and hot baths, purging and knitting needles; resort to illegal, 'back-street' abortionists using soap and saline injections; and other means were ubiquitous: the tide of suffering and loss of life was immense.[18] The pill; access to easier, less judgemental, and more reliable forms of pregnancy testing; and the availability of safe, legal abortions allowed women, potentially, to take much more control over their lives.[19]

It is hardly surprising that the pill stirred up so much controversy when first introduced. Moralists of a conservative disposition were aghast that men might be freed from responsibility for the consequences of sex; that women could now 'sin' and get off scot-free. In North America, a young Helen Gurley Brown became an overnight celebrity when she published *Sex and the Single Girl* (1962), urging young unmarried women to cultivate financial independence and suggesting that they try men out, sexually, before marrying them.[20] An early draft of the book included a section on contraception, although this was thought too contentious, and was therefore left out of the final publication.[21] A year later Mary McCarthy's novel *The Group* made the *New York Times* bestseller list.[22] It focused on single women and their relationships, and contained an unforgettable description of one character,

Dottie, seeking out a sympathetic woman doctor who was prepared to fit unmarried women with diaphragms or Dutch caps. When Dottie's lover proves himself changeable and a thoughtless cad, she kicks the birth control kit under a park bench, unused and still in its pristine packaging. The book's frankness caused a sensation and it was banned in some countries, including Ireland and Australia.

In Britain, censorship relaxed after the collapse of the Crown's case against Penguin Books for obscenity over the publication of D. H. Lawrence's novel *Lady Chatterley's Lover* in 1960.[23] Respected literary authorities found the book tender and moral in its full-frontal approach to sex. It was still easier to get away with sexual openness if the sex was linked to love. But an uncoupling of sex and love was evident in new kinds of advice literature inclined to treat sex as appetite, something which only involved morality to the extent that the participants in a relationship were respectful of each other as people. In 1968, Helena Wright's *Sex and Society* argued strongly for a change in attitudes to sex and marriage now that reliable contraception was available.[24] Wright was convinced that pre-marital sexual experiences could be educational and had the potential to strengthen later, lasting unions. Even more contentiously, she also defended extra-marital sexual relationships, which she believed could buttress marriages, if partners could rid themselves of jealousy and possessiveness.[25]

Progressive attitudes of this kind coexisted with lingering popular conservatism and suspicion of the contraceptive pill. An almost-forgotten British film entitled *Prudence and the Pill*, which screened in 1968, featured five heterosexual couples, married and unmarried, all of whom were in some kind of emotional disequilibrium and some of whom were desperately keen to avoid

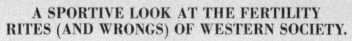

12. *Prudence and the Pill*. Film poster 1968

pregnancy.[26] The idea of an oral contraceptive seems distant and too good to be true. A sexual comedy of errors ensues in which 'Thenol' birth control pills are swapped, surreptitiously, for vitamin pills or aspirin, or vice versa: chaos follows, and all the women conceive. The film provides fascinating glimpses into class and culture at that time, illustrating a degree of incomprehension and a desire for, and yet a deep resistance to, contemporary change. Upper-class stockbroker Gerald (David Niven) is unhappily married, with a mistress on the side, and he's harassed by a need to sort out the mess caused by his chauffeur having impregnated the housemaid. 'In the entire history of the world', he claims, 'no man has ever had pleasure out of a woman without having to pay for it'. The film seems to prove him right on this, but there's a strong undercurrent of things shifting irreversibly, of a younger generation who might indeed 'get away without paying', and who were incubating entirely different attitudes to sex and sexual mores.

The idea that you might have to 'pay the price' for sexual pleasure was strongly ingrained in the culture of the 1950s. It underlay the era's often unforgiving attitudes to women who 'got into trouble' and to the men who got them there. Sometimes this attitude got in the way of an acceptance of the new forms of birth control because it was thought not good for the young that they should have things so easy—to indulge in 'free love'—and not have to strive for self-control. These attitudes persisted into the 1960s and 1970s. Writer Janice Galloway, growing up in Scotland in the early 1970s, records that she and her then boyfriend visited the latter's family doctor hoping to get a prescription for the pill. Janice was doing well at school, and though the young couple considered themselves engaged, they wanted to wait until she had completed her examinations and they had managed to save some money before getting married.[27] Both were over sixteen. They were trying to act responsibly. However, the doctor they consulted was a Catholic, and he gave them short shrift: he bluntly instructed them either to get married straight away or to abstain from any kind of physical intimacy. Not long afterwards Janice realized she had become pregnant. Luckily, her own doctor was more sympathetic, and it was arranged for her to have an abortion.

Janice lived with her mother and sister, who were supportive at this point, her mother confessing that she herself had been pregnant at the time she married: the baby had died and she had carried the experience as a guilty secret ever since. Janice's sister Cora had walked out on an unhappy relationship, abandoning her small infant son. Janice had grown up in a household in which men were assumed to be unreliable. They came and they went, and women hardened themselves, struggling to cope on their own. Pregnancy could spell disaster. 'Anything, my mother told me, was better than *paying the price* and the price for children, as everyone knew, was the ruination of a future, the end of your life', Galloway recollected, some years later.[28]

Janice never imagined that she herself would be 'caught out' by an unwanted pregnancy. Though highly intelligent, as an adolescent she had her illusions: 'Being *caught out*', she had imagined, 'was for other, less canny people. I was, or so I imagined, in the clear.'[29] Even so, she considered herself extraordinarily lucky to have been a young woman in the early 1970s. She had not had to resort to back-street abortion or to extreme methods of trying to terminate a pregnancy as her mother had.

> That my adolescence coincided with the advent of mass-produced, reliable contraception was an all-round bonus. For that alone, my

sister called me spoiled and my mother, repeatedly, assured me I didn't know I'd been born.[30]

For a generation who had wrestled with the complications of 'barrier' methods of contraception, and the often terrible, life-threatening implications of trying to prevent the birth of unwanted children, the pill seemed almost miraculous. Historian Hera Cook observed that the pill 'shifted the associations of contraception away from the red and pink, slime and rubber of condoms and caps, sex and genitals'.[31] It was discreet, it was hygienic, and it worked. It could take young women, as well as their parents, some time to come to grips with this and stories such as Janice Galloway's were common. Young women—even highly intelligent ones—were often reluctant to look too prepared in encounters with young men. Premeditated sex might imply a level of experience, a sophistication, or a 'hardness' which they did not feel nor want to project. When asked for a prescription for the pill, doctors—especially if Catholic or conservative—might be judgemental and discouraging. They were within their rights to refuse. Student health centres in universities in the late 1960s and 1970s were often staffed by doctors who took a liberal, tolerant approach to student sexuality. Even so, studies at the Universities of Sussex and Aberdeen in the early 1970s revealed that a disturbingly high proportion of female undergraduates with active sex lives were taking no precautions against unwanted pregnancy.[32]

This situation only began to change as free, effective oral contraceptives became more widely available, and their use more acceptable. Attitudes to sexual experimentation among young unmarried people were changing fast, and women were learning, though sometimes all too slowly, to look after themselves. By 1969, nearly half of all women then aged twenty-three in Britain had used oral contraceptives. Twenty years later, in 1989, it was estimated that more than 80 per cent of women born between 1950 and 1959 had used the pill for contraception.[33] Hera Cook has suggested that the social changes associated with women taking responsibility for contraception may have been even more marked in Britain than in North America.[34] This is because in the 1950s, more than two thirds of American women were estimated to be using female-controlled methods (such as the diaphragm), compared with only one seventh of English women. Such methods allowed young women to adopt a less fatalistic attitude, to plan, and to take more control over their own lives.

Novels written by women between the late 1950s and the 1970s provide telling insights into the way changing social and sexual mores impacted on the lives of young women.[35] The crop of earlier novels structured around middle-class women's frustrations, above all, their sense of being caged in by role expectations and a certain lifestyle, of having to live with unfaithful husbands and being powerless to do anything about it, receded. A new group of texts investigated the predicaments of younger women. They almost invariably deal with the gaps and distinctions between sex and love. Penelope Mortimer's *Daddy's Gone A-Hunting* spans earlier and later genres in dealing with mother–daughter relationships, providing a gloss on social change.[36] When Angela, Ruth Whiting's daughter and a student at Oxford, finds she is pregnant by a boyfriend with whom she very quickly realizes she is not in love, she is terrified, but knows she wants to terminate the pregnancy. This is set in the 1950s, when abortion was still illegal. The boyfriend proves himself egocentric and useless, and Angela turns to her mother. Although Ruth is depressed and apathetic, she is galvanized into action by her daughter's desperation, and she negotiates her way through the maze of clandestine, difficult, and expensive arrangements necessary to help her to secure an abortion. Ruth's confusion of emotions over all this, and her sadness, are contrasted with Angela's determination and robust sense of self, both of which are strengthened by her ordeal. But the older woman doesn't hesitate, and there is no moral judgement: Angela's predicament has to be resolved on her own terms.

American novelist Rona Jaffe's *The Best of Everything* (1958) offered an extraordinarily perceptive picture of the changing social world of young women in New York around mid-century.[37] These women were caught between 'traditional' expectations of marriage and family life, and the expanding world of work and opportunity in the city. The book begins by introducing Caroline Bender, a highly intelligent young woman whose fiancé had recently broken off their engagement to marry someone else. Her world is shattered, and she takes a job in publishing out of 'emotional necessity' as much as economic need. The novel traces the fortunes of Caroline and four of her female friends, all of whom have somehow expected to be 'completed' by marriage, and all of whom struggle with the idea of themselves as independent women, working to support themselves. The women have to deal with exploitative men both at work and in their personal lives, and they are forced to question their own illusions about the indissolubility of sexual desire, integrity, and love. One character (April) is almost destroyed when her lover forces her into having an abortion and then abandons her. Another is driven crazy by her own sexual jealousy and possessiveness. Caroline's relationships with men are anything but straightforward: those she is sexually attracted to don't offer themselves as 'husband material'; she finds it impossible to fancy the one man who is keen to marry her. Gradually, Caroline comes to be more focused on her own abilities and career. She comes to see life differently: work ambitions and female friendships become much more important. Writing a new introduction to her novel, which was reprinted in 2005, Jaffe attributed its initial popularity to the fact that she had written about things which had rarely been spoken about in the late 1950s. For her the book had been about 'how your dreams change, how your life changes'. Her narrative resisted the escape hatch of a clear ending: it was quintessentially a novel about growth, and change.[38]

The conflicts generated by rapid change are eloquently explored in the novels of English author Andrea Newman, in which young women who are able to benefit from higher education and have the means to control their fertility try to make sense of their emotions, relationships, and behaviour. They often make a hash of it. Newman's characters move towards separating love and sex: sometimes they have to do this in order to survive. In *A Share of the World* (1964), the central character, Lois, has arrived at university considering herself engaged to Peter, a boy she sleeps with and had become involved with back home.[39] When he dumps her she is lost. She is at the same time destabilized by the breakdown of her parents' marriage, by her mother's unhappiness, and especially by her father's new relationship with a much younger woman. Lois tries to numb her emotions and to force herself into exploring new relationships, sexually exciting but never fully satisfying. One of these relationships is with a married male tutor in college—rules against this kind of thing didn't exist in the early 1960s. Lois's girlfriends and fellow students all stumble in the dark, foundering over their romantic predicaments and decisions about sex: they recognize that things are changing, and sometimes wish they weren't. Anne, who is engaged and feels safe about it, considers that she's luckier than Lois in feeling securely attached, but concedes that 'it's lovely and smooth if you marry your first lover, but if you don't, what then?'[40] Marty, highly intelligent and sophisticated on the surface, urges Lois to take care with contraception, especially when Lois confesses that being prepared for sex with someone she hadn't already met 'made her feel cheap'. But then it is Marty who gets pregnant by a charismatic but exploitative lover, and who has to undergo a miserable abortion.

There are no happy endings here. Indeed, it is striking how many novels about female students in this period end with abortions, rather than with marriage. At the end of A Share of the World, Lois is left without any clear sense of direction. Her university exams are over: she's got a lower second class degree. With no obvious career plan in mind she goes home to help her mother. But she still has some of her illusions left, which she clings to, rather desperately. The book ends with her seeking to reassure herself that she is bound to meet the right person to share her life with one day: 'after all, people nearly always do, don't they?'[41]

This new generation of female novelists often represented their female characters as rudderless, unsure about careers and career options, and inclined, still, to invest rather too much of themselves in the dream of meeting the right man. In Margaret Drabble's A Summer Birdcage (1962), Sarah and her sister Louise are two clever girls who have graduated from Oxford: 'over-educated, and lacking a sense of vocation'.[42] They are both hazy about what to do with their lives. Louise marries someone rich and successful who she doesn't love, and soon embarks on a passionate affair with a less successful man to whom she is strongly physically attracted. Her sister looks on disapprovingly while the marriage falls apart. Sarah muses on the unattractive prospects that she feels women are doomed to face: children, hobbies such as embroidery, and then, almost inevitably, a 'sagging mind'.[43] She can't think of anything she can really do with her life except to become a writer: she'd enjoyed writing essays as an undergraduate and would have liked to go on doing so indefinitely. These young women are still imbued with the prejudices of their time in that intellectual seriousness seems deeply unsexy. Sarah contemplated academic research while at Oxford but didn't pursue it, convinced that 'You can't be a sexy don'.[44] We learn that she would quite like to marry an intelligent, academic type, but wasn't drawn to the uncertain status of being a don's wife. Thinking seriously about her future tended to make her panic.

In slightly later novels, such as Margaret Drabble's *The Millstone* (1965) and Andrea Newman's *Alexa* (1968), we begin to meet female characters with more autonomy and independence.[45] Rosamund Stacey in *The Millstone* is the daughter of middle-class intellectual parents and she herself is absorbed in her academic research. Her parents had drilled her in self-reliance to the point that she 'believed dependence to be a fatal sin'. Rosamund finds work easier to succeed at than relationships; she's sexually inhibited, in spite of projecting a surface impression of sophistication. When she finds herself pregnant as the result of a chance encounter, she considers abortion but is half-hearted about going about it. In the end she decides, pretty much by default, to have the child. She does not tell the father, with whom she has only a slender acquaintance: she thinks that it would not be right, in the circumstances, to burden him with a sense of obligation. Rosamund finds it impossible to imagine herself in the role of a conventional middle-class wife, like her sister-in-law, Clare. Even her own mother, we learn, had a serious job of her own, in social work. There is a wonderful passage in the book where Rosamund comes across Clare in Selfridges, and finds herself calculating just how much time she must waste on shopping, dinner parties, and endless visits to dry-cleaners and hairdressers. As the pregnant Rosamund leaves her disapproving sister-in-law in the store's food department, Clare is described as 'bending over the counter, pointing at a dressed pheasant with a plum-gloved hand'.[46] The connections between luxury goods, lack of purpose, and the life of the middle-class housewife are made all too apparent. *The Millstone* ends with an optimistic vision of women's capacity for independence, with Rosamund growing clearer about her values and coping well. After a serious illness, her baby is thriving. She is an adoring single mother with scholarly achievements and a solid CV, well placed for a secure job in academia.

In *Alexa*, Andrea Newman goes still further in depicting self-reliance and sexual confidence in an unmarried, economically independent woman writer who thinks and behaves very much as men were commonly supposed to behave. The fictional Alexa has no trouble at all in recognizing her own sexual needs, in initiating sexual encounters, and in distinguishing between sex and love. Alexa, the privileged daughter of avant-garde parents, is joyful and enjoys her work: her life is contrasted with that of her married friend, Christine, who once had ambitions to excel as a concert pianist, but whose ambitions and sense of purpose have evaporated in the course of a conventional marriage to a pedantic schoolteacher. Christine is exhausted by her children and domesticity. Alexa offers to take over her domestic duties for a while, allowing Christine a period of respite in her elegant London flat. What happens, predictably, is that Christine's husband becomes obsessed with the glamorous Alexa. His feelings are shambolic. He deplores Alexa for her 'unfeminine' boldness, is jealous of her for her success as a writer, and desires her for her body and free-spirited sexiness. The text offers a sharp vision of contrasting lifestyles, showing that women have choices, deftly unpicking and scrutinizing many of the assumptions and prejudices about their sexual behaviour and aspirations in the late 1960s.

Newman's novels are in many ways ahead of their time: it's easier to imagine Alexa existing in the 1980s rather than the 1960s. Published in 2007 but set in the 1970s, Charlotte Greig's *A Girl's Guide to Modern European Philosophy* is a coming-of-age novel about a student at the University of Sussex.[47] Reading this in conjunction with the earlier novels gives a sense of just how much things had changed for young women at university since 1950. In the 1950s, women students commonly lived in single sex halls of residence where their social lives, and particularly their relationships with young men, were policed by the university authorities, mainly through the rules and strictures imposed by women wardens, principals, and 'moral tutors'. Universities, still burdened by having to act *in loco parentis* to undergraduates, were terrified by the potential scandal associated with student pregnancies. Women undergraduates who did become pregnant were often expected—or required—to abandon their studies and to leave the university. Married female students were still unusual, and might be required to forfeit their grants. Some fifteen to twenty years later, students were regarded as adults and their sex lives were seen as their own responsibility. Student health centres routinely provided help with contraception and abortion, and many universities offered crèche facilities and other forms of assistance to student parents and even single mothers.

While reflecting these changes in attitude and provision, Greig's novel represents young women as undergoing similar conflicts to those experienced by an earlier generation. Because she was writing in 2007, when a more open attitude to sexuality was common, she is able to describe these more frankly. In the novel, Susannah isn't sure about what she wants out of relationships and finds herself physically drawn to, and sexually involved with, two men—neither of them wholly satisfactory. One is a sophisticated, well-established local antiques dealer, who she comes to realize is probably bisexual. The other is a young male undergraduate: sexy, but emotionally attached to an earlier girlfriend. Though she is taking the pill, Susannah slips up and misses a few tablets. She finds herself pregnant but isn't sure who the father is. Agonizing about what to do, she seeks advice from female friends, a male tutor, and both boyfriends; she even attempts to wrest guidance from the philosophy books on her reading list. The turning point in Susannah's experience and in the novel as a whole is when she realizes that there isn't a man—or any form of male authority figure—who will give her the answer. She is going to have to decide for herself what to do. Her young lover Rob is too immature not to be frightened by the responsibilities of marriage and parenthood. She herself has doubts about whether she wants—or has the courage to become—a single mother. There's a reminder that the new 'permissiveness' of the 1970s was more in evidence in some parts of the UK than others. Susannah's home is in South Wales, and she knows that, were she to choose to have a child as an unmarried mother, her own mother would be devastated; her chapel-going aunt and uncle deeply shocked and 'ashamed to show their faces ever again in the congregation'. 'Down in Swansea', she explains, 'we were still living in the fifties, if not the nineteenth century—at least in my family, anyway'.[48]

In both Britain and North America it was young, white, and middle-class females, mainly those who were privileged enough to leave home and go to college or university, who were most affected by the new freedoms of the 1960s and 1970s. And it was these women whose expectations often contrasted strongly with those of their mothers. Mothers of an earlier generation, who might have come to terms with social prescriptions about femininity and a domestic existence, didn't always inspire their daughters. A longish tradition of feminist writing testifies that lessons in self-sacrifice could alienate or elicit resentment in girls who hungered after some kind of achievement or independence in their own lives. Much earlier in the century, Virginia Woolf had argued that a women writer had to kill off 'the angel in the house'—that guilt-inspiring ideal of dutiful femininity often modelled by a mother—if she was to make any progress in her vocation.[49] In the eyes of French feminist Simone de Beauvoir, women were particularly compromised and trapped by motherhood.[50]

In 1976, American poet and feminist writer Adrienne Rich published her tour de force, *Of Woman Born: Motherhood as Experience and Institution*, in which she asserted:

> Many daughters live in rage at their mothers for having accepted, too readily and passively, 'whatever comes'. A mother's victimization does not merely humiliate her, it mutilates the daughter who watches her for clues as to what it means to be a woman...The mother's self-hatred and low expectations are the binding-rags for the psyche of the daughter.[51]

Nancy Friday's *My Mother/Myself: The Daughter's Search for Identity*, first published in 1977, offered another biting critique of the psychological legacy mothers bequeathed to daughters. Its tone was angry. 'I have always lied to my mother', Friday confessed at the beginning of her first chapter. 'And she to me.'[52] Feelings of anger and resentment were common in second-wave feminist writing about motherhood, in large part because society was changing so fast, widening the gulf in experience and attitudes between generations. British writer Linda Grant, describing her youthful self, recorded that in the early 1970s

> I was a feminist, I was a Marxist, I wanted the world turned inside out, but principally I wanted more than anything else not to be like my mother: to marry, to have children, not to have a career or any kind of significant working life.[53]

Some younger women found themselves so deeply ambivalent about motherhood that they were unsure whether they wanted to have children themselves. English journalist Mary Ingham published a soul-searching account of the dilemmas over marriage and children faced by a group of women born just after the Second World War who had been her classmates at a girls' grammar school in the early 1960s. Her book, *Now We Are Thirty* (1981), was subtitled 'Women of the Breakthrough Generation'—signalling her awareness of just how much the pill, the sexual revolution, and new opportunities in education had influenced the lives of this generation of younger women.[54] Their expectations were completely different from those of their mothers, most of whom had been fearful about sex before marriage lest it 'got them into trouble' and marked them out as 'second-hand' or 'damaged goods'. Many of the younger women had gone to university, and experimented with sex in a way their mothers would never have dreamed of. 'Student rooms all over the country were to become the battle/testing/playgrounds for the determination of the New Morality', Ingham commented, wryly.[55]

Despite this, there was a strong tone of uncertainty in Ingham's book. She was writing at the time at which many of her contemporaries were beginning to 'settle down' and have babies, or at least agonizing over whether they should be doing so. Her own uncertainties about motherhood haunt and shadow the last chapter of her book. There was unease about whether more 'permissive' attitudes to sexual experience had damaged relationships between the sexes. In a book called *The Failure of the Sexual Revolution* (1974), philosopher and psychoanalyst George Frankl had contended that sexually liberated, independent women were exacerbating a crisis in masculinity among young men, and that the new blurring of sex roles was weakening the magnetic charge of male–female attraction.[56] Ingham found herself worrying about this, and also about whether the pill made sex too easy for people to flit from partner to partner rather than developing deep, committed relationships.[57] Maybe women risked too much by sleeping around, to the detriment of their reputation and their security, whereas men 'simply got what they wanted without the usual attendant fuss and blackmail, manipulation and persuasion'?[58]

Some feminist writers were indeed arguing that the sexual revolution had simply liberated men to sleep around and licensed them to exploit women even more than in the past. This argument was propounded most forcefully by those inclined to believe that men, as oppressors, were beyond reforming. The radical feminist writer Sheila Jeffreys, for instance, whose views were most fully expressed in her polemic of 1990, *Anti-Climax: A Feminist Perspective* on the Sexual Revolution, had little faith in heterosexual relation-ships, which she saw as characterized by power and control.[59]

Feminism itself was multi-faceted, rather than a monolithic sys-tem of ideas, and the analysis of women's oppression generated a number of different approaches and sometimes competing ortho-doxies. There was common ground in questioning the sexual div-ision of labour, in the challenge to sex roles, in exposing and condemning rape and domestic violence, and in the desire to pro-mote women's autonomy and independence. There was disagree-ment among feminists over the extent to which women's interests differed according to their social class or the colour of their skin. Many—probably a majority—of feminists believed that a blur-ring of sex roles, a move away from traditional relationships of dependence and independence, would immeasurably improve relationships between men and women. Women would become stronger and less vulnerable through economic independence; men would be less burdened by the responsibilities of being sole breadwinners and 'providers'. Rethinking gender stereotypes would allow women to express ambition and initiative, men to feel more at ease with sensitivity and emotion. There was far reaching, radical potential in the attempt to uncouple 'sex' from 'gender'; a distinction of central importance to second-wave fem-inists because it suggested that differences between men and women might be a result of upbringing and 'social conditioning', rather than being ineradicable or in some way 'fundamental', as if they were ultimately grounded in biology. In this context, British sociologist Ann Oakley's ground-breaking study Sex, Gender and Society (1972) quickly became a classic.[60] Oakley drew upon work in biology, anthropology, and sociology to argue that culture rather than bodily endowment shapes what we regard as 'masculine' or 'feminine', and showed that there is a great deal of overlap between the attributes of men and women.

Second-wave feminism flourished in Britain among a generation of women who had benefited from the educational reforms of the post-war period, especially those young women who had been high achievers in secondary school and gone on to higher education. Their expectations had been raised through education, and after graduating, they were often shocked to encounter pervasive sexism in the worlds of work and training. If they had assumed that they would find jobs and opportunities appropriate to their level of formal qualification and skills, then they were frequently disappointed. Marriage—and especially motherhood—curtailed these opportunities still further. This gap between expectations and opportunities made for a great deal of personal frustration. Pat Thane and her colleagues Kate Perry and Amy Erickson, working on a large-scale study of the lives of women who graduated from Girton College, Cambridge, through the twentieth century, found that the women who graduated in the 1960s were the cohort most conflicted and likely to express frustration over their lives.[61] These women were more likely to have expected equal opportunities than their predecessors, but they were almost routinely disappointed. A significant proportion of this cohort expressed frustration over lack of career opportunities and the conflicts between career and family responsibilities: many of them clearly identified themselves as feminists.[62]

Roughly the same age as the women of the 'breakthrough generation' whose lives were documented by Mary Ingham, some of these Girtonians graduating in the 1960s came to see women's liberation as a political priority. As journalist Kira Cochrane later observed in the British newspaper *The Guardian*, 'a generation was finding its voice'.[63] The first National Women's Liberation Conference in Britain was one result. It took place at Ruskin College, Oxford in February 1970. The organizers were unsure how many women would attend, imagining that the event would attract one or two hundred people: some five hundred women, sensibly equipped with sleeping bags, turned up.[64] Discussions ranged over family, motherhood, women's work, and equal pay, and the tone was heady and optimistic. Four goals were identified at this time: equal education, equal pay, free contraception and abortion 'on demand', and twenty-four-hour nursery provision. Two further demands were added to the agenda at the sixth National Conference, held in Edinburgh in 1974. The fifth goal was legal and financial independence for all women; the sixth, the right to a self-defined sexuality and an end to discrimination against lesbians.

Women's needs as both workers and mothers were seen as central to the project for liberation from the beginning. The efflorescence of feminist writing and scholarship on these subjects in the 1970s and 1980s reflects this. Ann Oakley broke new ground with both scholarly and accessible studies of housework and motherhood—two subjects which had received very little attention from academic sociology or history in the past. *Housewife*, published in 1974, offered an uncompromising critique of domesticity and its effect on women. Arguing that it wasn't enough to ask men for more 'help' in the home, Oakley contended that what was required were different forms of family living.[65] In her books on motherhood, *Becoming a Mother* (1979), *Women Confined* (1980), and *From Here to Maternity* (1981), Oakley drew on female experiences of childbirth and motherhood. She drew attention to ways in which a male-dominated hospital environment might compound women's feelings of loss of control, leading to misunderstanding of the experiences of exhaustion and loss of agency which could lead to post-natal depression.[66] Oakley's work was influential, both widely read and feeding into projects to allow women more say in how they wanted to give birth and in how they might seek to transform the conditions of family and domestic life.

The tendency to more open discussion of sexuality in the 1960s and 1970s was reflected in renewed public interest in earlier research by Alfred Kinsey, and in more recent studies by William Masters and Virginia Johnson. It spiralled with the publication of popular sex books which sold in record quantities in both Britain and North America, such as Alex Comfort's *The Joy of Sex* (1972).[67] Second-wave feminism generated its own tradition of writing about female sexuality. *Our Bodies, Ourselves*, originally published by the Boston Women's Health Collective in 1971, became available in a British edition, edited by Angela Phillips and Jill Rakusen, and published by Penguin in 1978. It was widely read and reprinted almost annually in the early 1980s.[68] As the title suggests, the book was essentially a self-help manual, urging women to take responsibility for their own health and decisions about reproduction, and not to be over-awed by medical expertise and institutional procedures defining female 'patients' as relatively powerless and passive.

Conventional attitudes to sexuality and understandings of women's sexual pleasure were also brought into question in the 1970s. Ann Koedt's classic essay 'The Myth of the Female Orgasm' challenged the Freudian-influenced orthodoxy that women who climaxed through clitoral stimulation were in some way immature or 'frigid'; penetrative, heterosexual sex didn't always make for orgasm.[69] In *The Hite Report on Female Sexuality* (1976), Shere Hite claimed that barely one third of the women in her sample (some 3000 answered her questionnaires) enjoyed fairly regular orgasms through penetrative sex with men.[70] This uncoupling of the idea of female sexual pleasure from the idea of masculine phallic performance was both radical and controversial. It was seen by some as offering legitimation for the pleasures of lesbianism. But it also had the potential to liberate men from anxiety about masculine performance.[71] Women writers were asserting claims to a new authority and expertise on the subjects of female sexuality, sexual pleasure, and sexual fantasy, and in the 1970s and 1980s, books on these subjects sold well.[72] The growth of feminist publishing houses such as The Feminist Press (founded in New York, 1970), Virago (London, from 1973), and The Women's Press (London, founded 1978) facilitated the diffusion of a rich crop of feminist texts on sex and sexual politics at this time.[73] Some of these ventures, such as Sheba Press (founded in the UK in 1980), made a commitment to diversity, in particular to publishing non-white authors. [74]

Feminist ideas snowballed in the 1970s and 1980s: the burgeoning of feminist publishing was both cause and effect. Equally if not more important in disseminating new ideas about women was the rise of 'educational feminism'. Career openings for women were still limited in the 1970s: many of the women graduating in the 1960s and 1970s were still pulled or pushed into teaching, whether or not they owned to having any strong desire for the work. These graduate women teachers brought new expectations about girls into schools, often questioning the bias of traditional curricula and approaches. They worked in the first instance against 'sexism', and later for what came to be called 'girl-friendly' schooling.[75]

In the past, women in the UK had often gone into teaching via teacher training colleges, which accepted entrants with only two 'A' level passes when universities required three.[76] Qualifying as a teacher did not require graduation, and the teacher training certificate carried less status than a university degree. Many male teachers were graduates, whereas many certificated women with years of experience found themselves excluded from any prospect of promotion: stuck in junior roles as their male graduate colleagues climbed up the ranks. There was a blossoming of adult education in both England and North America in the 1980s, as women who had been discouraged from studying for degrees earlier in their lives returned to college and university for a 'second chance' at education.[77]

These 'women returners' swelled enrolments in adult education and the ranks of part-time students in the Open University, established in 1969 with a mission to widen access to higher education in Britain. Women returners were often avid learners, restless and bored by domestic responsibilities, and keen to explore wider worlds. They could be a potent force for social change. It is no coincidence that mature women students feature so largely in the literature of the period, such as Marilyn French's *The Woman's Room* (1977), one of the key literary texts of second-wave feminism. In the novel, Mira and some of her friends leave suburban domesticity for Harvard, seeking more solid identities as individuals.[78] In the UK, the film *Educating Rita* (1983), based on an earlier stage play by Willy Russell, featured a working-class hairdresser who seeks personal growth through studying English Literature through the Open University.[79] Both *The Woman's Room* and *Educating Rita* drew attention to the frustrations experienced by women whose ambitions and sense of self had been stifled early in life, though neither text offered easy answers for the future.

The education of girls was transformed in these years, in that ideas about equal opportunities triumphed over a long-standing tradition of belief that girls needed to be educated differently from boys, usually with an emphasis on some kind of special feminine incapacity or need for training in housework and domesticity. In England, the policy of a defined, national curriculum to be taught in all state schools facilitated this.[80] The move towards equal opportunities was further strengthened by feminist attempts to promote a better deal for girls, with attention to informal as well as formal aspects of the curriculum. This involved paying attention to how girls were treated in the classroom as well as what they were formally taught, and encompassed studies of how girls' aspirations were shaped in the family, as well as in contact with their peers. Feminists were much bothered by messages in children's reading books which encouraged girls into passivity, and particularly by happy-ever-after messages in fairy tales.[81] Several studies offered critiques of 'sexism' in children's literature. There were attempts to re-write traditional stories with feisty heroines who didn't automatically melt at the sight of a prince. Robert Munsch's The *Paper Bag Princess* (1980) proved a lasting success.[82] It featured a smart and resourceful princess and a tiresome, silly prince. The book was endorsed by the National Association of Women, and feminists loved it.

Judy Blume's *Forever* (1975) was unquestionably one of the most significant books written for girls in that decade. Revolutionary in its treatment of teenage sexuality in a non-preachy but nevertheless responsible way, it reassured girls that sexual feelings and

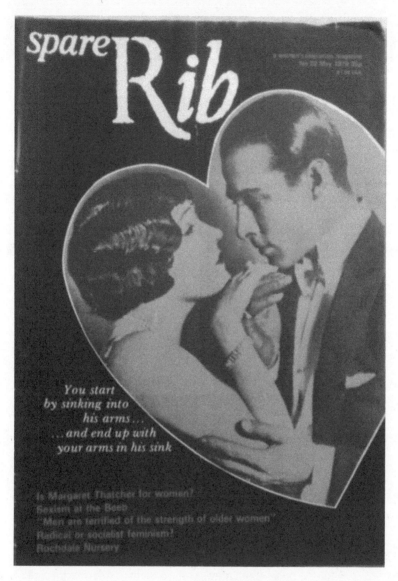

13. Feminist magazine *Spare Rib* aimed to disillusion starry-eyed romantics, 1979

14. *Spare Rib*, sceptical about men's commitment to role-sharing, 1982

15. Women's dreams…and realities: Women's Liberation poster from *Spare Rib*, 1970s

sexual curiosity were normal and didn't necessarily—or even that often—go hand in hand with enduring love.[83] It showed that healthy relationships were based on respect but that expectations of long-term commitment, in the young, could be unrealistic: relationships were to be explored as one grew up. The book has proved a lasting success, though it has always been controversial, and there have been many attempts to censor it since first publication. In a recent edition, Blume has gone on record noting that were she to write the book today, she would show its heroine, Katherine, making sure that her boyfriend used a condom as well as herself taking the contraceptive pill: over the preceding three decades, sexually transmitted diseases (especially HIV) had become more of a threat.[84] But the book's main message to girls was both radical and clear: if they were going to become sexually active, then rather than relying on fate or boyfriends, it was crucial that they should take responsibility for themselves.[85] The advice has stood the test of history.

Notes

1. Rowbotham, Sheila, *Promise of a Dream: Remembering the Sixties* (London: Allen Lane, 2000).
2. Diski, Jenny, 'A Long Forgotten War', *London Review of Books*, vol. 22, no. 13, July 2000, 9–10, https://www.lrb.co.uk/v22/n13/jenny-diski/a-long-forgotten-war, accessed 4/08/2018.
3. Gerrard, Nicci, 'Woman of Substance', *The Observer*, 23 July 2000, https://www.theguardian.com/books/2000/jul/23/biography.niccigerrard, accessed 4/08/2018.
4. Titmuss, R., 'The Position of Women: Some Vital Statistics', in *Essays on 'The Welfare State'* (London: Allen and Unwin, 1958).
5. For the UK see Office for National Statistics (ONS) Marriages in England and Wales; for USA, see data from Census Bureau, cited in

Kurtzleben, Danielle, 'Think We're All Getting Married Too Late? Think Again', *US News*, 14 February 2014, https://www.usnews.com/news/blogs/data-mine/2014/02/14/think-were-all-getting-married-super-late-think-again, accessed 09/04/2019.

6. Kurtzleben, 'Think We're All Getting Married Too Late?'

7. Frank Sinatra, first recording of the song 'Love and Marriage' 1955. Music by Jimmy van Heusen, lyrics by Sammy Cahn. There were many later recordings, and the song was a great hit in the 1950s.

8. A good starting point for the UK would be Cook, Hera, *The Long Sexual Revolution: English Women, Sex, and Contraception 1800–1975* (Oxford: Oxford University Press, 2004); see also Brown, Callum, 'Sex, Religion and the Single Woman, c. 1950–75: The Importance of a "Short" Sexual Revolution to the English Religious Crisis of the Sixties', *Twentieth Century British History*, vol. 22, no. 2, 2011, 189–215. For North America see, *inter alia*, Pétigny, Alan, 'Illegitimacy, Postwar Psychology and the Reperiodization of the Sexual Revolution', *Journal of Social History*, vol. 38, no. 1, October 2004, 63–79.

9. See for instance Jeffreys, S., *Anticlimax: A Feminist Perspective on the Sexual Revolution* (London: The Woman's Press, 1990).

10. See, for instance, Evans, Sara, *Personal Politics: The Roots of the Women's Liberation Movement in the Civil Rights Movement and the New Left* (New York: Alfred Knopf, 1979). For a broad-ranging history see Freedman, Estelle, *No Turning Back: The History of Feminism and the Future of Women* (New York: Ballantine, 2002).

11. See Rosen, Michael and Williams, Emma-Louise, 'Secondary Modern', *History Workshop Journal*, 24 January 2013, http://www.historyworkshop.org.uk/secondary-modern/, accessed 5/08/2018. Many areas had more generous provision for boys than for girls at the secondary level.

12. See Spencer, S., 'Reflections on the "Site of Struggle": Girls' Experience of Secondary Education in the Late 1950s', *History of Education*, vol. 33, no. 4, July 2004, 437–47; also Attar, Dena, *Wasting Girls' Time: The History and Politics of Home Economics* (London: Virago, 1990); Dyhouse, C., *Students: A Gendered History* (London: Routledge, 2006); see especially 'Women and the "New Universities of the 1960s"', 100ff.

13. Tyler May, Elaine, *America and The Pill: A History of Promise, Peril and Liberation* (New York: Basic Books, 2010), vi.

14. Cook, *The Long Sexual Revolution*, 268; Bridge, Sarah, 'A History of the Pill', *The Guardian*, 12 September 2007, https://www.theguardian.com/society/2007/sep/12/health.medicineandhealth, accessed 09/04/2019.

15. Mohr, James C., *Abortion in America: The Origins and Evolution of National Policy* (New York: Oxford University Press, 1979); Reagan, Lesley J., *When Abortion was a Crime: Women, Medicine and the Law in the United States, 1867–1973* (Berkeley: University of California Press, 1998); Brookes, Barbara, *Abortion in England, 1900–1967* (London: Routledge, 1988); Brooke, Stephen, '"A New World for Women?" Abortion Law Reform in Britain during the 1930s', *American Historical Review*, vol. 106, no. 2, April 2001, 431–59

16. See references above; also, for United States, Solinger, Rickie, *Pregnancy and Power: A Short History of Reproductive Politics in America* (New York: New York University Press, 2005), and for Britain, Paintin, David, *Abortion Law Reform in Britain, 1964–2003: A Personal Account* (Stratford-on-Avon: BPAS, 2015).

17. Fisher, Kate, *Birth Control, Sex and Marriage in Britain 1918–1960* (Oxford: Oxford University Press, 2006), 5, 6, 12.

18. Stopes, M., *Mother England: A Contemporary History*, 'Self Written by those Who Have Had No Historian' (London: John Bale, Sons and Danielsson, 1929); Kandiah, Michael D. and Staerck, Gillian (eds), *The Abortion Act of 1967* (Institute of Contemporary British History Witness Seminar, 2002).

19. For feminist involvement with pregnancy testing in Britain see Olszynko-Gryn, Jesse, 'The Feminist Appropriation of Pregnancy Testing in 1970s Britain', *Women's History Review*, online 11 July 2017, https://doi.org/10.1080/09612025.2017.1346869, accessed 7/11/2019.

20. Brown, Helen Gurley, *Sex and the Single Girl* (London: Frederick Mueller, 1963).

21. Szalai, Jennifer, 'The Complicated Origins of " Having it All"', *The New York Times Magazine*, 2 January 2015, https://www.nytimes.com/2015/01/04/magazine/the-complicated-origins-of-having-it-all.html, accessed 6/08/2018.

22. McCarthy, M., *The Group* (New York: Harcourt Brace, 1963).

23. See Robertson, Geoffrey, 'The Trial of Lady Chatterley's Lover', *The Guardian*, 22 October 2010, https://www.theguardian.com/books/2010/oct/22/dh-lawrence-lady-chatterley-trial, accessed 6/08/2018; Rolphe, C., *The Trial of Lady Chatterley: Regina v Penguin Books, Ltd*: transcript of the trial (Harmondsworth: Penguin, 1961).

24. Wright, Helena, *Sex and Society* (London: Allen and Unwin, 1968), especially 114 ff.

25. Ibid. 117.

26. *Prudence and the Pill*, 1968, directed by Fielder Cook and Ronald Neame, starring Deborah Kerr and David Niven.
27. Galloway, Janice, *All Made Up* (London: Granta, 2011).
28. Ibid. 303.
29. Ibid.
30. Ibid.
31. Cook, *The Long Sexual Revolution*, 278.
32. Ryle, A., *Student Casualties* (London: Allen Lane, 1969), 120, 124; McCance, C., and Hall, D. J., 'Sexual Behaviour and Contraceptive Practice of Unmarried Female Undergraduates at Aberdeen University', *British Medical Journal*, 7 June 1972, 694–700.
33. Cook, *The Long Sexual Revolution*, 268.
34. Ibid. 267.
35. Hera Cook's D Phil. thesis has an interesting discussion of contemporary novels reflecting on changes in women's lives: see her 'The Long Sexual Revolution: British Women, Sex and Contraception in the Twentieth Century' (D. Phil. Thesis, University of Sussex, 1999).
36. Mortimer, Penelope, *Daddy's Gone A-Hunting* (London: Michael Joseph, 1958).
37. Jaffe, Rona, *The Best of Everything* (first published 1958, this edition London: Penguin, 2011).
38. Ibid. xi.
39. Newman, Andrea, *A Share of the World* (London: Panther, 1965).
40. Ibid. 52.
41. Ibid. 191.
42. Drabble, Margaret, *A Summer Bird-Cage* (London: Weidenfeld and Nicolson, 1962), 6.
43. Ibid. 25.
44. Ibid. 126.
45. Drabble, M., *The Millstone* (London: Weidenfeld and Nicolson, 1965); Newman, A., *Alexa* (London: Triton, 1968).
46. Drabble, *The Millstone* (this edition, Harmondsworth: Penguin, 1968), 83.
47. Greig, Charlotte, *A Girl's Guide to Modern European Philosophy* (London: Serpent's Tail, 2007).
48. Ibid. 264–5.
49. Virginia Woolf spoke of the need for a woman writer to kill the 'Angel in the House' (i.e. the image of self-sacrificing femininity) in a paper on 'Professions for Women' written for the Women's Service League in 1931. See Showalter, Elaine, 'Killing the Angel in the House: The

Autonomy of Women Writers', *The Antioch Review*, vol. 50, no. 1–2, Winter–Spring 1992, 207–20.

50. Patterson, Yolanda Astarita, 'Simone de Beauvoir and the Demystification of Motherhood', *Yale French Studies*, vol. 72, 1986, Special Issue 'Simone de Beauvoir: Witness to a Century', 87–105.

51. Rich, Adrienne, *Of Woman Born: Motherhood as Experience and Institution* (London: Virago, 1977), 243.

52. Friday, Nancy, *My Mother, Myself: The Daughter's Search for Identity* (London: Fontana, 1979), 1.

53. Grant, Linda, *Remind Me Who I Am, Again* (London: Granta, 1998), 38.

54. Ingham, Mary, *Now We Are Thirty: Women of the Breakthrough Generation* (London: Eyre Methuen, 1981).

55. Ibid. 108. For further thoughts on the generational differences between daughters and their mothers in this period see Abrams, Lynn, 'Liberating the Female Self: Epiphanies, Conflict and Coherence in the Life Stories of Postwar British Women', *Social History*, vol. 39, no. 1, 2014, 14–35.

56. Frankl, G., *The Failure of the Sexual Revolution* (London: Kahn and Averill, 1974).

57. Ingham, Chapter 8, 'Sole Survivors'.

58. Ingham, 166.

59. Jeffreys, S., *Anticlimax: A Feminist Perspective on the Sexual Revolution* (London: The Woman's Press, 1990).

60. Oakley, Ann, *Sex, Gender and Society* (Middlesex: Temple Smith, 1972).

61. Thane, P., 'Girton Graduates: Earning and Learning, 1920s–1980s', *Women's History Review*, vol. 13, no. 3, 2004, 347–61.

62. Ibid. 357.

63. Cochrane, Kira, 'Forty Years of Women's Liberation', *The Guardian*, 26 February 2010, https://www.theguardian.com/lifeandstyle/2010/feb/26/forty-years-womens-liberation, accessed 6/08/2018.

64. Ibid.

65. Oakley, Ann, *Housewife* (London: Allen Lane, 1974).

66. Oakley, Ann, *Becoming a Mother* (Oxford: Martin Robertson, 1979); *Woman Confined: Towards a Sociology of Childbirth* (Oxford: Martin Robertson, 1980); *From Here to Maternity: Becoming a Mother* (Harmondsworth: Penguin, 1981).

67. Kinsey, Alfred C., Pomeroy, Wardell B., and Martin, Clyde E., *Sexual Behaviour in the Human Male* (Bloomington: Indiana University Press, 1948); Kinsey, A. et al., *Sexual Behaviour in the Human Female* (Bloomington: Indiana University Press, 1953); Masters, W. H., Johnson,

Virginia E., and Kolodny, Robert C., *Masters and Johnson on Sex and Human Loving* (London: Macmillan, 1986). Comfort, Alex, *The Joy of Sex: A Gourmet Guide to Lovemaking* (London: Quartet, 1972).

68. Boston Women's Health Collective, *Our Bodies, Ourselves: A Book By and For Women* (New York: Simon and Schuster, 1973); edition edited by Angela Phillips and Jill Rakusen, London: Penguin, 1978.

69. Koedt, Anne, *The Myth of the Vaginal Orgasm* (New York: New York Radical Feminists, 1968); reproduced at Chicago Women's Liberation Union (CWLU) Herstory Project, https://www.cwluherstory.org/classic-feminist-writings-articles/myth-of-the-vaginal-orgasm, accessed 7/08/2018; see also Gerhard, Jane, 'Revisiting "The Myth of the Vaginal Orgasm": American Sexual Thought and Second Wave Feminism', *Feminist Studies*, vol. 26, no. 2, Summer 2000, 449–76.

70. Hite, Shere, *The Hite Report: A Nationwide Study of Female Sexuality* (first edition 1976, this edition New York: Seven Stories Press, 2004), see especially Introduction.

71. On this theme see Hall, Lesley A., *Hidden Anxieties: Male Sexuality 1900–1950* (Cambridge: Polity, 1991), which insightfully draws upon letters written by men to Marie Stopes.

72. See, for instance, Nancy Friday's writing on women's sexual fantasies: Friday, N., *My Secret Garden: Women's Sexual Fantasies* (London: Quartet, 1975).

73. Virago for instance caused a stir by publishing Mills, Jane, *Make It Happy* (London: Virago, 1978), while The Women's Press published Shulamith Firestone's *The Dialectic of Sex: The Case for Feminist Revolution* in 1979. For a detailed consideration of the work of the feminist presses see Riley, Catherine, 'The Intersections between Early Feminist Polemic and Publishing: How Books Changed Lives in the Second Wave', *Women: A Cultural Review*, vol. 26, no. 4, 2015, 384–401; also Forster, Laurel, 'Spreading the Word: Feminist Print Cultures and the Women's Liberation Movement', *Women's History Review*, vol. 25, no. 5, 2016, 812–31.

74. On the history of Sheba Press see https://mith.umd.edu/womensstudies/ReferenceRoom/Publications/about-sheba-press.html, accessed 7/08/2018.

75. See, for instance, Whyte, J., Kant, L., Deem, R., and Cruicksank, M. (eds), *Girl-Friendly Schooling* (London: Methuen, 1985).

76. Edwards, Elizabeth, *Women in Teacher Training Colleges: A Culture of Femininity* (London: Routledge, 2001).

77. Perry, Pauline, 'Hope Fulfilled or Hope Deferred?' in Masson, M. R. and Simonton, D. (eds), *Women and Higher Education: Past, Present and Future* (Aberdeen: Aberdeen University Press, 1996).

78. French, Marilyn, *The Women's Room* (New York: Simon and Schuster, 1977).

79. *Educating Rita* (1983), British film directed by Lewis Gilbert with screenplay by Willy Russell. Starring Julie Walters and Michael Caine.

80. Arnot, M., David, M., and Weiner, G., *Closing the Gender Gap: Postwar Education and Social Change* (Cambridge: Polity Press, 1999).

81. *Sexism in Children's Books: Facts, Figures and Guidelines* (London: Writers and Readers Publishing Co-Operative, 1976; Zipes, Jack (ed.), *Don't Bet on the Prince: Contemporary Feminist Fairy Tales in North America and England* (Aldershot: Gower, 1986); Haase, D. (ed.), *Fairy Tales and Feminism: New Approaches* (Detroit: Wayne State University Press, 2004). See also Stones, Rosemary (ed.), *More to Life than Mr Right: Stories for Young Feminists* (London: Piccadilly Press, 1985).

82. Munsch, Robert, *The Paper Bag Princess* (Toronto: Annick Press and Discus Books, 1980).

83. Blume, Judy, *Forever* (London: Gollancz, 1976). See Sarah Crown, 'Teen Spirit', *The Guardian*, 8 June 2005, https://www.theguardian.com/books/2005/jun/08/booksforchildrenandteenagers.sarahcrown, accessed 7/08/2018; Alexandra Alter and Kathryn Shattuck, 'What Judy Blume's Books Meant', *New York Times*, 1 June 2015, https://www.nytimes.com/2015/06/02/books/what-judy-blumes-books-meant.html, accessed 7/08/2018.

84. http://www.judyblume.com/books/ya/forever.php, accessed 7/08/2018.

85. See Crawford, Marisa, 'Judy Blume Taught a Generation of Young Girls to be Feminists', *Broadly, Vice Magazine*, 3 April 2018, https://broadly.vice.com/en_us/article/bjp77m/judy-blume-feminism-generation-young-girls, accessed 7/08/2018.

5

HAVING IT ALL? IDENTITY, WORK, CHOICE

In 1981 Colette Dowling published *The Cinderella Complex: Women's Hidden Fear of Independence*, which attracted column space in *The New York Times* and quickly became an international best-seller.[1] The book focused on what Dowling called 'the lie in the promise' of dependency.[2] Too many women still wanted to be looked after, she submitted: they dreamed of meeting a Prince Charming who would protect them in wedded bliss.

The 1970s had brought new freedoms and possibilities of personal development for women, Dowling acknowledged, but these freedoms could be frightening. It could be hard to overcome years of feminine conditioning, to distance oneself from male authority figures, to abandon fantasies of being rescued from the buffetings of the workplace and the ruthless power and money struggles of the external world. Domesticity could look like a cosy retreat: it was easy to be seduced by home comforts into 'a world of cherry pies and bed quilts and freshly ironed summer dresses'.[3] Dowling knew this, she confessed, because she had been there herself. When her first marriage failed, she had to learn to stand on her own two feet. Later, in a new relationship, she had been surprised to observe herself slipping back into habits of dependency.

Her new partner was a writer, and Dowling found herself gradually reverting to 'woman's traditional role of helper. Putterer. Amanuensis. Typist of someone else's dreams.'[4]

Dowling recalled Simone de Beauvoir's warning that women in heterosexual relationships tended towards submissiveness in order to avoid the strain involved in embracing an authentic existence.[5] This was similar to what sociologist Jessie Bernard had described as the process of 'dwindling into a wife': a shrinking of the self in order to make marriage easier.[6] In the course of her research on marriage, Bernard reported that she had come across women who had been competent and independent in their youth, but whom long years of marriage had effectively deskilled. When such women were eventually freed from looking after children, or were widowed, they could feel helpless and lacking in confidence.[7] Dependency in marriage was too easy, an infantile rather than an adult state, because a dependent woman didn't have to fend for herself. She could burden the man with responsibility for providing.

The 'Cinderella complex', Dowling concluded, was:

> A network of largely repressed attitudes and fears that keeps women in a kind of half-light, retreating from the full use of their minds and creativity. Like Cinderella, women today are still waiting for something external to transform their lives.[8]

Much of this, she thought, was based on fear: a fear of being left alone and of not being able to cope, a fear of looking unattractive as a female. But the 'good wife' who was applauded for her self-lessness and for her dedication to her family should not be regarded as a saint, Dowling insisted, but seen in her true colours, as 'a clinger'. Women needed to overcome their fears of loneliness and inadequacy, and to rescue themselves: they had to marshal their courage and 'spring free'.[9]

In Britain, a couple of years before the first publication of *The Cinderella Complex*, *Guardian* journalist Jill Tweedie had written a book called *In the Name of Love*, in which she advanced similar arguments.[10] Tweedie's conviction was that true love could not exist in conditions of inequality. Dependency—particularly economic dependency—eroded self-respect and made it impossible for the dependent party (in heterosexual relationships at the time, almost always the woman) to achieve any real self-knowledge or separate form of identity. Tweedie drew on her personal experience (she had married three times) as well as her wide reading in this book, and it was richly embellished with references to contemporary feminist writing, such as Marilyn French's *The Women's Room*. The personal odyssey of French's heroine, Mira, Tweedie pointed out, had particular resonance for contemporary feminists because her independence was so hard won; she had to learn to accept loneliness as a better alternative to 'the poison apple of love'.[11]

Bleak as this might sound, the message of Tweedie's book was fundamentally optimistic. Her third marriage, she assured her readers, had proved happy and companionable, and was based on mutual independence and respect. In the second edition of her book, which appeared in 1988, Tweedie included an addendum which she entitled 'Ten Years On', in which she attempted to take stock of the achievements of women's liberation over the previous decade. Progress had been slower than one might have expected or hoped, she confessed, particularly in respect of women's earning power and their opportunities for promotion. The social damage done by the spread of HIV/AIDS had been a major setback.

Even so, she thought that the outlook of young women at the end of the 1980s contrasted very positively with that of their predecessors: 'many more take for granted, without fuss or celebration, a self-respect and an autonomy unknown to most of their mothers, and to most women still, outside the West', she concluded.[12]

The gains made in terms of women's independence between 1970 and 1990 were dramatic. In Britain, the Equal Pay Act of 1970 and the Sex Discrimination Act of 1975 were important landmarks. Legislation against sexual discrimination had particularly far-reaching effects in education, directly or indirectly helping to bring down the barriers which had previously excluded women from elite institutions of higher education through quotas or all-male colleges.[13] The proportions of women studying at the Universities of Oxford and Cambridge, and taking up training in the medical or veterinary schools, rose. Before 1975, university graduates had characteristically received advice on employment and professional training from separate men's or women's careers advisory services or employment bureaux. Jobs were seen as gendered. Women graduates of that era often recalled the sense of hopelessness they felt after consulting with these services: they were generally offered teaching or secretarial training and were warned that openings for women in broadcasting, advertising, or publishing—those areas which seemed alluring to many women—were as rare as hen's teeth.[14]

After 1975, things improved. The range of jobs taken up by women graduates widened and the proportion reluctantly herded into teaching fell.[15] Meanwhile, schoolgirls continued to benefit from the trend towards 'girl-friendly' schooling and the gender-neutral national curriculum. Their aspirations and ambitions began to change. In 1972, British social investigator Sue Sharpe had carried out a study of Ealing schoolgirls, in which she had found that the majority of her sample (67 per cent) had wanted to leave school as soon as possible and to get married.[16] In a follow-up study at the beginning of the 1990s, Sharpe found that the situation had changed dramatically: by then the majority of girls wanted to stay on at school to improve their chances of employment.[17]

By the end of the 1990s, educational researchers Madeleine Arnot, Miriam David, and Gaby Weiner were able to publish a book entitled *Closing the Gender Gap*, showing how the far-reaching social and legislative changes of the post-war world had brought about a new equality in provision for girls and boys in schools in Britain.[18] Girls' success in examinations had improved significantly, with their performance often drawing equal to, or exceeding, that of boys. Indeed, instances where female pupils were 'outperforming' their male peers had generated new forms of anxiety among some educationalists about whether now it was boys rather than girls who were 'underachieving' and whose school experiences called for particular scrutiny and possibly remedial treatment.[19] These concerns about boys' educational performance falling behind that of girls generated something of a panic in North America and many parts of Western Europe.[20] By the 1990s, there was increasing disquiet about relative gender performance (often intersecting with class and ethnicity) in higher education as well as in the schools. In 1996, for the first time in history, the proportion of women undergraduates in British universities equalled (and was soon to exceed) that of men.[21]

It wasn't just a question of doing well in school, going to university, and getting better jobs. Young women were turning their backs on the pattern of working for a few years before getting married, and leaving work, if not at marriage, then almost certainly when a first child was born. Increasingly, in both Britain and North America, women were hanging on to their jobs even when they became mothers. Having invested in education and training, it seemed a waste to risk leaving the labour market: any promotion at work was likely to have been hard won and it was well known that older women found it difficult to re-enter the workplace after raising families. High incomes were needed for the purchase of housing: in Britain, a dramatic rise in property values towards the end of the century made it almost mandatory, in some parts of the country, for two earners to combine forces to support a family home. Quite aside from these considerations, it became clear that many women, whether married, in partnerships, mothers, or not, simply *wanted* to go on working.

Many women derived a sense of identity, status, and personal satisfaction from their work. At the same time, it could be draining to combine a busy work schedule with domestic tasks unless these tasks were shared. Shirley Conran's *Superwoman*, first published in the UK in 1975, quipped that 'life was too short to stuff a mushroom'. 'What is a home?' she asked, suggesting that 'A home is a myth. A home is the Forth Bridge, one long, never-ending cleaning job which nobody notices until you don't do it.'[22] The book was in part a compendium of ideas for streamlining the running of a home so that women would no longer feel ground down by its demands. Conran later confessed that she'd received a mass of complaints: stay-at-home wives had felt insulted by what they saw as her devaluation of the work of home-making, whereas some feminists objected to the very idea that running a home was a woman's responsibility in the first place.[23] Nevertheless, the book sold well.

Surveys of the time spent on household tasks and childcare showed that men were beginning to do more in the home.[24] In the 1950s, the sight of a pram-pushing father had been rare. By the end of the 1970s, it wasn't so unusual to see men with buggies or carrying infants strapped to their backs or chests in slings. The term 'New Man', much used in the 1980s, suggested someone who rejected traditionally 'sexist' attitudes, who was willing to do his share around the house, and who was more in touch with the sensitive and emotional side of his personality. He wasn't altogether a figment of the journalistic imagination: some men were indeed sharing childcare, helping in nurseries and crèches, and supporting wives and partners in their own work ambitions. They were precursors of a long-term trend. Studies carried out by the University of Oxford's Centre for Time Use Research show that over the past fifty years men have consistently increased their share of work in the home, even though they still on average put in less time on domestic tasks than women do.[25]

Women have long complained that men see them as primarily responsible for the management of the home, with male partners represented as 'helping' rather than taking charge; others find it hard to delegate tasks which they believe that they themselves will carry out more thoroughly and efficiently. At the end of the twentieth century, sociology professor Jonathan Gershuny coined the ungainly term 'Allerednic syndrome' (Cinderella backwards) to describe the predicament of highly trained women who gave up work after the birth of a child, or who were reduced to exhaustion by the double burden of domesticity and work outside the home.[26] In the fairy tale, the prince married the scullery maid and turned her into a princess; in modern times, Gershuny suggested, the danger was that the prince might marry a princess only to turn her into a scullery maid. Women sought to avoid this fate through a series of strategies: negotiating the sharing of tasks with partners where possible; the seeking out of crèches and nurseries; enlisting the help of parents; and, where they could afford it, the employment of nannies, babysitters, and cleaners.

In relationships where both partners were equally committed to work outside the home, the whole territory of responsibility for childcare and domestic work could be fraught with difficulty. The most common image used by working mothers to describe coping with the tensions in their lives was that of 'juggling'. The use of the term in this context was ubiquitous, and it has been so through the whole of the last century. In her novel *The Creators*, for instance, published in 1910, British novelist May Sinclair analysed the predicament of her fictional heroine Jane Holland, who struggled to combine her work as a writer with the demands of family life. Jane's performance was likened to that of a highly skilled juggler, sometimes marvelling at her own dexterity, but shot through with tension and anxiety about taking her eye off the ball.[27]

Almost a hundred years later, writer and journalist Allison Pearson used the Concise Oxford Dictionary's definition of the verb 'to juggle' as an epigraph to her novel about city fund manager and working mother Kate Reddy, *I Don't Know How She Does It* (2002).[28] The definition highlighted dexterity/anxiety but also hinted at the deceit and fraudulence which is sometimes associated with the term. Pearson's novel—which sold well—was adapted into a film, starring Sarah Jessica Parker as Kate Reddy, in 2011.[29] Reviews of the film were mixed, not least because Kate's life on screen appeared so privileged. In *The Guardian*, critic Xan Brooks commented acerbically that the film was 'guaranteed to strike a chord with every harassed working Mum who's found herself lumbered with a full-time nanny, oodles of cash, a four-story Boston townhouse and a supportive husband with flexible working hours'.[30]

Stories about the difficulties of motherhood, whether combined with work or not, proliferated in the 1990s and in the first decade of the new century. In Britain, Rachel Cusk's *A Life's Work: On Becoming a Mother* (2001) offered a dark and unsettling account of how having a baby could erode a woman's identity. Kate Figes' *Life after Birth* (1998) and Naomi Wolf's *Misconceptions* (2001) were also eloquent about the drama—and sometimes trauma—involved in childbirth and the conflicts and ambivalent emotions involved in becoming a mother.[31]

British novelist Helen Simpson's collection of edgy, bittersweet short stories, *Hey Yeah Right Get a Life* (2000; published in the United States as *Getting a Life*), offered kaleidoscopic perspectives on the problem of maintaining a sense of self when trying to deal with the unrelenting neediness of families and small children.[32] One mother in Simpson's stories, Dorrie, despairs at the 'sequestration' of her hours and fears that any further incursions on her time 'would send her beside herself': 'Loss of inner life, that's what it was; lack of any purchase in the outside world, and loss of all respect; continuous unavoidable Lilliputian demands; numbness, apathy and biscuits. She was at the end of her rope.'[33]

Another story highlights the stark contrasts between the lives of a modern, professional career woman with children and the more average, stay-at-home mothers marooned in the suburbs and trying to escape a kind of death-by-drowning in mundane domestic cares. In another tale, a teenager looks with unabashed horror on the lives of struggling mothers and determines that her own life will follow a very different pattern.[34]

Perhaps every generation of feminists has to demythologize motherhood. Two novels from this period which stood out for their astute and often comic treatment of problems faced by women who were successful in their careers and tried to combine high-flying jobs with mothering were Maeve Haran's *Having It All* (1991) and the aforementioned novel by Allison Pearson, *I Don't Know How She Does It*.[35] Both focus on the lives of fictional characters who are highly privileged: Liz Ward, in *Having It All*, is a programme controller for a television company; Kate Reddy, in *I Don't Know How She Does It*, works as a fund manager in the City. Both women project an image of themselves as confident, Armani-suited Glamazons, regularly chauffeured around London to business meetings where they deliver slick presentations and offer razor-sharp interventions, smoothly taking executive decisions in their stride.

Keeping up this performance requires the juggling of nannies and childcare, schedules and relationships, business contacts and school timetables. Inside, the women live in fear of being caught out: by patches of baby sick on their sleekly tailored business suits, by ladders in their tights, by children being sent home with nits in their hair, by having forgotten school sports days or nativity plays at Christmas time. They lie about their family responsibilities to bosses and colleagues, lest these bosses and colleagues scent weakness: any lack of commitment or ambition at work might prove fatal, effectively condemning them to 'the mummy track'. Though dog-tired, the women stay awake at night making lists in their heads: shopping lists, memos to deal with plumbers and dry cleaners, school homework, birthday cakes and vaccinations, hair appointments, obligations to in-laws, and reminders to purchase tins of pet food. On top of all this, they fervently remind themselves that they must not forget the importance of having sex with their husbands, however exhausted they are: their marriages must not be allowed to crash.

In both of these novels marriages *do* threaten to collapse under the strain of all this, although the sexual politics of the situation are dealt with differently by the two writers. In Haran's novel, Liz's husband, also a high-flier, is shown as relishing his wife's worldly success and her competence at work. He doesn't want Liz to be a dependent *Hausfrau*, associating this with memories of the joyless, self-sacrificial stance once adopted by his own mother. Kate's husband Richard, in Pearson's book, is represented as much more equivocal about his wife's career. His background is such that he comes to feel unmanned by not being the main breadwinner in the family.

Though written ten years apart, there are many similarities between these novels. In both, the female characters are overwhelmed, less by the demands of work itself than by the requirements of performing in a workplace where the rules are made by men. In both books, the women, stressed and exhausted, abandon their high-pressure jobs for a while. They spend brief periods at home, caring for children, but then realize that full-time domesticity isn't sufficient to satisfy them. Both turn to other ventures, specifically forms of business activity and commercial ventures where they have more control over their working hours and conditions of employment. Liz, in Haran's novel, throws her energies into 'Womanpower', a company which organizes part-time work opportunities for women. Allison Pearson's Kate helps to rescue a company where women workers manufacture dolls' houses. Tellingly, both books have sub-plots which are in effect revenge fantasies. Before bowing out of their jobs, the central female characters collude with their female colleagues to bring misogynist bosses or co-workers to their knees. Both texts are eloquent about the strains, but also the tender joys, of relating to small children. And, equally, both convey a great deal about the exhilarations of the workplace, the satisfactions of competence, of teamwork, and of creativity and purpose; the pleasures of working with colleagues; the heady experiences of ambition and power.

These books have often been criticized for self-indulgently detailing the dilemmas and the consumer habits of a highly privileged elite of women workers. The women in Haran and Pearson's books are successful and rich. From the 1980s, high-flying businesswomen and female politicians were becoming more common, their lifestyles often attracting gossipy and fascinated attention in the press. In North America, the careers of Geraldine Ferrano, Nancy Pelosi, Condoleezza Rice, and Hillary Clinton broke new ground in politics; in the business world their counterparts included Carly Fiorina, Mary Barra, Indra Nooyi, Gini Rometty, Sheryl Sandberg, and others. In Britain, Margaret Thatcher moved into Downing Street in 1979; Anita Roddick, Nicola Horlick, Carolyn McCall, and others made their mark in the worlds of business and the media. The careers of successful women inspired many, but they also attracted speculation and envy. How did such women manage, if they were mothers? Did these women really 'have everything'? Did their children suffer? There was a good deal of *Schadenfreude* in all this.

Susan Faludi's influential *Backlash: The Undeclared War against American Women* (1991) saw cultural obsession with stories of burnt-out working women who retreated back into the home as a major facet of the backlash against feminism in the 1980s.[36] In the British edition of her book, Faludi instances the popular reception of Maeve Haran's *Having It All* as a clear example of this backlash in the UK.[37] Much was made of the fact that Maeve Haran had drawn upon her own experience in writing the novel—she herself had worked in television and had decided to abandon the inflexible demands of the job in order to establish a new career as a writer. This had proved harder than she had expected, and the much-lauded 'six-figure advance' that she received for *Having It All* came about after a great deal of trial and error, over which she tells us she suffered 'a dark night of the soul'.[38] When the book was launched, the publisher (Michael Joseph) made a sustained effort to stir up controversy, billing the question of whether or not women could cope with demanding, pressurized jobs as 'the hot topic of 1991'.[39] British journalist Julie Burchill, forever keen on fomenting controversy, was quoted as having dismissed the book as 'more morally repellent than pornography', while reviewers in the *Sunday Times* and *The Times* had seen it as 'a depressing read with a defeatist message' and 'part of a conspiracy to shame women back to the nursery'.[40] Perhaps the shrewdest review was by Libby Purves in *The Times*. 'Brace yourselves', she urged working mothers, because 'a gang of ruthless publishers' was out to puncture their confidence with a novel about a TV executive 'who runs out on a vital meeting to cheer on her son in his school sack-race'.[41] Our heroine then resigns, and 'flounces off to a country cottage and makes patchwork cushions and posies of Michaelmas daisies like a proper woman'.[42]

And to some extent the publicity worked, with a reviewer in *The Independent* announcing that 'Maeve Haran has broken rank, and a good thing too' and Angela Neustatter making vague digs at 'female fascism', as if feminism had dragooned women into the workplace and never defended their right to choose.[43] In reality, neither in their fiction nor in their own lives did Haran or Pearson ever seriously recommend giving up work—they were simply pointing out that the lack of flexibility and family friendliness in a male-dominated workplace made life difficult if not nearly impossible for mothers. In Pearson's *I Don't Know How She Does It*, Kate confesses that the idea of *not* having an income of her own scares her: she realizes that she needs her own money 'the way I need my own lungs'.[44] She feels that 'giving up work is like becoming a missing person. One of the domestic Disappeared', joking that 'The post offices of Britain should be full of Wanted posters for women who lost themselves in their children and were never seen again'.[45] Maeve Haran's decision to give up her job in television was a gamble: she wanted to write, and she had applied herself to the task of trying to identify the formula for a best-seller with energy and determination.[46] Her fictional character, Liz, similarly seeks fulfilling work which allows her the flexibility to combine motherhood with creativity, and without sacrificing an income. In Allison Pearson's more recent novel, *How Hard Can It Be?* (2017), a sequel to *I Don't Know How She Does It*, we meet Kate Reddy again: her children are now older and she is desperate to return to the world of regularly paid work.[47] Her age is against her, but through a combination of chutzpah and lying she manages to get herself re-employed by her former firm of investment managers, even working again on the fund which she had herself, some years earlier, set up. In spite of all the odds, she makes a success of this.

Many mothers in Britain and North America—probably the majority—work full time out of sheer economic necessity. Kate Reddy's triumphant return to high-paid work in the City may read like a wish-fulfilment fantasy, but it touches on problems faced by the countless women in less glamorous jobs who struggle with family responsibilities, the demands of teenagers and ageing parents, the inflexibilities of male-dominated career patterns, and age-related discrimination against women in the workplace. Allison Pearson's books sell because so many women 'carry the puzzle of family life in their heads'.[48] The books further pinpoint some of the problems faced by couples in long-term marriages; the power imbalances that may be caused by different earning abilities, the challenges of the menopause, and the not infrequently conflicting ties of parenthood, loyalty, fidelity, and sexual desire. Pearson writes about these subjects with humour, a light touch, and a comforting amount of optimism. The real-life equivalents of Liz Ward and Kate Reddy often battle with conspicuously fewer resources and against more challenging odds; nevertheless, the fictions—where they don't irritate—can serve to reassure.

The phrase 'having it all' was first associated with the title of a book by *Cosmopolitan* editor Helen Gurley Brown: *Having It All: Love, Success, Sex, Money; Even if You're Starting with Nothing*, first published in 1982.[49] Brown is said to have hated the title. Her biographer, Jennifer Scanlon, describes how she had been pushed into using it by her publisher.[50] The title—almost an accusation—suggests greed and entitlement, whereas Brown had wanted her text to convey encouragement to the downtrodden.[51] Critics have regularly pointed out that Brown herself, who had no children, seems to have believed that combining child-raising with success in a paid career was something of a tall order. However, since the 1980s, the phrase 'having it all' has consistently been associated with the 'demands' of feminism, and it has generally been deployed (with more than a touch of moral disapproval) to suggest that feminists, in 'wanting everything', are basically unreasonable. As Jennifer Szalai has pointed out in an article in *The New York Times*

Magazine, this 're-writing of recent history that blames the woman's movement for women's troubles' is effectively part of the 'backlash' identified by Susan Faludi: 'To say that women expect to 'have it all' is to trivialize issues like parental leave, equal pay and safe, affordable child care: it makes women sound like entitled, narcissistic battle-axes while also casting them as fools.'[52]

It is difficult to see the phrase disappearing, precisely because it serves as a rebuke in the minds of those who would argue that feminism has 'gone too far'. In reality, of course, there is still a great deal further to go if societies are to ease the predicaments of both mothers and fathers in the workplace.

For women's independence as wage-earners and their presence in the workplace are now such an established feature of Western societies that attitudes to the sexual division of labour which were taken for granted in the 1950s have begun to disappear. Novels reflect this. From the late 1970s, particularly, we begin to see the depiction of new types of female characters whose identity derives as much (or more) from their work as from their relationships. Barbara Taylor Bradford's hugely successful novel *A Woman of Substance* (1979) tells the story of Emma Harte, a resourceful girl born into poverty in the North of England, a domestic servant who starts off unpromisingly by finding herself pregnant by the son of her employer.[53] Let down by her lover, Emma decides to shift for herself. Over the years she transforms herself into a resourceful and competent businesswoman. Her relationships with men are anything but straightforward, but neither her life nor her happiness are dictated by romance. Emma herself is a powerful woman and her whole life is an adventure.

Novels by Shirley Conran, especially *Lace* (1982), and Judith Krantz's *I'll Take Manhattan* (1986) similarly explore the idea of women finding strength and self-definition through their work, and through friendships with other women, as much as through relationships with men.[54] Relationships with men improve, in these books, when women discover their own sense of purpose in fulfilling work, rather than seeing men as a solution to life's problems. This message was hammered out repeatedly in feminist literature after 1970. In an early novel by Fay Weldon, *Down Among the Women* (1971), the author maps changes through generations.[55] Her central character Scarlet, who has come from difficult beginnings into a relatively serene, married middle age, finds herself defending her life and the lives of her friends from the sceptical criticisms of her free-thinking daughter, Byzantia. Byzantia accuses her mother of defining 'success' in terms of stable relationships with men. Scarlet retaliates by suggesting that stable relationships with men might be seen as a *symptom* of success rather than a cause. Byzantia's riposte is that the very investment of so much energy and hope in relating to men might be seen as pathological, a symbol 'of a fearful disease from which you all suffer'.[56]

Data from the Thirtieth British Social Attitudes Survey, collected in 2013, highlighted marked changes in people's attitudes to gender roles in the UK since the 1980s.[57] In the mid-1980s, close to half of those questioned might be said to have supported conventional gender roles, where the man was seen as the main breadwinner and the woman's role in the family seen mainly in terms of caring. Since then there has been a steady decline in the numbers of people thinking like this. By 2012, only 13 per cent of those questioned defended the idea of traditional sex roles. The authors of this section of the survey (Jacqueline Scott and Elizabeth Clery) showed that this transformation of attitudes had gone hand in hand with a significant rise in women's labour market participation. The assumption that both partners in a heterosexual relationship would go out to work was found to be particularly strong among the younger cohorts. Where young children were concerned, however, it was still often assumed that women would work part time—and women still tended to do more work than their male partners around the home.[58] Even so, these changes were hugely significant, and underpinned the equally marked changes in women's sexual behaviour that the British National Surveys of Sexual Attitudes identified as having taken place through the same time period.[59] Women's sexual behaviour, in terms of onset of sexual activity, number of partners, and a weakened connection between sexual activity and reproduction, was increasingly falling into line with that of men.[60]

If women were becoming more independent, both economically and sexually, did this imply an end to what Colette Dowling had identified as 'the Cinderella Syndrome'? Social and cultural change is often uneven, for many reasons. Social inequalities in both the UK and North America continued to shape women's life chances, and middle-class status in particular generally went along with educational advantages and the kind of cultural capital that made it easier to enter certain forms of privileged employment. Race and ethnicity were factors which intersected with class, making it difficult to generalize too widely about gains in autonomy and economic or educational progress. There were also generational variables. Younger women were perhaps less susceptible to the belief that finding a perfect, princely, provider-type partner was the best solution to life's problems. But while women still, on average, earned less than men, this traditional dream of finding a rich protector was hard to eradicate.

British historian Zoe Strimpel has shown how the fast-changing sexual mores of the late twentieth century generated anxiety and unease about the economic aspects of courtship.[61] Who should pay for drinks or dinner on a first date? If women were 'liberated', should men expect them to go halves? Or would a woman judge a date who failed to pick up the tab as mean-minded and lacking in chivalry or masculine generosity? Old certainties about these gendered scripts were challenged at a time when the practices of courtship or dating were already being radically reshaped by a proliferation of advertising in newspaper 'lonely hearts' columns, by computer applications, and subsequently by digital technology and online dating.

Expectations changed unevenly and some women insisted (often with a stubborn pride) that their outlook remained traditional. In Britain, Colette Sinclair, who wrote a book describing her exhausting two-year search for Mr Right in the 1980s, was unapologetic about her criteria for selecting a soulmate.[62] He had to be nice-looking, sexy, well-off, and prepared to be a good father to her young daughter, Moya. Around thirty years old at the time of writing, she already had three failed marriages (based on 'half romantic, half mercenary needs') behind her. Sinclair's detailed descriptions of her first dates with potential partners in England and in the US show her highly sensitive to issues such as choice of venue, restaurant, clothing, and assumptions about who should bear the cost of dinner. Her default choice of venue for a first meeting tended to be Brighton's elegant and expensive Grand Hotel, although she began to fear that the staff, familiar with her meeting so many different men on the premises, would assume that she was a prostitute. Sinclair wanted—and expected—a man to keep her in luxury, seeing this as his 'natural' role (and her entitlement): she was critical of what she identified as new, 'American' expectations that wives should go out to work.[63] Still single at the end of her book, she longed for another marriage because experience had taught her that 'a woman's status is very dependent on having a husband': she missed 'the social security, the shared moments', the 'envious looks' from other women who had yet to find a mate. Even so, she admitted that she was beginning to learn that 'life without a man isn't the end of the world'.[64]

Women in the late twentieth century could live highly independent lives. At a fantasy level, though, the idea of meeting and marrying a man who might offer a rescue from the bruising experiences of a workaday life and take care of you forever might still remain alluring. The huge success of the film *Pretty Woman* (1990) can probably be explained in these terms.[65] Film critic Owen Gleiberman was one of the first to identify the film as a modern Cinderella story, with elements of Pygmalion thrown in.[66] Although his initial review of *Pretty Woman* was hostile, Gleiberman conceded that the movie might just catch on, shrewdly predicting that 'With its tough-hooker heroine, it can work as a feminist version of an upscale princess fantasy'.[67] The film features weary, workaholic, but devastatingly handsome businessman Edward Lewis (Richard Gere) falling for gorgeous Hollywood sex worker Vivian Ward (Julia Roberts). In what way might it be seen as a *feminist* version of the Cinderella story? Vivian is no passive victim: her independence and agency is made clear early in the film when she proves herself a better driver than Edward (she handles a Lotus Esprit with confidence and verve).

But the film is shot through with contradictions. Vivian won't be patronized—apart from when she goes on a wild spending spree round the boutiques of Rodeo Drive brandishing Edward's credit card. Who rescues whom? Edward is represented as a victim of overwork, exhausted and endangered by the values of corporate ruthlessness. Vivian dreams of fairy-tale rescuers, of knights on white horses, but when Edward acts this out, metaphorically, by climbing onto the roof of a white limousine in order to reach her, she retorts that *she* 'rescues him, right back'. We're left in no doubt that the film is about dreams: 'Welcome to Hollywood! What's your dream?...This is Hollywood, land of dreams.' Reality was a little different—and by the 1990s, even illusions were changing.

Notes

1. Dowling, Colette, *The Cinderella Complex: Women's Hidden Fear of Independence* (London: Fontana, 1981).
2. Ibid. 11.
3. Ibid. 15.
4. Ibid. 16.
5. Ibid. 17.
6. Bernard, Jessie, *The Future of Marriage* (New York: World Publishing, 1972), xvi, 38–9.
7. Ibid.
8. Dowling, *Cinderella Complex*, 31.
9. Ibid. 78.
10. Tweedie, Jill, *In the Name of Love* (London: Macmillan, 1988).
11. Ibid. 183.
12. Ibid. 189.
13. Dyhouse, Carol, *Students: A Gendered History* (Abingdon: Routledge, 2006), esp. 108–13.
14. Ibid. 114–17.
15. Ibid.

16. Sharpe, S., 'Just Like a Girl': How Girls Learn to be Women (London: Penguin, 1976).

17. Ibid. 2nd edn, 1994.

18. Arnot, M., David, M., and Weiner, G., Closing the Gender Gap: Postwar Education and Social Change (Cambridge: Polity Press, 1999).

19. See, for instance, Elwood, J., Maw, J., Epstein, D., and Hey, V. (eds), Failing Boys? Issues in Gender and Achievement (Milton Keynes: Open University Press, 1998); Francis, Becky, Reassessing Gender and Achievement: Questioning Contemporary Key Debates (Abingdon: Routledge, 2005), esp. chapter 7.

20. See, for instance, Gender and Education Association, http://www.genderandeducation.com/resources-2/the-boys-underachievement-debate/, accessed 17/04/2019.

21. Dyhouse, Students: A Gendered History, 207.

22. Conran, S., Superwoman: Everywoman's Book of Household Management (London: Sidgwick and Jackson, 1975).

23. Jenny Johnstone for The Daily Mail, 4 August 2012, http://www.dailymail.co.uk/news/article-2183474/Shirley-Conran-Superwoman-author-confesses-If-I-turn-time-I-wouldnt-children.html, accessed 17/04/2019.

24. University of Oxford, Centre for Time Use Research data; see, inter alia, Altintas, Evrim, and Sullivan, Oriel, 'Fifty Years of Change Updated: Cross-National Gender Convergence in Housework', Demographic Research, vol. 35, no. 16, August 2016, 455–70.

25. Ibid.

26. Gershuny, J. and Robson, K., 'The Sad Tale of Allerednic: The Social Position of British Mothers after First Birth, and Future Research with European Data', Conference Paper, European Sociological Conference, Helsinki, Finland, August/September 2001, https://www.iser.essex.ac.uk/research/publications/504426, accessed 17/04/2019.

27. Sinclair, May, The Creators: A Comedy (London: Hutchinson, 1910), 349; discussed in Dyhouse, C., Feminism and the Family in England, 1880–1939 (Oxford: Blackwell, 1989).

28. Pearson, Allison, I Don't Know How She Does It (London: Vintage, 2003).

29. I Don't Know How She Does It, film, 2011, director Douglas McGrath.

30. Brooks, Xan, 'I Don't Know How She Does It', review, The Guardian, 15 September 2011, https://www.theguardian.com/film/2011/sep/15/i-dont-know-how-she-does-it-film-review, accessed 13/08/2018.

31. Cusk, Rachel, *A Life's Work* (London: Fourth Estate, 2001); Figes, Kate, *Life after Birth* (London: Viking, 1998); Wolf, Naomi, *Misconceptions: Truth, Lies and the Unexpected on the Journey to Motherhood* (New York and London: Doubleday, 2001).

32. Simpson, Helen, *Hey Yeah Right Get a Life* (London: Jonathan Cape, 2000); published in United States as *Getting a Life* (New York: Alfred A Knopf, 2000).

33. Simpson, *Hey Yeah Right Get a Life*, 54.

34. Ibid. See stories entitled 'Burns and the Bankers' and 'Lentils and Lilies'.

35. Haran, Maeve, *Having it All* (first published Penguin, 1991, this edition London: Pan, 2014); Pearson, *I Don't Know How She Does It*.

36. Faludi, Susan, *Backlash: The Undeclared War against American Women* (London: Vintage, 1992).

37. Ibid. 15, 113–14.

38. Haran, Maeve, *Weekend*, 'Inside Story', *Daily Mail*, 20 August 1994, 36–7.

39. Faludi, 113–14; Picardie, Justine, review of Maeve Haran, *Having It All*, *The Independent*, 22 July 1991, 17.

40. Ibid. See also Hill, Jane, 'Lash Back in Anger: Have Feminists Fired a War on Women?' *The Guardian*, 24 March 1992, 21; Neustatter, Angela, 'Women: To Have and To Hold Forth: The publication of Maeve Haran's Novel *Having It All*, with its suggestion that women could solve the work-versus-kids dilemma by cutting back on their careers, has infuriated feminists', *The Guardian*, 11 July 1991.

41. Purves, Libby, 'Which Way to the Promised Land?' *The Times*, 19 June 1991, 12 (Times Digital Archive, accessed 21/08/2018).

42. Ibid.

43. Neustatter, 'Women'; Picardie, review.

44. Pearson, *I Don't Know How She Does It*, 176.

45. Ibid.

46. Haran, 'Inside Story'; see also Yvonne Roberts interview with Maeve Haran, 'From Mother to Daughter: Twenty Years on, Having It All is Still Just a Work of Fiction', *The Guardian*, 8 June 2014, https://www.theguardian.com/lifeandstyle/2014/jun/08/having-it-all-maeve-haran-daughter, accessed 17/04/2019.

47. Pearson, Allison, *How Hard Can It Be?* (London: Harper Collins, Borough Press, 2017).

48. Pearson, *I Don't Know How She Does It*, 190.

49. Brown, Helen Gurley, *Having It All: Love, Success, Sex, Money, Even If You're Starting with Nothing* (New York: Simon and Schuster, Linden Press, 1982).

50. Szalai, Jennifer, 'The Complicated Origins of "Having it All"', *The New York Times Magazine*, 2 January 2015, https://www.nytimes.com/2015/01/04/magazine/the-complicated-origins-of-having-it-all.html, accessed 17/04/2019.

51. Helen Gurley Brown had wanted her publisher to use the title 'The Mouseburger Plan'. Szalai, 'The Complicated Origins', 4.

52. Ibid. 5.

53. Bradford, Barbara Taylor, *A Woman of Substance* (Bath: Chivers, 1979).

54. Conran, Shirley, *Lace* (London: Sidgwick and Jackson, 1982); Krantz, Judith, *I'll Take Manhattan* (London: Bantam, 1986).

55. Weldon, Fay, *Down Among the Women* (London: St Martin's Press, 1972).

56. Ibid. 216.

57. British Social Attitudes, no. 30, http://www.bsa.natcen.ac.uk/latest-report/british-social-attitudes-30/gender-roles/attitudes-have-changed-but-have-behaviours.aspx, accessed 21/08/2018.

58. Ibid.

59. See British National Survey of Sexual Attitudes (Natsal), Surveys 1 (1990–1), 2 (1991–2001), and 3 (2010–12) 2013, http://www.ucl.ac.uk/news/news-articles/1113/26112013-Results-from-third-National-Survey-of-Sexual-Attitudes-and-Lifestyles, accessed 21/08/2018.

60. Ibid. See comments by Professor Kay Wellings.

61. Strimpel, Zoe, 'In Solitary Pursuit: Singles, Sex War and the Search for Love, 1977–1983', *Cultural and Social History*, vol. 14, no. 5, 2017, 691–795.

62. Sinclair, Colette, *Man Hunt: The Search for Mr Right* (London: Sidgwick and Jackson, 1989).

63. Ibid. 205.

64. Ibid. 208.

65. *Pretty Woman*, 1990, director Gary Marshall, Buena Vista Pictures, starring Julia Roberts and Richard Gere.

66. Glieberman, Owen, '"Pretty Woman": Twenty Years after My Most Infamous Review (Yes, I Gave it D), Here's My Mea Culpa—And Also My Defense', *Entertainment Weekly*, 24 March 2010, https://ew.com/article/2010/03/24/pretty-woman-my-most-infamous-review/, accessed 21/08/2018.

67. Ibid.

6

UGLY SISTERS? FOLK-DEVILS
AND FEMINISM

Social experiences—and understandings about gender scripts, or what it meant to be a man or a woman—changed radically between the 1970s and the 1990s. This demonstrably unnerved contemporaries, fuelling what has been described as backlash and a whole series of moral panics. The spread of the HIV virus and deaths from AIDS in the 1980s served further to reinforce pessimism about the outcomes of the sexual revolution. Was Western society experiencing a moral meltdown, witnessing the erosion of all modesty and decency and a terrifying destruction of family values? Unsurprisingly, feminism—linked by cause and effect with social change, though by no means its sole instigator—regularly came in for blame. Feminists were often the butt of humour or satire: some of it good-humoured, some not. Just as suffragettes at the beginning of the twentieth century had been depicted as ugly, man-hating harridans, 'Women's Libbers' in Britain and America were relentlessly represented as big-bummed, hairy-legged, and asexual, eschewing all femininity and keen to cut up men. Britain's satirical magazine *Private Eye* ran a regular column, 'Loony Feminist Nonsense', in the 1980s, in which 'wimmin' were shown as baying for male blood. A typical cartoon depicted a lumpy-looking, long-suffering male stripped down to

16. Private Eye's *Book of Wimmin,* 1986

his vest and pants and lashed to a stake like a version of the martyred Saint Sebastian, ringed by gleeful Amazons armed with bows and arrows who were using him for target practice; or Orpheus, cornered by Maenads.[1]

If many of those who celebrated the feminist awakening of the 1970s had put their faith in change that would improve relationships between men and women, by the 1990s even some of the more sympathetic observers seemed to be having doubts. British writer Linda Grant, growing up in Manchester in the 1960s and 1970s, had welcomed the heady changes of that time. In 1994 she published a book, *Sexing the Millennium: Women and the Sexual Revolution*.[2] Grant explained that although she had originally set out 'to chart a social history of the pill', the book had become a 'personal quest to find out what had happened to herself and her generation'.[3] What she found perplexing was her sense that 'since the sexual revolution, relations between men and women seem to have turned murderous'.[4] Though she owned that she was dispirited by contemporary evidence of continuing violence against women, Grant refused to abandon faith in the potential of sexual freedoms for underpinning new forms of strength in women and a more humane, progressive society.

In his wide-ranging *Modern Love: An Intimate History of Men and Women in Twentieth-Century Britain* (2003), historian Marcus Collins charted the rise and fall of what he termed 'mutuality', which he defined as 'the notion that an intimate equality should be established between men and women through mixing, companionate marriage and shared sexual pleasure'.[5] Collins saw 'mutuality' as having replaced nineteenth-century assumptions about the relationship between men and women. These earlier assumptions had been based on the idea of 'separate spheres', where men were seen as presiding over public space, women as belonging in the home. He suggested that new ideas about mutuality, intimacy, and equality between men and women made fair progress in the first half of the twentieth century up until encountering a serious road block in the form of second-wave feminism. Between 1945 and 1990, Collins claimed, mutualism was eclipsed and derailed by second-wave feminists' insistence on autonomy, their identification of marriage as oppressive, and a rejection, by some radical feminists, of heterosexuality in favour of political lesbianism.[6] However, he does concede that other feminists saw a compatibility between mutuality and feminism, and 'refused to choose between their politics and their personal relationships with men'.[7]

Collins's book might be seen as giving a distorted picture, in that it downplays long-standing feminist faith in sexual equality as having the potential to improve the lives of both men and women, as well as their relations with each other. This faith in sexual equality had an important material dimension which Collins also underplays: the challenge to the idea of women as completely dependent on a male breadwinner. Western feminism has always recognized economic dependence as closely bound up with autonomy and power, thus visions of sexual equality have gone hand in hand with ideas about how to tackle women's economic powerlessness and vulnerability. This concern underpinned early twentieth-century visions of 'the endowment of motherhood', feminist campaigns for family allowances to be paid direct to the mother, and some second-wave feminists' (arguably rather unrealistic) demands for 'wages for housework' in the 1970s.[8] Most consistently, though, feminism has defended women's rights as independent wage earners, and with this the need for a changing division of labour in both workplace and home.

Distortions and stereotypes can set hard. As the twentieth century drew to a close, the very word 'feminism' could raise hackles. Some argued that feminism had played itself out. Young women frequently disowned it, even in university environments. That so many would preface any explanation of personal viewpoints on gender-related issues with 'I'm not a feminist, but...' became a kind of cliché for defensive, ambivalent attitudes, rendered muzzy by language and cultural representation.

There was much bandying about of the term 'postfeminism' in the 1990s, a label vague in meaning but often used by the media to suggest that feminism was now irrelevant, was played out, and had had its day. Feminists working in the field of cultural studies, such as Angela McRobbie and Charlotte Brunsdon, considered why feminism might be heard as 'as a censorious voice', troubling young women who did not want to appear unfeminine or hostile to men.[9] For fans of *Buffy the Vampire Slayer* and *Ally McBeal*, Brunsdon suggested, second-wave feminism could look dated, and its adherents might be 'demonized as personally censorious, hairy and politically correct'.[10] McRobbie pointed out that historicizing feminism, that is, relegating it to the past, made it feel safer.[11] But those who investigated young women's attitudes to feminism around the turn of the century often encountered a paradox. They found widespread sympathy for feminist goals: for equal opportunities and equal pay, for improved childcare, for a tightening of laws against sexual abuse and harassment. There was also a genuine appreciation of what a previous generation of feminists had achieved. But such sympathies and awareness could be tinged with unease about identifying with feminism as a political movement in the present. In North America, for instance, sociologist Pamela Aronson found that many young women had a tendency to sit on the fence when asked whether they saw themselves as feminists: they did not want to be perceived as anti-men.[12] And there were other studies of younger women's attitudes which found little or no evidence for anything which could be called 'postfeminism', and suggested that a new generation of women showed strong support for feminist goals, finding feminism of continuing relevance in their lives.[13]

The archives of the Mass Observation Project in Britain provide a wealth of material on attitudes to social change, gender, and feminism in the 1990s. The Mass Observation Project was launched in 1981. It set out to continue in the traditions of its predecessor, the social research organization known as Mass Observation, which had originally been founded in 1937 by a group of individuals keen to explore the anthropology of everyday life.[14] The new project went about things by issuing a regular series of 'directives', or open-ended questionnaires on selected topics, to a panel of volunteer writers. The aim was to collect a rich—if not strictly representative—database of opinions, attitudes, and experiences on various subjects which would offer insights into life in modern Britain. Many of the Mass Observers on the panel were born before 1960, and they were well placed to reflect upon the nature of change over time.

Among the always somewhat eclectic topics Mass Observers were asked to write about were a directive in 1990 enquiring about 'Close Relationships' and, in the following year, a directive entitled 'Women and Men' that suggested that they focus on gender and feminism. As always, the respondents were given prompts in the form of loose questions or suggestions, such as (in the case of the 1990 directive): 'Love: what does the word mean to you?' or 'What makes for a good marriage?' The following year's queries included 'Do you think there have been significant changes over the past few years in what we expect from men and from women? If you think there have been changes, please describe them (with real examples if possible) and say (a) whether you approve, (b) whether they have affected you personally, (c) whether they have gone far enough—or too far?' Respondents were also questioned about their understandings of the terms 'New Man', 'Liberated Woman', and 'Feminism'. As ever, they were encouraged to write completely freely on these subjects.

The overwhelming impression one gets from reading through the replies to the Close Relationships directive is that respondents agreed that there had been massive changes during their lifetimes. They described the repressiveness of their youth, when, as one elderly female respondent described, 'the word sex was never used', 'divorce was a dirty word', and pregnancy before marriage was an unforgiveable sin, which her father 'would never have forgiven her for'.[15] A younger female writer, who had been at college in the early 1960s, remembered that even then it had been unusual to have sex before marriage. The girls in her college had conducted a 'poll of virgins', and only two of her peers had admitted to no longer describing themselves as such.[16] A friend, she recalled, had been expelled for becoming pregnant. When she protested against the injustice of this, she herself had been threatened with expulsion. Both of these women thought that the modern acceptance of young people living together before getting married was a sensible practice, and they saw easier access to birth control and the availability of safer abortion as blessings.

These were common sentiments. Several of the older women recalled friends and acquaintances who had suffered clandestine abortions. One remembered a seventeen-year-old friend who, having found herself pregnant by an American soldier, had sought a 'back-street' abortion which had killed her.[17] An elderly widow recorded that she had worked in a hospital as a ward sister before the legalization of abortion: she could recall three young women having died through botched abortions, two more having been seriously disabled, and even more who had suffered chronic conditions as a result of their experiences.[18] None of the women writing in response to the directive regretted the advances in birth control or its availability. One observed wryly that she had had two children in two years without contraception and, had it not been available, she might well have had another twenty-four by the time of writing.[19]

There was a great deal of support among older respondents for the idea of young people living together. This was often seen as an opportunity to explore sexuality, but more importantly as a way of testing compatibility: a sensible precautionary practice before marrying. A seventy-year-old woman concluded: 'On the whole I think the modern custom of living together before marriage is excellent. You jolly well know what you are getting!'[20] A younger woman thought it essential to cohabit before committing, explaining that in her view this was 'nothing to do with sex, but I think that only by living with someone can you see if you can live with them—is he a slob, is she grumpy in the mornings, does he do his fair share of housework?'[21] One younger writer observed that living together had now become the norm: to marry without a period of cohabitation might be seen as risky, 'almost like breaking convention'.[22]

Some of the older women writers mentioned their regret that they had known so little about sex when they had been young. They felt that they had 'missed out' on sexual pleasure. A female respondent who had been married and divorced twice regretted that 'I didn't even know I had a clitorus [sic] until I was over 46 years old'.[23] Other women respondents recorded that the availability of safe contraception had allowed them to live adventurous sexual lives, both before and after marriage. A sixty-three-year-old respondent told Mass Observation that she had loved her husband as a man and as the father of her children during a thirty-year marriage, but that her strongest sexual relationships had been with lovers.[24] She had learned through experience that it was possible to love more than one man at the same time, and did not herself feel anything like sexual jealousy. She had been thankful to be of a generation able to rely on contraception and the possibility of abortion:

> Contraception via the FPA [Family Planning Association] enabled me to plan both my pregnancies and to limit the size of my family to two. It also enabled me to take the risk of extramarital sex and to have a lover long after it would have been advisable to have children.[25]

Older women sometimes confessed that in looking back, they had found themselves questioning why they had married so young. One respondent, who had given birth just before her sixteenth birthday and who later married, now felt that she had made a mistake in having tried to use the man involved as 'an escape route from a miserable home life'.[26] Another wrote: 'I got married because girls did—it legitimated sex, allowed one to leave home, set up house and have babies.'[27] Now divorced, with an active sex life but no wish to remarry, this writer no longer considered these reasons valid. A lingering sense of regret about the ways in which having married so early in life may have constrained opportunities for personal growth and pleasures underlay some of the replies from widows who had stayed in marriages, but who often confessed (somewhat guiltily) to enjoyment of new freedoms after their husbands had died. 'I know this must sound awful, but

I enjoy being a widow', wrote one seventy-year-old. 'I like not having to dish up a meal at set times, pleasing myself what time I go to bed at night, and best of all, having a double bed all to myself.' She added: 'I love being able to do what I want when I want and how I want, which I have never been able to do before.'[28]

There were many ways in which female respondents to the Close Relationships directive thought that women's lives had improved since the 1950s. Alongside control over childbearing, opportunities for a greater degree of economic independence were seen as crucial. Some women remembered the indignity of having to beg for housekeeping money from husbands who were opposed to their wives going out to work. Women welcomed the wider opportunities for employment, particularly insofar as these gave them more choices. One woman thought that there was still some way to go here, but that:

> Once women have the economic independence and can show that they can survive even with children in tow, this will give others more confidence to make *choices* in their lives that would have been absolutely unthinkable to their mothers.[29]

Similar sentiments were expressed by another older woman, who reflected:

> So many of my mother's generation stayed married, literally, for bed and board. They hadn't been trained or prepared sufficiently to support themselves in a time of trouble, either widowhood, or a disastrous marriage. Many women of my generation were in that situation also. It is terrible.[30]

Many respondents believed that the relationships between men and women had also improved, alongside the strengthening of women's position. A factor singled out as important here was the abolition of National Service, which was seen as having exacerbated divisions between the sexes. In one particularly thoughtful response to the directive, one woman wrote:

> When I grew up there was not much alternative to marriage for girls. It seems to me that girls now have everything they want, but I am sure there are different problems for them. I think young men now are much more understanding and willing to share everything with their wives. When I was married most men had been in the army or were doing National Service and this made a deep division of the sexes. After National Service was stopped the men were different.
>
> Army life coarsens men and devalues women, now young men seem to like and appreciate women more and they are real partners, not as they used to be, either on pedestals, dolls, or slaves to men.[31]

This woman was optimistic about the drift of recent history: in her view, increased sexual freedoms, more genuine equality, and possibilities of financial independence for women made for more respectful and balanced relationships. To her, 'Relationships in the 1990s seem almost ideal', although she admitted that 'she was looking from the outside' and that young people might feel differently.[32]

Some of the men who responded to the Close Relationships directive were more guarded in judging the impact of recent social change. A few confessed to feeling confused by changing—and sometimes blurred—expectations about masculinity. A widower looked back on his marriage (he and his wife had married in 1947) and reflected on the assumptions that he had made about a husband's role:

> We both grew up during an era when women's role in the home was more dominant than today. Although conscious of placing my

wife upon a pedestal, nevertheless, I never thought that I should share either cooking or housework. I always thought that if I did the washing up I was behaving honourably. Even when she also worked, I still accepted that my dinner would be ready upon my arrival home from the office.[33]

There was a touch of frustration in such accounts: some husbands weren't altogether sure what their wives expected of them anymore. One man reflected uneasily and slightly resentfully about his experience of a long marriage:

I am aware that I have never been able to be the sort of person my wife would have liked me to be—sweet-talking, demonstratively loving, conventionally dressed, outgoing socially, continually appreciative, helpful in the house foreseeing what should be done before having to be told—but I think the media has a lot to answer for here in creating expectations beyond the capability of the average mere male. And now in later life she is led to expect a fulfilling sex life from an ageing husband with a much reduced libido, conveniently forgetting how he had to restrain himself in his prime for fear of an unwanted pregnancy in days before the pill.[34]

This man conceded that things had improved between him and his wife more recently: 'At last, after being remarkably insensitive to my feeling of inadequacy, she has come to terms with it, and is now very understanding.' Concluding, he suggested: 'The whole business of sex for the male of my generation has been influenced by Romantic literature, theatre and cinema.' He thought that women's new expectations of men had made life increasingly difficult.[35]

Some older men emphasized that they had been brought up to assume that men had stronger sexual appetites than women, and that they had been astonished to learn, often rather late in life, that this was by no means always the case. Respondents sometimes regretted that they hadn't known this in their younger days. One divorced male came over as wide-eyed when he described himself as having been spoiled for choice. He marvelled at having met 'ladies who were very prim and proper but never-the-less very keen on having sex'.[36] He had lived on his own for a few years after parting from his wife, and

> during that time had trouble with not-so-young ladies wanting to sleep with me. What surprised me mostly was that these ladies were educated and in responsible jobs. Even so, they had no inhibitions about getting their man. In my younger days it was the man who had to do the chasing.[37]

This writer comes across as a little unsure about the 'femininity' of female sexual agency when he expresses relief in having met the woman who was to become his second wife, who he was relieved to describe as 'by no means a man-chaser'.

Some male respondents wholeheartedly welcomed the changes of recent decades. One writer who had clearly reflected a great deal on the history and nature of close relationships submitted that 'the concept of love is not just historically variable but stretched, vague, dubious, spiky. It is often the mask for self-love, or a desire to control another person.'[38] He described himself as 'a romantic egalitarian'. What he himself sought in any relationship was equality: 'I dislike a power imbalance, or a guru-disciple symbiosis.' This writer was of the opinion that gay liberation had 'helped heteros such as myself, uncomfortable with normative masculinity but nervous or ignorant for so long about the alternatives'. In short, he believed that both 'feminism and the gay intervention' had 'made it possible to rethink masculinity'.[39]

The majority of both male and female responses to the Close Relationships directive were positive about the social changes which had reshaped marriage since the Second World War. However, the responses to the Mass Observation directive on Women and Men, one year later in 1991, present a very different picture. This second directive similarly probed people's attitudes to gender equality, but writers were also encouraged to share their thoughts about 'liberated women', 'new men', and feminism. These prompts tended to polarize responses and unleashed a torrent of antagonism, particularly from older women writers, towards feminists and feminism.

There was perceptible ambiguity in some of these responses. A number of women declared themselves eager to see more equality between the sexes, but hostile to feminism. Feminists were seen as 'too militant' and 'aggressive'. Their political stance was often dismissed as unproductive on the grounds that their tactics were held to have alienated men. One woman, who described herself as retired, independent, and very much 'a liberated woman', nevertheless condemned feminists:

> I don't think a feminist is the same [as a liberated woman]. She belongs to the same ilk that burned its bras years ago. (I never thought much of that idea—an uplift made you feel good!). She seems to be aggressive unnecessarily about all sorts of matters, trivial or important, which of course brings out aggression in the opposition. As my stepfather used to say, 'You catch more flies with honey than with vinegar' and so I doubt if any changes in favour of women have been brought about by feminists.[40]

Feminists were berated for being unfeminine or 'rampant man-haters', for 'ranting and raving about men'.[41] One woman described

them as 'the butch type who decide to become bricklayers'.[42]
Another confessed:

> I am unsure what a 'New Man' or a 'Liberated Woman' are, but I do
> feel that a feminist is far from female. To me such a person is hard,
> calculating, and wants the best of both the male and female world.
> I do not like feminists (i.e. Germaine Greere!) [sic][43]

Crude, unflattering stereotypes very similar to those rehearsed in
the anti-suffragist literature of the 1900s were all too evident.
Speaking of feminists, one man sneered: 'isn't it strange that these
are usually Amazonian or plain-as-a-pikestaff types who have no
man of their own?'[44] A woman who had been successful in her
career and who expressed her approval of 'liberated women'
nevertheless sketched a virulent caricature of feminists as 'stri-
dent and unreasonable', 'dressing to repel, putting on vast quantities of weight and neglecting to comb their usually filthy looking
hair'.[45] Another female writer's hostility to feminists was even
more vitriolic. In her opinion, feminists were humourless, end-
lessly whingeing on about the wrongdoings of men. They used to
throw nagging wives in the duckpond years ago, this writer added,
menacingly.[46] If they couldn't be ducked as witches then perhaps
feminists should all be sent off to a desert island, she suggested,
where she had no doubt that they would all go on fighting among
themselves but nobody would have to listen to them anymore.

This kind of folk-devilling of feminists, casting them in the role
of witches or pantomime Ugly Sisters, was largely absent in the
responses of the younger women. Younger women were less well
represented on the Mass Observation panel generally, but several
of them had no compunction in declaring themselves feminists at

the outset. Interestingly, it was altogether less evident in the replies of men. One or two of the men who submitted hostile representations of feminism qualified these with comments which showed an awareness of media representations and stereotypes. A male respondent who described an image of feminists as 'butch and arrogantly flat-chested', for instance, took pains to point out that this was a viewpoint common in the media, but one which he himself didn't share.[47]

There were women, too, who were keen to distance themselves from the sea of negative representations. One woman admitted: 'I still think of "feminist" as a derogatory term and have a stereotype image of an unattractive, aggressive, hectoring, narrow-minded man-hater', but went on more thoughtfully to confess:

> I don't actually know anyone fitting this description, but I do know happy, confident, ambitious and attractive females who work hard to make a success of careers and relationships without being over-bearing—or, on the other hand, doormats![48]

Another woman similarly found herself questioning stereotypes, so that her views became clearer in the course of answering the directive from Mass Observation. A divorcée, she welcomed new opportunities for work and independence but thought that there was still some way to go: 'women are not on the winning side yet.' 'I didn't think until I wrote this that I was a feminist', she reflected, 'but now I think I am', adding: 'I don't have to have hairy legs or hate men to be a feminist, do I?'[49]

Writers gave a wide range of responses to questions about the 'New Man'. Most understood the term to refer to a man who shared domestic tasks and family responsibilities. Few male respondents were as openly hostile to this idea as the observer who wrote: 'Yes, the "new man" does exist. Wimp would be the best way to describe him.'[50] Several women expressed scepticism. 'I am inclined to believe he is a figment of someone's imagination', wrote one woman.[51] Another was more contemptuous: 'What is a New Man? No idea. If he is anything like the old man you can keep him, Suspect it is all bull.'[52] Others were more reflective. One emphasized that the idea of 'the new man' was a little misleading because family-minded men had always existed: her own father, she remembered, had been just as tender and caring as her mother.[53] One gay respondent suggested that the idea of the new man was essentially a heterosexual concept: he thought that gay men found much less difficulty in committing to equality around the home.[54] For several writers the idea of the new man remained an ideal, and one which was tied up with the idea of female liberation. An observer who identified herself as a feminist elaborated in fulsome detail:

> To me, New Man is a man who rejects the image of macho masculinity in favour of self-discovery, honesty, compassion, vision and integration. He is someone who seeks wholeness both for himself and the world. Yes, he does exist, and I know lots of them, mostly in the 30 to 50 age group. He is very definitely not a wimp, devaluing himself or putting himself in an inferior position to women (as I have heard New Man described) but a person seeking equality and this is also what being a liberated woman is all about—self-discovery, honesty...and freedom to be oneself.[55]

That younger men were—in the main—considered to be less wedded to 'macho' stereotypes inclined some women to a belief that society was moving in the right direction, even if there was still a long way to go before true equality could be held to exist. But others felt that the rapidity of recent change was causing confusion: 'Men and women should know what is expected of them', wrote one such woman, 'but it is very muddled at the moment. This is causing a lot of divorce, heart attacks and discontent as well as unemployment.'[56] A handful of men spoke similarly of confusion, complaining that when they acted in a way that they supposed reflected good manners or 'gentlemanly behaviour' they were running a risk of being dismissed as patronizing, sexist, or male chauvinist pigs.[57]

Some of the attitudes represented in the Mass Observation directives resonate with Susan Faludi's extensive analysis of the backlash against feminism in the 1980s. However, the most vituperative attacks on feminists in this body of evidence came from women rather than from men, and they were less an expression of any conviction that feminism 'had gone too far' than a form of shadow-boxing with crude stereotypes of feminists as unnatural monsters, aggressive and bristling with antipathy towards men. It is as if there was a need to project anxiety and hostility onto scapegoats. This served to reinforce the writers' confidence in their own femininity, to reassure themselves, perhaps, that they might continue to bask in the light of masculine approval. At the same time, most of these women were well aware of the improvements in women's position over the previous decades and they welcomed these improvements, tending to underplay the extent to which they might be attributable to feminism.

The attitudes reflected by the panel of Mass Observers cannot be taken as representative of British society as a whole, but they nevertheless furnish insights into what was probably a common position of many in the 1990s: that is, a basic acceptance that many of the social changes affecting relationships between men and women had been for the good. Women not uncommonly expressed a belief that women's progress towards equality still had some way to go, but this was often went hand in hand with a certain protectiveness towards men, and a palpable desire to avoid behaviour that might fuel sexual antagonism.

Most writers welcomed the fact that women had more choices than in the past. And apart from the one or two observers inclined to dismiss the 'new man' as 'a wimp', most saw more caring and sharing between the sexes in the domestic arena as a good thing. Many women judged younger men to be more confident in relationships and role sharing than their elders. Although some of the men commented on difficulties in adjusting to new expectations about manhood, others welcomed these changes. There was scarcely any evidence of what one might describe as a full-blown 'crisis of masculinity' in this sample.

Nonetheless, discussions about a new 'crisis in masculinity' proliferated in the last decade of the twentieth century. These discussions were wide-ranging. There were attempts to blame feminism for having upset the balance of the sexes. Girls were doing so well at school, it was often argued, that they were outperforming boys: the boys being reduced to sullen and resentful non-compliance or aggression and hostility in the classroom.[58] 'Laddish' and sexist behaviour was encouraged by a new genre of men's magazines described as 'lads' mags': *Maxim*, *Zoo*, *Nuts*, and *Loaded*. Young men, it was suggested, no longer knew how to behave as lovers, husbands, or fathers.[59] Selfish individualism drove young mothers into doing without men, others complained, with fathers reduced to walk-on parts as weekend visitors, in danger of losing credibility with their own children.[60] Fathers' groups were founded and flourished on both sides of the Atlantic, some more militant and misogynist than others: since the courts were widely seen as giving preference to mothers in custody cases, most of these groups were dedicated to extending men's rights in care, control, and access to their natural children.[61] In North America, guru of the men's movement Robert Bly's vision of the Wild Man inspired nostalgia for some imaginary lost essence of primeval masculinity.[62] Men, like women, comforted themselves with myths, legends, and fairy tales in the forest.

There were very different views about just how real, or how severe, this turn-of-the-century crisis in masculinity actually was. In North America, Susan Faludi followed up her work on the backlash against women with a study of dispossessed men: *Stiffed: The Betrayal of the American Man* (1999).[63] This focussed mainly on the plight of blue-collar, working-class men threatened by unemployment at a time of rapid industrial change. It was often compared to the 1997 British film *The Full Monty*, directed by Peter Cattaneo: a major commercial success, which showed men as dignified and resourceful in the face of job loss and personal crises. The film celebrates male camaraderie without hostility to women.[64] In Britain, *The Guardian*'s film critic Jonathan Romney characterized the film as political in the gentlest way, though its ending, he submitted, was 'all feel-good fairy-tale'.[65]

There were marked regional variations in unemployment in the 1980s and 1990s. In Britain's industrial north, men who had been brought up to think of themselves as providers and who now found themselves out of work suffered disproportionately. In both Britain and North America, the growth of information technology-based industries were shaping new forms of work identity for both men and women.

One important consequence of the perceived crisis affecting men was a new interest in the history of masculinity. When social historian Peter Stearns published *Be a Man! Males in Modern Society* in 1979, he was breaking new ground: masculinity had been taken for granted and it certainly wasn't a subject thought worthy of historical scrutiny.[66] The work of British historian John Tosh did much to change things. Tosh's detailed investigations into masculine experience and ideas about nineteenth-century manhood helped to establish a new historical field.[67] Reflecting upon developments in the field in 2005, Tosh observed wryly that fifty years ago, any 'mention of manhood was most likely to signal a pep talk about courage and duty addressed to teenage boys'.[68] Yet the gendered study of men had to be considered 'indispensable to any serious feminist historical project'. The importance of histories of gender was that they showed how social expectations of men and women were linked, and by showing how these expectations had changed through time, they strengthened faith in the possibilities of more change in the future.

Studies of masculinity, both historical and contemporary accounts, have proliferated since the 1990s, leading to reviews of clusters of books on similar themes in academic journals and a steady stream of often alarmist headlines in the press. One particularly vexed account was Irish psychiatrist Anthony Clare's book *On Men: Masculinity in Crisis*, first published in 2000.[69] Clare, a well-known and popular radio broadcaster, writer, and TV personality in the UK, contended that men were in serious trouble. Chapter headings such as 'The Dying Phallus' and 'Farewell to the Family Man' are indicative of the book's tone. Clare was an engaging writer, drawing freely on his own personal experience in addition to backing up his argument with rich scholarly references. Reflecting on his own upbringing, he confessed that he saw with hindsight that learning to be a man had been all about competition and pretending to a confidence he had rarely (if ever) felt: he had become accustomed, like his peers, to suppress any sign of vulnerability. He had learned further that as a man, whatever career he chose would be of key importance, because he would have to earn enough to support a wife and family. Only in recent years had he begun to question these tenets, and to see himself as having been shaped by social assumptions in a specific historical context.

Drawing on historical writing by John Tosh and social and historical studies of fatherhood by Adrienne Burgess and others, Clare's argument was that recent history had undermined men as fathers and that they were often effectively squeezed out of family life.[70] Though he was sympathetic to feminism, he thought that relationships between the sexes had deteriorated: divorce was ever more common, and the importance that society put on motherhood had led to an undervaluing of men's role in the family. The result was that many children lost contact with their fathers:

> For a growing number of children in the developed world, Father was no longer even a shadowy figure, playing a walk-on role in the portrait of family life; he had become a memory, in many instances airbrushed right out of the family picture.[71]

This was unwarrantedly pessimistic. It isn't easy to get a clear picture of longer term trends in divorce rates in Britain and North America for a whole variety of reasons. Different age groups show different patterns, and marital breakup has been highest among the 'baby boomer' generation, continuing into later life.[72] Younger cohorts show lower divorce rates, but this reflects the trend towards cohabitation rather than marriage in the first place. There is controversy among demographers and statisticians keen to draw lessons from history.[73] While divorce rates rose dramatically in the 1970s, some have argued that they levelled off after the 1980s, others that they have continued to rise. A recent report from Britain's Office for National Statistics (ONS) points out that in 2016, there were 8.9 divorces of opposite sex couples per 1000 married men and women, an increase of 4.7 per cent since 2015; however, divorce rates in 2016 were 20 per cent lower than their recent peak in 2003–4.[74] The ONS also reports that numbers of lone-parent families in the UK have been decreasing in recent years (from 3 million in 2015 to 2.8 million in 2017), and that the proportion of lone-parent families with dependent children has stayed roughly the same (around 25 per cent) for a decade. Yet none of this tells us anything about fathers or the quality of parenting. Though most 'lone parents' are female, we can't assume that fathers are completely out of the picture. Nor can we assume that married couples are more committed parents than those who cohabit without any legal ceremony.

There is a quite a lot of evidence, on the other hand, to suggest that men have become increasingly involved with their children. There have been important cultural and social shifts since the end of the Second World War. Men are now frequently present at the birth of their offspring. Only about 10 per cent of fathers attended the birth of their children in 1960, the process of labour being seen as primarily a woman's business: by the 1990s, more than 90 per cent of fathers witnessed their children's entry into the world.[75] Working men now have opportunities—even if limited—for paternal leave. They carry babies in slings and backpacks and push buggies, without being routinely sneered at for their efforts. In North America, Robert L. Griswold and Ralph LaRossa have explored the emergence of more emotionally committed, hands-on forms of fatherhood in the later decades of the twentieth century, and more recently, historian Laura King has published a detailed history of fatherhood in modern Britain.[76] These studies highlight new expectations about men and parenting. Far from Anthony Clare's bleak vision of being squeezed out of family life, the research shows that fathers are increasingly expected to play a central part in it.

When Phil Hogan, a journalist writing for Britain's *Observer* newspaper, began a weekly column about his experience of day-to-day parenthood in the 1990s, he was breaking new ground.[77] He later recalled that his editor of the time had described it as 'a woman's column, written by a man'.[78] Hogan remembered a distinct sense of making it up as he went along, but subsequently took pride in the sense of having shared hands-on childcare since the birth of his first son in 1988:

> At least I was up there with the 'new' men of 1988, attending ante-natal classes and helping to choose a buggy (the new word for pushchair) at Mothercare. We found ourselves bandying terms like 'amniocentesis' and 'dilation'. We learnt that a pregnant woman might dine on liver and Guinness (I am not sure if this is still the advice of doctors) and worked at the secrets of controlled breathing and lumbar massage. We were given our lists of things to take to the hospital—sandwiches, a drink, a crossword—to help pass the hours while our wives or girlfriends rehearsed the primal groaning that would grow more and more unearthly towards the final push.[79]

Not everyone was sympathetic. Hogan recalled 'being jeered at by builders one morning as I hurried along to the childminder's with Baxter [his eldest son] in his sling'.[80] But a decade later conditions were very different. Newspaper columns by male journalists recording the joys and challenges of everyday parenting had caught on:

The Observer's Tim Dowling followed in Phil Hogan's footsteps.[81] Women still took responsibility for the bulk of childcare, but fathers were much more likely to be involved with everyday routines.

The changes across Britain and North America were uneven. A study of men's changing commitments to family and work in New York by sociologist Kathleen Gerson in 1993 showed that around a third of her sample of men clung to traditional roles as providers, reluctant to involve themselves in what was still considered women's work.[82] Another third of her interviewees had tended to steer clear of marriage and family responsibilities altogether. But the final third of the men interviewed could be described as 'involved' fathers, who regarded the time that they spent with families and children as an important part of their identity.

Both men's and women's expectations and their ideas about their rights and responsibilities as parents were being transformed. Husbands divorced from wives were setting up fathers' groups and men's rights associations to campaign for more generous access arrangements and to challenge women's claims to sole custody. Where men did feel squeezed out of liberal access to their young children, they were fighting back, and not always in a militant, headline-grabbing fashion: there has been a growing acceptance of the idea that children benefit from regular contact with fathers as well as mothers. Being involved in the day-to-day care of children was less and less likely to be viewed as unmanly behaviour. In 1987 British art retailer Athena Reproductions published a poster featuring a shirtless male model holding a young baby. Spencer Rowell's photograph of a sensitive, caring man had huge appeal: more than five million copies of the poster were sold. Adam Perry, the model for this iconic image of the New Man, confessed himself overwhelmed, and found his life irrevocably

17. Spencer Rowell's photograph of a sensitive, caring man for Athena Reproductions, 1987

changed, by the torrent of female adulation that resulted.[83] New Men with a commitment to hands-on child care were becoming seen as both attractive and desirable. Footballer David Beckham had the names of his children tattooed on his body. Women's dreams of family life were changing and many now hoped and expected to find partners who would take an equal part in parenting. Some still complained that they shouldered more than their fair share of responsibility in looking after children, but the culture had nevertheless changed in ways that were basically consonant with the long-term goals of feminism.

Notes

1. Private Eye, *Book of Wimmin* (London: Private Eye, 1986). The illustration described, by Michael Heath, is featured on the cover.
2. Grant, Linda, *Sexing the Millennium: Women and the Sexual Revolution* (New York: Grove Press, 1994).
3. Ibid. 3–15.
4. Ibid. 3.
5. Collins, Marcus, *Modern Love: An Intimate History of Men and Women in Twentieth Century Britain* (London: Atlantic, 2003), 4.
6. Ibid. 167–206. See esp. 186.
7. Ibid. 199.
8. The literature on these subjects is voluminous. A good starting point is Pedersen, S., *Family, Dependence and the Origins of the Welfare State: Britain and France 1914–1945* (Cambridge: Cambridge University Press, 1995). See also Allen, Ann Taylor, 'Employment of Endowment? The Dilemma of Motherhood 1890–1914' in the same author's *Feminism and Motherhood in Western Europe, 1890–1970: The Maternal Dilemma* (New York: Palgrave Macmillan, 2005). On wages for housework see Malos, Ellen, *The Politics of Housework* (Cheltenham: New Clarion Press, 1995).
9. McRobbie, Angela, 'Young Women and Consumer Culture', *Cultural Studies*, vol. 22, no. 5, 2008, 531–50; Brunsdon, Charlotte, 'Feminism, Postfeminism, Martha, Martha and Nigella', *Cinema Journal*, vol. 44, no. 2, 2005, 110–16. See also Munford, Rebecca and Waters, Melanie, *Feminism and Popular Culture: Investigating the Postfeminist Mystique* (New Brunswick: Rutgers University Press, 2014); Scharff, C., *Repudiating Feminism: Young Women in a Neo-Liberal World* (Abingdon: Routledge, 2016).
10. Brunsdon, 'Feminism, Postfeminism', 112. The American TV series *Buffy the Vampire Slayer*, created by Joss Whedon and starring Sarah Michelle Gellar as Buffy, aired on The WB/UPN 1997–2003; *Ally McBeal*, created by David E. Kelley and starring Calista Flockhart, aired on Fox 1997–2002.
11. McRobbie, 'Young Women and Consumer Culture'.
12. Aronson, Pamela, 'Feminists or "Postfeminists"? Young Women's Attitudes towards Feminism and Gender Relations', *Gender and Society*, vol. 17, no. 6, December 2003, 903–22. See also Scharff, *Repudiating Feminism*.

13. See, for instance, Hall, Elaine J. and Rodriguez, Marnie Salupo, 'The Myth of Postfeminism', *Gender and Society*, vol. 17, no. 6, December 2003, 876–902.
14. For the history of Mass Observation see Hinton, James, *The Mass Observers: A History, 1937–1949* (Oxford: Oxford University Press, 2013) and Hubble, Nick, *Mass Observation and Everyday Life: Culture, History, Theory* (Basingstoke: Palgrave Macmillan, 2005).
15. Mass Observation Archive (MOA), Replies to Close Relationships Directive, 1990, S 474.
16. Ibid. A 1473.
17. Ibid. H 260.
18. Ibid. L 1991.
19. Ibid. R 2399.
20. Ibid. M 1375.
21. Ibid. T 1826.
22. Ibid. S 808.
23. Ibid. M 1536.
24. Ibid. M 2164.
25. Ibid.
26. Ibid. M 1201.
27. Ibid. M 1979.
28. Ibid. W 1505.
29. Ibid. A 1530.
30. Ibid. H 655.
31. Ibid. L 1884.
32. Ibid.
33. Ibid. T 2459.
34. Ibid. H 2269.
35. Ibid.
36. Ibid. M 1450.
37. Ibid.
38. Ibid. R 1671.
39. Ibid.
40. MOA Replies to Women and Men Directive, 1991, B 89.
41. Ibid. B 1391.
42. Ibid. C 706.
43. Ibid. D 1685.

44. Ibid. B 1654.
45. Ibid. S 1570.
46. Ibid. S 1089.
47. Ibid. S 2067.
48. Ibid. B 1215.
49. Ibid. S 1012.
50. Ibid. H 1543.
51. Ibid. B 89.
52. Ibid. B 1224.
53. Ibid. A 2168.
54. Ibid. G 2284.
55. Ibid. H 2447.
56. Ibid. C 1191.
57. See for instance, B 1654, MOA Replies to Women and Men Directive.
58. See, for instance, Sommers, Christina Hoff, *The War Against Boys: How Misguided Feminism is Harming Our Young Men* (New York: Touchstone, 2000).
59. See for example discussion by Simon Midgley in *The Independent*, 14 November 1993, https://www.independent.co.uk/life-style/is-this-man-confused-feminism-and-social-pressures-are-confounding-the-modern-male-true-or-false-1504236.html, accessed 23/08/2018. See also Knox, Robbie, ''90s Lad Culture Was Beautiful', *Huffpost*, 'Building Modern Men', 17/11/2015, https://www.huffingtonpost.co.uk/robbie-knox/lad-culture_b_8582284.html, accessed 23/08/2018. For interesting comparison with male responses to an earlier 'wave' of feminism see Kimmel, Michael S., 'Men's Responses to Feminism at the Turn of the Century', *Gender and Society*, vol. 1, no. 3, September 1987, 261–83.
60. See for instance Ladd-Taylor, Molly and Umansky, Lauri, *'Bad Mothers': The Politics of Blame in Twentieth-Century America* (New York: New York University Press, 1998); Thane, Pat and Evans, Tanya, *Sinners? Scroungers? Saints? Unmarried Motherhood in 20th-Century England* (Oxford: Oxford University Press, 2012); also Song, Miri, 'Changing Conceptions of Lone Parenthood in Britain: Lone Parents or Single Mums?' *European Journal of Women's Studies*, vol. 3, 1996, 377–97.
61. In the UK, a *Families Need Fathers* group was founded in 1974; *Fathers4Justice* dates from 2001. For the multiplicity of fathers' groups in North America founded between the 1970s and 2000 see entry by

Williams, Gwyneth I., in Baer, Judith A., *Historical and Multicultural Encyclopedia of Women's Reproductive Rights in the United States* (Westport: Greenwood Press, 2002), 81ff.

62. Bly, Robert, *Iron John: A Book about Men* (Boston: Addison Wesley, 1990).
63. Faludi, Susan, *Stiffed: The Betrayal of the American Man* (New York: W. Morrow and Co., 1999).
64. *The Full Monty*, British comedy, 1997, directed by Peter Cattaneo, screenplay by Simon Beaufoy. Set in Sheffield in the early 1970s.
65. Romney, Jonathan, review of *The Full Monty* in *The Guardian*, 29 August 1997, https://www.theguardian.com/film/1997/aug/29/1, accessed 23/08/2018.
66. Stearns, Peter N., *Be a Man! Males in Modern Society* (New York: Holmes and Meier, 1979).
67. Tosh, John, 'What Should Historians do with Masculinity? Reflections on Nineteenth Century Britain', *History Workshop Journal*, vol. 38, 1994, 179–202.
68. Tosh, John, *Manliness and Masculinities in Nineteenth Century Britain: Essays on Gender, Family and Empire* (Harlow: Pearson, 2005), 13.
69. Clare, Anthony, *On Men: Masculinity in Crisis* (London: Chatto and Windus, 2000).
70. Burgess, Adrienne, *Fatherhood Reclaimed: The Making of the Modern Father* (London: Vermilion, 1997).
71. Clare, A., *On Men: Masculinity in Crisis* (London: Arrow Books, 2001), 136.
72. Olson, Randy, '144 Years of Marriage and Divorce in One Chart', posted 15 June 2015, http://www.randalolson.com/2015/06/15/144-years-of-marriage-and-divorce-in-1-chart/, accessed 23/08/2018; Stepler, R., 'Led by Baby Boomers, Divorce Rates Climb for America's 50+ Population', Pew Research, Fact Tank, News in the Numbers, 9 March 2017, http://www.pewresearch.org/fact-tank/2017/03/09/led-by-baby-boomers-divorce-rates-climb-for-americas-50-population/, accessed 23/08/2018. For UK, see Office for National Statistics (ONS), Divorces in England and Wales, https://www.ons.gov.uk/peoplepopulationand community/birthsdeathsandmarriages/divorce.
73. See, for instance, Kennedy, Sheela and Ruggles, Steven, 'Breaking Up is Hard to Count: The Rise of Divorce in the United States, 1980–2010', *Demography*, vol. 51, no. 2, April 2014, 587–98.

74. ONS, Statistical Bulletin, Divorces in England and Wales, 2016, https://www.ons.gov.uk/peoplepopulationandcommunity/ birthsdeathsandmarriages/divorce/bulletins/divorcesinenglandand wales/2016op.cit, accessed 23/08/2018.

75. King, Laura, 'Hiding in the Pub to Cutting the Cord? Men's Presence at Childbirth in Britain, c.1940s–2000s', *Social History of Medicine*, vol. 30, no. 2, May 2017, 389–407.

76. Griswold, Robert L., *Fatherhood in America: A History* (New York: Basic Books, 1993); LaRossa, Ralph, *The Modernization of Fatherhood: A Social and Political History* (Chicago: University of Chicago Press, 1997).

    King, Laura, *Family Men: Fatherhood and Masculinity in Britain, c. 1914–1960* (Oxford: Oxford University Press, 2015).

77. Hogan, Phil, 'Him Indoors: How Fathers Grew Up', *The Guardian*, October 25, 2009, https://www.theguardian.com/lifeandstyle/2009/ oct/25/parenting-fatherhood-phil-hogan, accessed 23/08/2018.

78. Ibid. 4.

79. Ibid. 3.

80. Ibid. 4.

81. Dowling, Tim, "'I've Been Good and Bad, Caring but Useless": Tim Dowling on Two Decades of Fatherhood', *The Guardian*, 13 May 2017, https://www.theguardian.com/lifeandstyle/2017/may/13/tim-dowling-sons-growing-up-parenting-lessons-learned-teenagers, accessed 23/ 08/2018.

82. Gerson, Kathleen, *No Man's Land: Men's Changing Commitments to Family and Work* (New York: Basic Books, 1993).

83. Milmo, Cahal, 'The Curse of "Man and Baby": Athena, and the Birth of a Legend', *The Independent*, 16 January 2007, https://www.independent. co.uk/news/uk/this-britain/the-curse-of-man-and-baby-athena-and-the-birth-of-a-legend-432331.html, accessed 29/08/2019.

7

SINGLES CULTURE, *SEX AND THE CITY*, AND FURTHER WAVES OF FEMINISM

The final decades of the twentieth century, and the beginning of the twenty-first, saw what we might describe as the rise of 'singles culture' among young people in towns and cities. A number of factors contributed to this: the expansion of higher education and changes in the workplace; the increasing independence of women; housing conditions; and of course most recently, the technological changes associated with digitization, smartphones, and the growth of the internet. The growth of singles culture was also intimately connected with demographic changes, especially the delaying (or rejection) of marriage and the delaying (or rejection) of childbearing among young people. Increasingly, young women were putting off the early marriage and motherhood that their mothers and grandmothers had so desired. Their dreams and ambitions broadened to include experiments in singledom, dating, and other forms of relationships or cohabitation.

British historian Zoe Strimpel has emphasized that the period from the 1970s to the 1990s was a key time in the evolution of new attitudes to 'singleness'.[1] A state previously depicted as one of *lack*—the sense of someone being outside of, or standing 'in the shadow of', marriage, of *not* having a partner—gave way to a more positive interpretation of the lifestyle of a young person who was able to enjoy sexual freedoms and forms of hedonistic consumption in the city. There were inevitably sex differences in the way this single state was represented: young males were often portrayed as relishing these freedoms more than their female counterparts, who were widely assumed to be more urgently driven to marry and start a family before their 'biological clock' made this unlikely. Strimpel's research has explored changing practices of courtship, focusing on the growth of what she calls 'mediated dating' in the period between the 1970s and the rise of internet dating and smartphone dating applications in Britain after 2000.[2] These were decades in which previously accepted patterns of meeting opposite-sex partners changed radically: the dance-hall and the cinema faded in importance with the rise of bars, gigs, and restaurants in a new urban setting. Strimpel has traced the rise of dating agencies such as Dateline (founded in 1966) and its associated venture, *Singles* magazine (1997–2004), together with the rapid rise of the 'personal ad' in newspapers, ranging from ads in London's *Time Out* to the popular 'Soulmates' column in *The Guardian*.[3]

These social changes were both reflected and dissected in the popular culture of the 1990s. The American sitcom *Friends*, created by David Crane and Marta Kauffman, aired on NBC from 1994 to 2004, attracting large audiences as well as an impressive series of awards. Its representation of the daily lives of six twentysomething white, heterosexual friends living in Manhattan touched on many of the conditions and issues shaping the lives of affluent young workers in the city—meeting in coffee bars, sharing apartments, trying to make sense of work and emotional lives, struggling to understand the differences between romance and friendship.

British writer Helen Fielding's *Bridget Jones's Diary*, first published in book form in 1996, enjoyed massive success worldwide: it had sold more than two million copies by 2006. A film version, starring Renée Zellweger, Hugh Grant, and Colin Firth, followed the book in 2001, and there have been various sequels. *Bridget Jones's Diary* epitomized the ambivalence around female singledom at the turn of the century. Bridget has a successful career and loyal friends but is tormented by family friends and relatives who ask 'How is your love life, Bridget?', and is haunted by the fear that she will 'end up alone'. She struggles with her self-image, her weight, and her appearance; she wrestles with her sexual desire for inappropriate (that is, sexually available but emotionally unavailable) men, who aren't prepared to commit to anything like a permanent relationship with her. The book struck a chord with a whole generation of women. In a survey carried out by *The Guardian* in 2010, it was ranked as one of the ten novels that best defined the twentieth century. Six years later, a BBC *Woman's Hour* panel selected the fictional Bridget Jones alongside real (but, by then, deceased) former Prime Minister Margaret Thatcher as one of seven women who had most impacted on British women's lives over the preceding seventy years.[4]

The six-year run of HBO's hugely popular comedy-drama *Sex and the City* (SATC) (1998–2004), based loosely on Candace Bushnell's short novel of the same name, dramatized the lives of four female friends in New York City. It focused less on these women's working lives than on female friendship and self-image, romantic predicaments, and patterns of consumption: particularly expenditure on fashionable clothing and highly expensive shoes. Lead character Carrie Bradshaw (Sarah Jessica Parker) obsesses over the elusive 'Mr Big': like Bridget Jones, she enjoys the sexual freedoms available to women in the city but romanticizes the unobtainable. The women in *SATC* are glossier than Bridget Jones, but (with the exception of the boldly autonomous Samantha Jones) equally likely to find themselves ambivalent about their single state. Bridget's insecurities about not having a 'serious' boyfriend, and her resentment of those who pity her, lead to late-night binge-drinking with her friend Shazza, during which they drunkenly curse 'smug, narrow-minded married people'.[5] Irritated by a newspaper feature on the loneliness of young city-dwelling singletons, Bridget and her friends fantasize about retaliating with a piece on the misery of the narrow lives of the 'smug marrieds', imagined as young wives who return from work exhausted but 'have to peel potatoes and put all the washing on while their porky bloater husbands slump burping in front of the football demanding plates of chips'.[6] 'Hurrah for singletons', shouts a tipsy Bridget after one late-night drinking session prompted by being stood up, yet again, by her elusive lothario: the flaky, philandering Daniel.

In *Bridget Jones's Diary*, men bent on avoiding emotional entanglement with the women they sleep with are dismissed as 'fuckwits'. Candace Bushnell's original text of *Sex and the City* homed in directly on detachment and defensiveness among young unmarried workers in New York, conveying a pervasive mood of anxiety and unease about relationships and commitment.[7] She refers to men who avoid commitment to female partners as 'toxic bachelors'. Carrie instances her friend Capote Duncan, once 'one of the most eligible bachelors in New York', as an example. Capote had dated a whole series of beautiful, smart, successful women, and everyone assumed that at some point he was bound to fall in love with one of them. But he never did. He was adamant that he didn't want 'a relationship', she explained:

> Doesn't even want to try. Isn't interested in the romantic commitment. Doesn't want to hear about the neurosis in somebody else's head. And he tells women that he'll be their friend, and they can have sex with him, but that's all there is and that's all there's ever going to be.
>
> And it's fine with him. It doesn't even make him sad anymore the way it used to.[8]

Carrie confesses that she understands her friend's cynicism. Recently, she'd found herself saying that she didn't want a relationship because 'at the end, unless you happened to get married, you were left with nothing'.[9] Carrie and her women friends feel smug because they are 'hard and proud of it', fully aware of the emotional cost of having got to that point:

> this place of complete independence where we had the luxury of treating men like sex-objects. It had taken hard work, loneliness, and the realization that, since there might never be anyone there for you, you had to take care of yourself in every sense of the word.[10]

The tone is brittle and bleak—much more so in Candace Bushnell's text than in the TV adaptation that followed it. In the HBO series of *SATC*, the irony is tempered by more humour and romanticism. The friendship between the four women is also underlined, crystallizing into one of the strongest messages of the series as a whole, and encapsulated in the much-quoted remark made by Charlotte in response to Carrie's expression of wistfulness at not having a man in her life who cares for her, of having no soulmate. 'Maybe we should be each other's soulmates', Charlotte suggests, 'and then we could let men be just great nice guys to have fun with'.[11]

Inspirational though this remark has proved for many, there is nonetheless a lingering sadness around discussions of the prospects of unmarried women in *SATC*.[12] In the book, a male lawyer observes that there is a 'window of opportunity' for women to get married in New York, 'somewhere between the ages of twenty-six and thirty-five'. Thereafter: 'They've been around too long. Their history works against them.'[13] This idea, together with that of women's 'biological clocks' ticking, with the danger of time running out should they want to have children, haunts these texts of the 1990s. But it coexists with expressions of the women characters' unease about the prospects of being holed up in the suburbs with small children. In Bushnell's text, Carrie cringes with revulsion at the antics of friends who she perceives parenting has turned into 'Psycho Moms'. These mothers are shown as fretting about their offspring's interaction with nannies and neurotically installing hidden cameras to monitor what is going on in every moment they are separated from their children.[14] The whole business of breastfeeding and 'baby massage', strollers and playgrounds, seems uninviting. In the episode in *SATC* where the women reluctantly go along to a former friend's baby shower, they are all desperate to leave and get back to their single lives in the city.

The themes of these texts and programmes, and particularly those of *SATC*, echo those explored in Rona Jaffe's 1958 novel about urban working women, *The Best of Everything*.[15] But there are also significant differences, which reflect the extent to which society had changed between 1958 and the 1990s. In Jaffe's novel, work and sex are areas of both risk and adventure for young women, who had previously envisaged their adult lives as contained entirely by marriage. You only became 'a career girl' if you failed to secure a fiancé. Most of the girls travelling daily into New York offices saw themselves as merely passing time: 'They go to their typing pool or their calculating machines as to a waiting place, a limbo for single girls who are waiting for love and marriage.'[16] Typical of this was Jaffe's character Mary Agnes, who saw work as a stop-gap, her aspirations for the future contained entirely in her 'cedar hope chest' and epitomized in her plans for the perfect wedding. Some of the girls might nurture ridiculously unrealistic dreams about their future: Jaffe depicts her character April as arriving in New York, her head stuffed with fantasies of becoming a famous actress, 'fed by visions of beautiful women no-one had ever heard of wearing white mink and diamonds and being escorted by handsome older men'.[17] The possibilities of seeing paid work as rewarding, or as an important part of one's identity, were remote. Central character Caroline Bender comes to see her job in publishing as important and to develop a sense of personal competence and ambition, but this development takes time and is presented as one of the main themes of the novel.

Sex, in *The Best of Everything*, is an area fraught with danger for young women. Sexual harassment is shown as ubiquitous, a routine hazard in the workplace. April's combination of pretty, country looks and naive romanticism ensure that she attracts predatory men: she quickly becomes a target for office gropers ('garter-snappers') and unrepentant philanderers. April falls deeply in love with Dexter Key, a handsome young man of good family who is emotionally manipulative and unscrupulous: he fakes commitment to her as a ploy to get her into bed with him, but has no intention whatsoever of marrying her. When April discovers that she is pregnant, Dexter coolly and efficiently arranges for her to have an abortion before abruptly dumping her altogether. Caroline's friend Gregg falls for a worldly, successful writer who is blasé about sex. She tries at first to be sensible about contraception, realizing that she's on a slippery slope which could lead to 'the Home for Unwed Mothers'.[18] But her confidence ebbs with his sophistication and his detachment: she crumbles psychologically and turns into a neurotic, clingy stalker. Sexual entanglement is risky for these women because they lack autonomy and bargaining power—too much depends upon 'securing' a man. Only Caroline comes through as a new type of independent woman, with the confidence to articulate her needs and desires. This growth in autonomy takes time and has its costs. 'When I'm twenty-six, if I'm not married by then, I'm going to take a lover', Caroline muses out loud to April, early in the book.[19] The girls find this a daring but nevertheless rather shocking prospect. By the end of the book, the still unmarried Caroline has acquired a measure of worldliness and sexual experience and we leave her agreeing to go on vacation to Las Vegas with a glamorous male celebrity, who we are given to understand will most probably become the next in a series of lovers.

By the 1990s, representations of young city women's lives had changed, in that work and sex were much more taken for granted and could be treated more lightly and casually, even if they were still depicted as primary aspects of experience and concern. The germs of singles culture which had been apparent in Jaffe's text had developed into a recognizable pattern. Parents receded from importance in narratives of young peoples' lives: peer groups and the ties of mixed-sex friendship had become much more prominent. Pitching the idea for a TV series that would become *Friends* to

NBC, writers Marta Kauffman and David Crane explained that the show would be about:

> Six people in their early 20's who hang out at this coffee house. An after hours insomnia cafe. It's about sex, love, relationships, careers...a time in your life when everything is possible, which is really exciting and really scary. It's about searching for love and commitment and security...and a fear of love and commitment and security. And it's about friendship, because when you are young and single in the city, your friends are your family.[20]

Friends has been much derided by critics who point to the fantasy elements of its setting: the impossibly large and glamorous apartments, the unconvincing work lives, the unlikely affluence, the apparent lack of diversity in New York City. But the series still managed to 'capture lightning in a bottle', resonating with elements of increasingly common experience.[21] The sharing of flats and apartments in towns and cities was now commonplace, even between young people of both sexes, which would have been socially unacceptable in the 1950s. Higher costs of renting, and rocketing house prices in many urban settings, ensured that flat-sharing would remain a feature of metropolitan culture. Young, middle-class women could increasingly be assumed to be independent, the beneficiaries of higher education, and capable of holding down responsible jobs. Bridget Jones is a graduate and works in the media. Miranda, in *SATC*, is a lawyer. The characters in *Friends*, *Bridget Jones's Diary*, and *SATC* are stronger and more autonomous than most of those in *The Best of Everything*: they are much less likely to be portrayed as hapless dupes or victims.

On the other hand, the treatment of working lives in these late twentieth-century texts and programmes can seem superficial when compared with that in Rona Jaffe's novel, partly because there is less attention to the workplace and much more emphasis on patterns of consumption. There is playful irony in Fielding's description of Bridget as trying (and usually failing) to concentrate more on her work than on possibilities for office romance: 'It is great when you start thinking about your career instead of worrying about trivial things—men and relationships', Bridget confides determinedly to her diary.[22] Relationships between the sexes as represented in these texts are much more informal and relaxed than they were fifty years earlier. Bridget flirts with the office lothario, Daniel (an attractive version of what Jaffe would have dubbed an office 'garter-snapper'), at work—but the reciprocity of the flirting and humorous tone pre-empts any serious reading of the relationship as one of sexual harassment. 'Premarital' sex could be assumed to be pretty much universal among young people by the end of the century: marriage itself had receded as a prospect for many, rendering the term itself old-fashioned if not obsolete. But if attitudes around sexuality had relaxed, those around experiences of love and commitment had arguably become more complicated than ever.

Feminist critics were sometimes harsh in their judgement of Bridget Jones and *SATC*, in spite of (or, in part, because of) their immense popularity among women readers and viewers. The women characters in these productions were criticized for lacking willpower, deplored for being too absorbed in body image, fashion, and consumption.[23] Historians keen on dividing the history of feminism into 'waves' often suggest a playing out of second-wave feminism and an entry into what might be designated as a 'third wave' of the movement around the 1980s.[24] It isn't easy to characterize this alleged 'third wave', because, as always, there was a range of differing viewpoints. Some have argued that this plurality of feminist positions was in itself a hallmark of 1980s and 1990s feminism, but neither first nor second-wave feminism had ever been completely monolithic or consistent: there had always been disagreement and divergences. Newish tendencies in the late twentieth century included an interest in identity, language, and 'intersectionality', the latter being a term coined by American legal scholar and civil rights activist Kimberlé Crenshaw in 1989 to emphasize the ways in which different experiences of race, gender, and social class could work together, positioning people differently in relation to their understanding of politics and social oppression.[25] Judith Butler's influential work *Gender Trouble: Feminism and the Subversion of Identity* (1990) argued that masculinity and femininity were performances rather than identities, and could not be thought of as innate in any way.[26] And the 1980s and 1990s were decades which saw a great deal of controversy among feminists about pornography.[27] Was pornography always oppressive of women? Were all heterosexual men capable of misogyny or even violence towards females?

Some of these controversies—particularly the debates over pornography—were acrimonious. In the context of late twentieth-century concerns about sexual abuse, AIDS, and the rise of 'lads' mags', they contributed to a sense of embattlement, and to pessimism about whether the differences between men and women were ultimately reconcilable. Two widely read books which fuelled thinking about the gulf between the sexes at this time were American linguistic professor Deborah Tannen's *You Just Don't Understand: Men and Women in Conversation* (1990) and relationship counsellor John Gray's *Men Are from Mars, Women Are from Venus* (1992).[28] Both studies emphasized gender differences in talking and thinking. For instance, they posited that for women, talking about emotions and difficulties tended to be more important than for men, who often preferred to escape from talk and to withdraw into themselves or into their 'man-caves' for distraction while working unconsciously or instrumentally on finding solutions. Tannen and Gray were criticized for exaggerating the differences between the sexes, but their observations resonated with large sections of the reading public and the books were phenomenally successful.[29] *You Just Don't Understand* rose to the top of the *New York Times'* best-selling list soon after publication, stayed on the list for nearly four years, and was translated into thirty-one languages worldwide. *Men Are from Mars, Women Are from Venus* was still selling well some ten years after publication.

Both Tannen and Gray's books were moderately optimistic, suggesting ways in which heterosexual couples might work on their relationships and intimacy through understanding these differences in styles of communication. But the mood of feminism generally in the 1990s could be difficult to read. There were observers who were concerned that feminist thinking had descended into sometimes abstrusely theoretical academic in-fighting, or a hard-line anti-pornography (and hence puritan and anti-male) stance that risked alienating younger women. The enthusiasm which had accompanied a flourishing of women's studies courses in Britain and America in the late 1970s and 1980s was beginning to wane, leading to discussion, though not to any agreement, about the implications of 'postfeminism'.

Disagreement about what was happening to young women reflected uncertainty about femininity. Was 'Girl Power' simply a slogan, a catchphrase of the popular culture of the 1990s, or did it reflect real social change, a generation of young women coming to maturity with a more developed sense of entitlement and more power and confidence than their predecessors?[30] The idea of femininity as a performance, which might be camped up with elements of irony or parody, subverting expectations and empowering the performer, was evident in the extraordinary cultural success of American pop idol Madonna. But not everyone was persuaded of the potential of basques, fishnets, and killer heels to liberate, especially outside of high-paid, celebrity circles. Madonna's hyper-femininity was controversial, if widely appealing.[31]

Naomi Wolf's best-selling book *The Beauty Myth*, first published in 1991, found an appreciative audience.[32] Wolf argued that the external constraints and corsets of Victorian femininity had given way, a century later, to a new set of pressures on women, largely internalized—she used the image of an 'iron maiden'—whereby they felt compelled to strive for beauty and perfection. She saw this as part of a backlash against the gains of feminism, a kind of conspiracy to keep women in their place. Appearance was everything: young women were bombarded with media images of flawless skin and perfect bodies; older women with images of dewy, wrinkle-free complexions and unrealistic youthful slenderness. Trying to measure up to these standards was leading to an 'epidemic' of anorexia, bingeing and purging, anxiety, and self-loathing, she contended. Wolf's statistics on eating disorders have been called into question, but her arguments appealed to many women, particularly younger women, who were anxious about their looks and bodies.[33]

If young women were seen as being constrained and inhibited by the pressure to *look* perfect, their behaviour was often castigated for the reverse. Reports of young girls dubbed 'ladettes' by the British press regularly drew attention to young women's *lack* of inhibition, their unconstrained drinking and brawling.[34] There was nothing new in such moral panics around girlhood, but a chorus of disapproval around so many aspects of feminine behaviour could make it difficult for young women to make sense of things. It wasn't always easy to see where feminism was going.

In Britain, Natasha Walter's *The New Feminism* (1998) was reasonably positive.[35] In areas such as education, Walter observed that girls were doing well. Women in the 1990s, she suggested, were freer and more powerful than their foremothers. They were forging new paths 'without any markers or goalposts', 'making up their lives as they go along'.[36] 'The feminist revolution' had brought 'phenomenal advances in education and employment, contraception and sexual mores, economic and cultural freedom'. There was some way to go yet, she conceded, but feminism could surely now allow itself 'a little celebration and a little laughter'.[37] Some forms of inequality—and particularly economic inequalities—were proving stubbornly hard to eradicate. But contemporary feminist academics did women no favours, Walter complained: they were too immersed in theory and out of touch with real lives. Identifying the personal and the political, she asserted, had led feminism into a dead end. What was needed was a new form of feminism that would 'unpick' the personal and the political, freeing itself 'from the spectre of political correctness', and leaving women alone to make their own decisions about personal issues, 'how to dress and talk and make love'.[38] The primary goal of the new feminism should be to attack 'the material basis of economic and social and political inequality'.

Just over ten years later, Natasha Walter had entirely changed her mind. 'I am ready to admit that I was entirely wrong', she wrote in *Living Dolls: The Return of Sexism*, which was published by

Virago in 2010.[39] Walter's new book contended that society had turned women into Barbie dolls, fobbing them off with an airbrushed, sexualized, and pink-and-pretty view of femininity and disastrously narrowing their choices. She worried that gender inequalities were increasingly justified as innate. But some reviewers raised an eyebrow at the subtitle—had sexism ever really gone away?[40]

The notion that sexual allure was being muddled up with empowerment, and commodification as a sex object confused with liberation, was by no means new. But these ideas were given new salience by turn-of-the-century discussions of pornography. A new word, 'pornification', entered the language, to suggest the increasing sexualization of society, or the normalization of explicit sexual imagery in the culture generally. Pornification was linked to the increasing availability of pornography on the internet. It was regularly deplored, especially in relation to its alleged effects on children. There was a great deal of concern about teenage boys' immersion in internet pornography, and its influence on their attitudes to girls. The subtitle of American writer Pamela Paul's book *Pornified: How Pornography Is Damaging Our Lives, Our Relationships and Our Families* (2005) is indicative of its approach.[41] Natasha Walter's concerns about the way in which young women were being seduced into crude forms of sexual display and objectification (stripping, certain forms of glamour modelling, pole dancing, etc), confusing these with 'liberation' and 'empowerment,' echoed some of the arguments rehearsed by American journalist Ariel Levy in her book *Female Chauvinist Pigs* (2005).[42] Levy had similarly deplored young girls' involvement in 'raunch culture', where, she argued, they confused genuine sexual freedom with forms of degrading sexual exhibitionism and slutty behaviour that effectively meant they were colluding with their own oppression. Debates around pornography tended to be polarized and vociferous, making it difficult to explore different categories of pornography and sexually explicit material and their uses, by women as well as men, or to ask questions about whether some kinds of pornography might have served a genuinely useful, even educative function.

Natasha Walter contended that a 'new hypersexual culture' redefined female success 'through a narrow framework of sexual allure' and that this was 'shrinking and warping the choices on offer to young women'.[43] But this might have been too gloomy a view, given young women's increasingly impressive performance in higher education in Western societies and their growing representation in a wide range of public positions and employment. Moreover, the early years of the twenty-first century brought a resurgence of interest, among younger women in particular, in feminism. Whether we want to saddle this with the label of a third, fourth, or even a fifth wave of the movement is immaterial: what was significant was that more and more young women seemed to be openly espousing feminism. The growth of the internet was an important contributory factor. Where 'Girl Power' had exhibited itself in fanzines in the 1980s and 1990s, it now became evident digitally, with global reach and implications. The sharing of experiences which had made 'consciousness-raising' such a potent political tool among feminists in the 1960s and 1970s had suddenly become easier than anyone could ever have imagined.

Blogs and websites which facilitated communication and the sharing of ideas between younger feminists included Catherine Redfern's (and later Jess McCabe's) www.thefword.org.uk from 2001, and American blogger Jessica Valenti's Feministing.com from 2004. Kat Banyard's campaigning ukfeminista.org.uk dates from 2010. The array of feminist websites which can be accessed by young women today is dazzling. With this came the potential for political activism on a new scale. The Slutwalk campaign, for instance, began in 2011 when a police officer in Toronto, Canada, suggested that girls might lessen the danger of being subjected to violent rape by not 'dressing like sluts'. It quickly exploded into a series of protest marches all over the world. Tired of hearing the victims of sex crimes blamed for their own sufferings, women in Canada, New York, London, and Melbourne took to the streets, many of them dressed in fishnet stockings, basques, and micro-skirts, refusing to be shamed as 'sluts', and hoisting banners declaring their right to expect protection as citizens and human beings whatever their choice of clothing.[44]

The speed with which feminist campaigning groups and individuals could gather support, and the scale on which this could happen, were new. Those who took to the internet to test ideas were sometimes surprised—if not overwhelmed—by the response. Laura Bates, for instance, a British feminist writer who set up the Everyday Sexism Project website (and its associated Twitter account, @EverydaySexism) in 2012, collected 'hundreds of thousands' of responses over the next few years from women who wanted to share their experiences.[45] These experiences came from all round the world, and they ranged from 'the niggling and normalized to the outrageously offensive and violent'. Bates also received a torrent of abusive messages, menaces, harassment, and even death threats.[46] Going public about this was a strategy which in itself made plain just how much women had to endure from 'everyday sexism' and misogyny, thus legitimating the continuing need for feminism. The same can be said of the more recent

#MeToo campaign, which was sparked by allegations of sexual misconduct on the part of former American film producer Harvey Weinstein in 2017. It quickly flared into an international movement against sexual harassment, particularly in the workplace.[47]

One of the most important aspects of these campaigns has been to highlight the continuing need for a feminism which will address the day-to-day problems women still face in their relations with men, in the family, and in the workplace. Feminism cannot any longer be seen as a body of theory which belongs mainly in the academy, to be argued over by academics. This process of normalization, of the growth of the need for an 'everyday feminism', can be best understood as having accompanied a long period of social change since the 1950s: particularly the gains women have made in education and the workplace, and in terms of self-respect and autonomy. Running parallel with these gains, the decriminalization and growing acceptance of homosexuality as normal rather than pathological, and society's increasing respect for the rights of lesbian, gay, bisexual, and transgender people, have served to further destabilize understandings of gender. It isn't at all easy to pronounce on the meanings of 'femininity' and 'masculinity' these days.

The widespread popular appeal of British writer Caitlin Moran's book *How to be a Woman* (2011) makes sense in this context. Young women needed to think about how they stood in relation to ideas about femininity and feminism, how to clarify their thoughts, and how to behave.[48] Moran's 'larky, joyful' tone assured them that feminism was just too important to be consigned to academic theory: it was at root a declaration of self-respect.[49] What on earth were women thinking if they rejected the idea of feminism, Moran asked? Were they opposed to equal pay? To having a vote? To not being the property of the men they married? To being free to wear jeans? Distorted perceptions of feminism in recent history had led some to assume that 'it was some spectacularly unappealing combination of misandry, misery and hypocrisy, which stood for ugly clothes, constant anger and, let's face it, no fucking', whereas all it really stood for was the right of women to be treated as human beings.[50] And feminism was good for men, too, Moran continued. Men had been ruling the world for some 100,000 years without a break, she quipped, and 'patriarchy must be *knackered* by now'.[51] All women wanted was to take some of the burden of responsibility off men so that they could go off and enjoy themselves a bit more.

Stories about how men have suffered as a result of women's gains in power and autonomy have increasingly been balanced out or contradicted by accounts from male writers who celebrate these changes, reinforcing the long-standing arguments of feminists that both sexes stand to benefit from more gender equality. Writing in the *Financial Times* in 2017, for instance, Janan Ganesh contended that the statistics which were usually summoned as evidence for a crisis of masculinity in the West—suicide rates, figures for drug use and crime—were more usefully linked to social class than to gender.[52] He submitted that younger, more educated males, particularly city-dwellers in London and New York, were enjoying lives of exceptional privilege. These men were enjoying freedoms beyond anything known by their fathers or grandfathers:

> Most mid-20th-century fathers never had a chance to marry a woman with her own career and hinterland, someone more stimulating than a Stepford Wife, or to confess to emotional frailty without derision, or to live alone without fear of gossip. Father-son envy must have multiplied as the world loosened up to accommodate

these things. If so, it was justified envy. The liberation of women was at least as freeing for men, but only if you came along at the right time.[53]

Interviewed about his book *Manxiety: The Difficulties of Being Male* for an article in Britain's *Daily Telegraph*, journalist and *GQ* editor Dylan Jones told editor Jonny Cooper that he thought that men had become more rather than less confident as a result of the changing position of women: as women had become less subservient, sexual relationships had become more balanced.[54] If anything like 'a crisis in masculinity' or 'manxiety' existed, he thought it mainly 'an overreaction to a welcome redressing of the balance of the sexes'. Both sexes stood to gain from this. The changing nature of women's dreams, their desire for fuller, more independent lives, and their hopes for more equal partnerships took some of the pressure off men, too.

Notes

1. Strimpel, Zoe, 'In Solitary Pursuit: *Singles*, Sex War and the Search for Love, 1977–1983', *Cultural and Social History*, vol. 14, no. 5, September 2017, 691–715. See also the same author's 'The Matchmaking Industry and Singles Culture in Britain, 1970–2000', thesis submitted for D. Phil., University of Sussex, 2017.
2. Strimpel, 'Matchmaking Industry and Singles Culture'.
3. Strimpel, 'In Solitary Pursuit'.
4. Irvine, Lindesay, 'The Last Word on the 20th Century's Most Defining Novels', *The Guardian*, 24 May 2007, https://www.theguardian.com/books/booksblog/2007/may/24/thelastwordonthe20thcent, accessed 05/04/2019; BBC Woman's Hour, December 2016, 'The Seven Women Who've Changed Women's Lives', http://www.bbc.co.uk/programmes/articles/PnqpZRvgbvMFBCtrwHhhTZ/the-seven-women-whove-changed-womens-lives, accessed 05/04/2019.

5. Fielding, Helen, *Bridget Jones's Diary* (London: Picador, 1996), 42.

6. Ibid. 244.

7. Bushnell, Candace, *Sex and the City* (London: Abacus, 2008).

8. Ibid. 4–5.

9. Ibid. 5.

10. Ibid. 41.

11. Charlotte's remark from TV version of *SATC*, season 4 episode 1.

12. Even a cursory websearch for this comment will show how inspirational it has proved to many. See, *inter alia*, Fleming, Dessidre, 'How SATC Proved that Our Girlfriends are Our Soulmates and Guys are Just People to Have Fun With', *ScoopWhoop*, 4 May 2018, https://www.scoopwhoop.com/sex-and-the-city-girlfriends-are-our-soulmates-boys-are-just-fun/#.a7wpyapmp, accessed 24/08/2018.

13. Bushnell, *Sex and the City*, 26.

14. Ibid. 157ff.

15. Jaffe, Rona, *The Best of Everything* (London: Penguin, 2011).

16. Ibid. 311.

17. Ibid. 21.

18. Ibid. 88.

19. Ibid. 59.

20. 'Friends: The Original Pitch for the TV Show', *Good in a Room*, https://goodinaroom.com/blog/original-pitch-tv-show-friends/, accessed 24/08/2018.

21. Rzadkiewicz, Olivia, 'Friends at 20: Gunther Remembers the "Lightning in a Bottle" Show', *The Telegraph*, 22 September 2014, https://www.telegraph.co.uk/culture/culturevideo/tvandradiovideo/11112986/Friends-at-20-Gunther-remembers-the-lightning-in-a-bottle-show.html, accessed 24/08/2018.

22. Fielding, *Bridget Jones's Diary*, 221.

23. For instance, Moore, Suzanne, 'Why I Hate Bridget Jones', *The Guardian*, 30 September 2013, https://www.theguardian.com/commentisfree/2013/sep/30/why-i-hate-bridget-jones, accessed 24/08/2018.

24. There have been many attempts to define and clarify the idea of successive 'waves' of feminism. See, for instance, Rampton, Martha, 'Four Waves of Feminism', https://www.pacificu.edu/about/media/four-waves-feminism, accessed 24/08/2018 or Grady, Constance, 'The Waves of Feminism, and Why People Keep Fighting over Them, Explained', Vox.com, 20 June 2018, https://www.vox.com/

2018/3/20/16955588/feminism-waves-explained-first-second-third-fourth, accessed 24/08/2018.

25. Crenshaw, Kimberlé, 'Mapping the Margins: Intersectionality, Identity Politics and Violence against Women of Color', *Stanford Law Review*, vol. 43, no. 6, July 1991, 1241–99; see also 'Kimberlé Crenshaw on Intersectionality, More than Two Decades Later', Columbia Law School website, https://www.law.columbia.edu/pt-br/news/2017/06/kimberle-crenshaw-intersectionality, accessed 24/08/2018.

26. Butler, Judith, *Gender Trouble: Feminism and the Subversion of Identity* (New York and London: Routledge, 1990).

27. The literature relating to feminism and pornography is immense and charged with controversy. See, for instance, Cornell, Drucilla (ed.), *Feminism and Pornography* (Oxford: Oxford University Press, 2000). For a thoughtful introduction to some of the issues, and a helpful bibliography, see Ciclitira, Karen, 'Pornography, Women and Feminism: Between Pleasure and Politics', *Sexualities*, vol. 7, no. 3, August 2004, 281–301.

28. Tannen, Deborah, *You Just Don't Understand: Men and Women in Conversation* (New York: Morrow, 1990); Gray, John, *Men are from Mars, Women are from Venus* (New York: HarperCollins, 1992).

29. See for instance Michael Kimmel lecture 'Mars, Venus or Planet Earth? Women and Men in a New Millennium', YouTube, https://www.youtube.com/watch?v=U-rpbihTvlY, accessed 24/08/2018.

30. See for instance Dyhouse, Carol, 'What Happened to Girl Power?' in *Girl Trouble, Panic and Progress in the History of Young Women* (London: Zed Books, 2013).

31. Churchwell, Sarah, 'Madonna at 60', *The Guardian*, 15 July 2018, https://www.theguardian.com/music/2018/jul/15/sarah-churchwell-on-madonna-power-success-feminist-legacy, accessed 24/08/2018; Schwichtenberg, Cathy, 'Madonna's Postmodern Feminism: Bringing the Margins to the Centre', *Southern Journal of Communication*, vol. 57, no. 2, April 2009, 120–31.

32. Wolf, Naomi, *The Beauty Myth: How Images of Beauty are Used Against Women* (London: Vintage, 1990).

33. Schoemaker, C. 'A Critical Appraisal of the Anorexia Statistics in *The Beauty Myth*', NCBI, *PubMed*, https://www.ncbi.nlm.nih.gov/pubmed/16864310, accessed 24/08/2018.

34. Dyhouse, *Girl Trouble*, 227–9.

35. Walter, Natasha, *The New Feminism* (London: Little, Brown, 1998).

36. Ibid. 2.

37. Ibid. 4, 6.

38. Ibid. 4, 52–3, 64.

39. Walter, Natasha, *Living Dolls: The Return of Sexism* (London: Virago, 2010), 8.

40. See for instance Jessica Valenti's review of Walter's *Living Dolls* in *The Observer*, 31 January 2010, https://www.theguardian.com/books/2010/jan/31/living-dolls-natasha-walter, accessed 25/08/2018.

41. Paul, Pamela, *Pornified: How Pornography is Transforming Our Lives, Our Relationships and Our Families* (New York: Times Books, 2005). See also Paasonen, Susanna, Nikunen, Kaarina, and Saarenmaa, Laura (eds), *Pornification: Sex and Sexuality in Media Culture* (Oxford: Berg, 2007).

42. Levy, Ariel, *Female Chauvinist Pigs: Women and the Rise of Raunch Culture* (New York: Free Press, 2005).

43. Walter, *Living Dolls*, 38.

44. Herriot, Lindsay, 'Slutwalk: Contextualizing the Movement', *Women's Studies International Forum*, vol. 53, November–December 2015, 22–30.

45. Bates, Laura, 'What I Have Learned from Five Years of Everyday Sexism' in *The Guardian*, 17 April 2017, https://www.theguardian.com/lifeandstyle/2017/apr/17/what-i-have-learned-from-five-years-of-everyday-sexism, accessed 25/08/2018.

46. Ibid.

47. Useful here is Burke, Louise, 'The #Me Too Shockwave: How the Movement Has Reverberated Around the World', *The Telegraph*, 9 March 2018, https://www.telegraph.co.uk/news/world/metoo-shockwave/, accessed 25/08/2018.

48. Moran, Caitlin, *How to be a Woman* (London: Ebury Press, 2011).

49. See for instance Emma Brockes's review of *How to be a Woman*, 'These Stilettos Are Not Made for Walking, Nor is the Thong', in *New York Times*, 26 July 2012, https://www.nytimes.com/2012/07/27/books/how-to-be-a-woman-by-caitlin-moran.html, accessed 25/08/2018.

50. Moran, *How to be a Woman*, 81.

51. Ibid. 308.

52. Ganesh, Janan, 'Masculinity Crisis? What Crisis?' *Financial Times*, 17 February 2017, https://www.ft.com/content/6f2355be-f36e-11e6-8758-687615182Ia6, accessed 17/04/2019.

53. Ibid.

54. Cooper, Jonny, 'Dylan Jones: Men Have Never Had It So Good', *The Telegraph*, 9 August 2016, https://www.telegraph.co.uk/men/thinking-man/dylan-jones-men-have-never-had-it-so-good/, accessed 25/08/ 2018; Jones, Dylan, *Manxiety: The Difficulties of Being Male* (London: Biteback Publishing, 2016).

8

FROM *CINDERELLA* TO *FROZEN*

In *How to be a Woman*, Caitlin Moran envisaged femininity, in the past, as having been routinely distorted by a sense of defeat, the awareness—and experience—of being a *loser*.[1] Feminism, on the other hand, was a route towards self-respect and well-being. Moran writes about her own experiences as a bright teenager growing up in the English Midlands in the 1980s, devouring books for inspiration, and seeking role models. She had become all too aware, she tells us, that many of her cultural heroines—Sylvia Plath, Dorothy Parker, Bessie Smith, and Janis Joplin—had struggled with depression and suicidal thoughts. 'I can't help but note that most of the women who hold their own with the men seem unhappy and apt to die young',[2] she recalled her adolescent self as thinking, and so she had begun to suspect that history had been 'poisonous to women'.[3] It had been when she came across Germaine Greer's *The Female Eunuch* that she began to envisage a way out of this predicament. The effect of reading this book, 'a total thrill', had been like someone 'triggering gold-glitter cannonade'.[4] Greer's brand of feminism was funny, literate, and joyful, and it convinced her that being a woman could be full of possibilities, an altogether 'amazing' thing to be.[5]

Thinking back further about how things had seemed before this epiphany, Moran recollected that what had bothered her most about womanhood when she was a young teenager had been the issue of princesses. In order to get anywhere in life she had somehow imagined that she had to transform herself, magically, and through some kind of psychic struggle, into a princess:

> That's how I'd get fallen in love with. That's how I'd get along. That's how the world would welcome me. The books; the Disney films; the most famous woman in the world being, when I was a child, Princess Diana: whilst there were other role models around, the sheer onslaught of princessalia every girl is subject to, wedges its way into the heart, in a quietly pernicious way.[6]

The royal wedding of Prince Charles and the young Lady Diana Spencer in 1981 had seemed like the perfect fairy tale, with women across the world glued to television screens, sighing over the details of dress, diamond jewellery, and the 'dreamlike life' that it was popularly supposed that Diana was marrying into. Moran tried to explain why she thought the secret fantasy of becoming a princess had been so debilitating, and how giving up on this fantasy had represented a landmark in her own liberation. For her, the dream of becoming a princess had been replaced initially by a fantasy of becoming a muse to some 'great artist': but these visions too had eventually given way to an acceptance of ordinariness, and with it a realization that who and what she would become was going to depend not on how she appeared, nor on whom she married, but essentially on her own efforts.[7]

Moran is writing on these subjects with the benefit of hindsight, but at the time of the 1981 royal wedding feminist sociologists had expressed similar concerns about the cramping effect of the spectacle on young girls' ambitions. In Britain, *The Times* news-paper had published an article written by Penny Perrick entitled 'A-level or glass slipper?', suggesting that Diana's influence might be harmful as a role model for young girls: she had meagre educa-tional qualifications and was supposed to have attracted the atten-tions of the prince on account of her youth, prettiness, and innocence.[8] Neither the attraction nor the fairy tale stood the test of time, of course—not least because the prince was in love not with his bride, but with an older and much more sophisticated married woman. After a long period of misery, mutual recrimin-ations, and infidelities, the royal couple divorced in 1996.

Though the reality of princessdom might not have seemed all that romantic, feminists were ruefully aware of the continuing appeal of Cinderella stories, and particularly of the allure of what came to be labelled 'princess culture'. Princess culture seemed to go straight to the heart of little girls, and the term was often deployed to include everything sugary, sparkly, and pink mar-keted for youthful feminine consumption. Associated with extreme forms of femininity—even caricatured femininity—it was sometimes referred to as 'girlie-girl culture'. It encompassed Disney Princesses, Barbie dolls, and fluffy and feathery tutus. It could include everything from the childishly innocent (glittery hair slides, tiaras, and rosebud velvet headbands) to the more obviously sexual (Playboy Bunny ears, sequinned basques, and fishnets). In Britain, writers such as Natasha Walter and *Guardian* journalist Polly Toynbee railed against what Walter saw as the insidious social forces turning girls into 'living dolls', and what Toynbee called the curse of 'girlification'.[9] Toynbee saw the moun-tain of pink tat piled up in retail stores such as Girl Heaven as poi-sonous and as damaging girls' brains. Walter saw exaggerated

18. Disney doll: Elsa from *Frozen*

femininity as part of a worrying process of sexualization that was intruding into childhood. In America, Lauren Greenfield's photographs provided evidence for young girls' obsessions with how they looked. Her images explore the many ways in which an often troubled preoccupation with bodies and appearance lie at the heart of adolescent femininity.[10] Were girls being socialized, yet again, into a sense of themselves as objects rather than being able to see themselves as desiring subjects?

One of the most comprehensive critiques of princess culture came from Peggy Orenstein, whose article 'What's Wrong with Cinderella?' first appeared in *The New York Times Magazine* in 2006 and was subsequently expanded into a book, *Cinderella Ate My Daughter: Dispatches from the Front Lines of the New Girlie-Girl Culture,* published by Harper Collins in 2011.[11] It seemed that pink was commercial gold, Orenstein noted, concerned about her own daughter's obsession with all things pink, pretty, and princess-like. Among the many examples of recent entrepreneurship in marketing princess-themed products to little girls, Orenstein focused particularly on the breathtaking success of Disney Consumer Products with its Disney Princess line, the brainchild of Andy Mooney in the early 2000s. She describes how Disney marketing executives set out to capitalize on young girls' fantasies about princesses with quite spectacular results. In 2006, after the introduction of the line, global revenues for Disney Consumer Products had shot up to $3 billion, from $300 million in 2001. At the time she was writing, Orenstein reported, there were more than 25,000 Disney Princess items on sale.[12] You could buy anything from Disney Princess Band-Aids to Disney Princess lip-balm; from Disney Princess crayons and notebooks to Disney Princess balloons, paper cups, and napkins. The 'stable' of Disney Princesses included favourite female characters from the early animated films: Cinderella, of course, from 1950; Snow White from 1937; and Aurora from Sleeping Beauty from 1959. 'Princesses' from more recent movies included Ariel, Belle, Jasmine, Mulan, and Pocahontas. Tinker Bell was originally allocated Princess status but was soon demoted. Tiana, Rapunzel, and Merida were added after Orenstein's *New York Times* article was written. After 2013 came Elsa and Anna from *Frozen*.

How much should mothers concern themselves over their young daughters' seeming addiction to princess culture? Orenstein approached the question from a number of angles. Maybe it was a historical reaction? Perhaps the fashion for princesses resuscitated 'the fantasy of romance' that had been dented somewhat by second-wave feminism? Maybe princess culture was superficial? After all, it wasn't unknown for girls dressed in pink satin to hack the heads off their Barbie dolls. Maybe it was just a phase that girls would grow out of? Orenstein's own daughter, tricked out like Ariel from Disney's Little Mermaid 'in a full-skirted frock with a gold bodice, a beaded crown perched sideways on her head', nevertheless reassured her Mom that she was determined to be a fireman when she grew up.[13]

While Orenstein and other writers and academics continued to ponder these questions, girl culture was not wholly static.[14] Cinderella herself appeared in more modern forms, as in the more ethnically inclusive and feminist 1997 Walt Disney TV version of the tale, based on Rodger and Hammerstein's musical (the third adaptation of their piece). The idea of a black Cinderella had appealed to Whitney Houston, who originally planned to star in the role. She later relinquished the part to pop star Brandy, with Houston as the Fairy Godmother.[15]

Disney Princesses weren't frozen in time, unchanging, or as if embalmed in cupboards in Bluebeard's Castle. They came and went and adapted with the times. These adaptations and what they signified in terms of role models, ethnicity, colonialism, and feminism fuelled a whole industry of popular cultural studies, reflected in publications such as Henry Giroux's classic *The Mouse That Roared: Disney and the End of Innocence* (1999), or more recently the nineteen essays in Douglas and Shea T. Brode's *Debating Disney: Pedagogical Perspectives on Commercial Cinema* (2016).[16] Most were in agreement that the first three Disney Princesses (Snow White, Cinderella, and Aurora) were what scholar of popular culture Mimi Nguyen pithily dismissed as 'spunkless specimens of yesteryear's Cold War gender roles'.[17] They sang through housework and adversity and dreamed of princes who would rescue them. The more recent heroines did better. In spite of their supermodel looks, they showed spirit, even if they ultimately sank into the arms of the princely male and the ditch of happy endings.

There is nothing inherently unfeminist about romance, of course, except when it triggers a loss of independent spirit and a collapse into passivity. The more recent Disney animations signal something of the opposite. Critics don't always agree about which are the most right-on of the Disney heroines. *Mulan*, for instance, questions gender stereotyping directly: the heroine is a cross-dressing Chinese woman who proves herself a bold female warrior. When the film was released in 1998, though, Janet Maslin pointed out in *The New York Times* that for all Mulan's courage and independence in rebelling against the royal matchmakers, she still falls for the General's son, Shang. The film is still 'enough of a fairy-tale to need Mr Right', Maslin complained.[18] But the Vietnamese-born Mimi Nguyen remembered the film as having been genuinely inspirational for her when she was growing up. 'An Asian tomboy defies convention, hoodwinks patriarchal authority and goes on to save the masses—the dominant narrative of my fantasy youth', she wrote.[19] Nguyen's account reminds us that the consumers of popular culture are discriminating: they can *select* what they find inspirational from a film or text through a process of renegotiation 'of picking, choosing and reimagining'.

Cultural critic Victoria Amador has argued that it is the Disney/Pixar film *Brave* (2012) that makes the most powerful statement of female agency.[20] In this film, tomboy Merida, like Mulan, rebels against being married off for dynastic reasons. The film's action revolves around three powerful women: Merida, her mother Elinor, and a witch. The men, Amador reminds us, are 'a collection of fighting bozos in kilts except for the three wee redheaded horrible triplet brothers and Merida's well-meaning father'.[21] Merida's stock-in-trade is action. She has little time for dreams. The end of the film sees her riding like the wind across the landscape rather than passively sinking into a male embrace—though she does reconcile with her conservative, controlling mother. Merida's body is less reminiscent of a supermodel than other Disney heroines, and she even has a normal-sized waist, although there were complaints that her appearance was later 'glamourized' in an attempt to sell more dolls and merchandise.[22]

There can be little doubt that Disney Princesses are more personable and have more about them these days. Tiana (in *The Princess and the Frog*, 2009) was the first African-American Disney Princess: she dreams not of a prince but of opening her own restaurant. Rapunzel, in *Tangled* (2010), is feisty. Her male counterpart, Flynn Rider, is initially a companion in adventure and derring-do rather than a love interest. He's a commoner, not a prince, and something of a criminal and ne'er-do-well to boot. Rather than relying on Flynn to save her, it is Rapunzel who rescues Flynn on a number of occasions. The directors of the film (Nathan Greno and Byron Howard) are alleged to have organized a 'Hot Man Meeting' with some thirty female colleagues, who were quizzed about what they found irresistible in a man so that Flynn could be crafted accordingly.[23] He emerged as a rogue, yet with a strong respect for women. In the end, it is Rapunzel who asks Flynn to marry her, rather than the other way around. More recently still, Polynesian Princess Moana from Disney's 2016 animation of that name is pure action heroine; she's inspired by her grandmother and a verdant nature goddess. There's no prince to complicate or detract from her purpose: her quest is entirely her own.

There has perhaps been less attention from film critics to the ways in which male characters have changed in Disney movies over the past half-century or so. Princes in the early animations didn't need personalities: they were hieroglyphs. Princely status and a fetching pair of tights (and maybe thigh boots) were sufficient to indicate desirability. By the time we get to *Beauty and the Beast* (1991), audiences were offered a bit more characterization. Belle reads books and makes choices. She isn't a victim, and she gets to see various kinds of masculinity in action: her benign and intelligent father, the dumb male chauvinist pig suitor Gaston, and the rough diamond Beast himself. But the plot still follows all the clichés of romance fiction, in that the Beast gets transformed by the love of a good woman. Like Mr Darcy in Jane Austen's *Pride and Prejudice*, he serves to reassure us (and particularly the girls in the audience) that rich men can respond to both *intelligence and spirit* in a woman.

In a paper published in *The Journal of Popular Film and Television* in 2008, critics Ken Gillam and Shannon R. Wooden explored the development of male protagonists in Disney/Pixar productions since 1990 such as *Cars*, *Toy Story*, and *The Incredibles*.[24] They argue that a common theme is that the men in these movies start by behaving as alpha males. They are competitive and thick-skinned. But the narrative in each case strips this model down to reveal an underlying loneliness and vulnerability. Gradually these characters learn, often through a significant homosocial relationship or through figurative emasculation, to appreciate the value of more sensitive, 'feminine' character traits. Effectively the films promote a model of what it is to be a 'New Man', teaching a kinder, gentler version of maleness.

Little girls revelling in dressing up like princesses don't always fantasize about princes. American photographer Blake Fitch's

19. Little princess from photographer Blake Fitch's project, *Dress Rehearsal*

sensitive photographs of young adolescent girls in princess outfits in her recent project, *Dress Rehearsal*, show these girls trying on femininity for size.[25] The artist's statement explaining her project emphasizes that the images reflect both the girls' exposure to gender expectations but also their own power and strength, as they try to make sense of what being a girl means in contemporary culture.[26] They are 'princess warriors' rather than passive dupes. What is important, Fitch emphasizes, is that the girls are learning to be heroines of their own story. Her images succeed in conveying a sense of these girls as thinkers, in settings where they appear to contemplate a somewhat thorny future: the mysteries of nature, their own physical powers, and the social meanings of romance. In these photographs the girls' dreaminess seems less about escape than about negotiating some kind of identity and pondering a way forward in their lives.

It can be argued that one of the ways in which princess culture and Cinderella stories have retained their stranglehold on the female imagination over the past half-century is through the lure of the white wedding. Little girls, it is often said, are conditioned from childhood to see marriage as a major life event and goal: the wedding as a girl's Big Day. Royal weddings in Britain and the entrepreneurial activities of the Walt Disney Company in North America have both exercised a potent influence on what feminists have sometimes labelled 'the wedding-industrial complex'.[27]

This 'wedding-industrial complex' stands for all the agencies promoting white weddings as the ultimate expression of love and romance, as well as representing them as the epitome of feminine achievement. According to some estimates, the average cost of a wedding in North America in 2017 was around $32,000, and the wedding industry as a whole (bridal magazines, venues, planners, caterers, outfits, hairdressers, drivers, limo hire, etc) was worth something in the region of $72 billion.[28] In the UK, the average cost of a wedding reached an all-time high in 2017 at around £33,000, with the industry as a whole worth £10 billion to the economy.[29] Expenditure on the average wedding has risen dramatically over the past few decades. In the US, the Disney Corporation has been a major player in the wedding industry, offering 'Fairy Tale Wedding' experiences in Disneyland and Disney World since the 1990s. Disney Cruise Lines have also fostered the trend for 'destination weddings' in exotic locations such as the Bahamas or Hawaii. Everything from wedding stationery to the bride's dress can be customized or chosen from the selection associated with each of the Disney Princesses: Aurora, Ariel, Tiana, etc. You can ride to meet your prince in a glass carriage drawn by white horses, should you so desire, and be accompanied by liveried trumpeters. Dedicated Disney wedding consultants are on hand to help you dream, plan, and coordinate your perfect day.[30]

Those invested in this industry constantly register concern about the declining popularity of weddings, as couples leave it longer to tie the knot, and many spurn marriage in favour of cohabitation. It is almost as if, as the number of couples marrying declines, more and more effort goes into the fantasy—as well as into commercial stimulation of the fantasy. British sociologist Julia Carter has suggested that as mores change and marriage becomes less necessary for social or normative reasons, it has become strengthened through appeals to tradition and romance.[31] Traditions are invented, and reinvented: they do not stand still. In their book *Cinderella Dreams: The Allure of the Lavish Wedding* (2003), Elizabeth Pleck and Cele Otnes argue that the rituals which have developed around expensive weddings in recent history embody a mix of hope and aspiration for participants, almost tantamount to a belief in magic, as well as affording opportunities for guilt-free, unfettered consumption.[32] 'Ready to start dreaming?' asks the Disney wedding website, offering virtual 'Dream Boards' and an invitation to contribute to their 'Ever After Blog'. It isn't difficult to dismiss the more extravagant details of lavish wedding celebrations—ice sculptures in the shape of swans or *putti*, the release of white doves or clouds of butterflies—as so much commercialized claptrap. Yet to do so, Pleck and Otnes contend, would be to miss the opportunity to understand the meanings embodied, particularly for women.[33]

The idea that a wedding is the most important event in a young woman's life, energetically promoted by bridal magazines and the wedding industry, goes deep. In a memorable episode of *Friends* from 1998, Monica tries to explain the dream of the perfect wedding to her brother, Ross, in the context of glitches in wedding plans which are upsetting his fiancée, Emily. Ross can't understand why Emily is making so much fuss about the arrangements. Monica explains that Emily, like other women, has probably been planning the wedding since she was five years old:

> Ever since she first took a pillow case and hung it off the back of her head. That's what we did! We dreamed about the perfect wedding, and the perfect place, with the perfect four-tiered wedding cake...[Monica tears up at this point and Ross has to pass her a Kleenex from the box helpfully chucked in his direction]...with the little people on top. But the most important part is that we had the perfect guy, who understood just how important all that other stuff was.[34]

It is hard to escape a suspicion that in some cases, and for some women, the bridal fantasy is more important than the husband. The word 'Bridezillas' entered the lexicon around the 1990s, a combination of 'bride' and 'Godzilla'. The Oxford English Dictionary dates its use in print from 1995, defined as designating 'a woman thought to have become intolerably obsessive or overbearing in planning the details of her wedding'.[35] A particularly bizarre twist on the idea of becoming a bride as the glorious apogee of feminine achievement comes from the modern Japanese phenomenon of the 'solo wedding': women can dress, primp, and preen as brides without the necessity for a groom, celebrating themselves and the fantasy of becoming a princess for a day. They may even commemorate their experience in an album of 'wedding photographs'.[36]

Popular cinema and reality TV shows have alternately celebrated and parodied the trend towards elaborate weddings: sometimes at the same time. Television documentary series such as *Bridezillas* in North America (from 2004) and *Big Fat Gypsy Weddings* (UK, from 2010; screened in North America as *My Big Fat Gypsy Wedding*) have attracted big audiences. Movies such as *Father of the Bride* (1991), *Four Weddings and a Funeral* (1994), and *Bridesmaids* (2011) have proved enduringly popular. An astonishing number of films have focused on weddings over the past thirty years, most of them romantic comedies, but some—like *Bridesmaids* (directed by Paul Feig and co-written by Annie Mumolo and Kristen Wiig)—with a subversive or critical edge.[37] Invented rather than inherited, wedding 'traditions' over the past half-century have become ever more elaborate. The hen party, for instance, barely existed in Britain before the 1970s. It is now commonplace, with tourist and hospitality industries in towns such as Brighton in East Sussex capitalizing on their popularity as venues. The sight of groups of tipsy women sporting lopsided wedding veils, tiaras, or fluffy antennae carousing through the main streets in such places is now commonplace. Frequently, one member of the party will be clutching a giant inflatable penis.

More upmarket versions of the hen party take place over the weekend in expensive spa hotels with lots of steam baths, facials, and 'pampering'. These forms of sociability both reflect and constitute social change. Hen parties have a shorter history than stag parties (which have been dated back to Ancient Sparta), and some would see them as reflecting women's growing independence and desire for parity with men.[38] They also reflect a more permanent female presence in the labour market. Some brides-to-be have disposable income to play with, although expenditure on hen parties and wedding celebrations can cause conflict between women: not all can afford this luxury. Hen parties further reflect the importance of same sex friendship and peer support in modern urban life, and the ways in which friendship networks have begun, at least to some extent, to displace family in the organization and control of marriage and wedding ceremonies.

But if the invented traditions around weddings reflect social and demographic change, they also offer a window into nostalgia for what can seem outdated and increasingly unrealistic expectations. Marriage today has lost the clarity of expectation that it carried in the 1950s. The old Ladybird reading books that children in Britain grew up with in that decade now make us laugh, and have acquired vintage chic.[39] Daddy goes to work; Mummy stays at home with Jane, who helps with laundry and cooking and makes her dolls perform domestic tasks. Was it ever that simple? The old gender role divisions have been blurred and symbols (briefcase equals work equals male, apron equals domestic equals female) no longer clearly signify. Marriages may still begin with both partners declaring love and commitment but we know that realistically, a significant proportion of them—probably some 40–50 per cent—will end in divorce.

If divorce rates have levelled off or even declined in recent decades, this is at least in part because the number of marriages has declined.[40] Recent figures from the Office for National Statistics in the UK confirm cohabitation to be a seemingly inexorable trend.[41] It may be that the tendency for those couples who do choose to marry to postpone doing so until they are in their late twenties or early thirties works in favour of more stable partnerships, since early marriage has always been associated with a higher rate of break-up. But many people in the West are living longer, and as they age, they may be tempted to leave unsatisfying marriages behind and try again, 'before it is too late', for love. Historians have long pointed out that over the past half-century or so, our expectations of marriage as a source of individual happiness and fulfilment have inflated to a point at which they are scarcely likely to be met. We too often want our husbands or wives to be 'soulmates' and to provide everything: love, romance, passion, compatibility, commitment, tolerance, understanding ... the list goes on and on. It is unrealistic to imagine that one partner can ever provide for all these needs, let alone do so consistently through a long lifetime.

Meanwhile the number of people living alone in the West has increased over recent decades. According to social scientist Eric Klinenberg, this trend—which is quite new in history—has gone hand in hand with the rise of affluence and state welfare provision.[42] Klinenberg estimates that in 1950 there were about four million Americans living alone: a little less than 10 per cent of all households were single-person households. By the time he came to write his book *Going Solo: The Extraordinary Rise and Surprising Appeal of Living Alone* (2012), more than thirty-two million people were living alone in the US, comprising around 28 per cent of households.[43] In the middle of the twentieth century, most single-person households were those of migrant workers in rural areas and the Mid-West. Half a century later, the pattern had changed. Single-person units were more characteristic of big-city living, and this was also the case in British and European cities. Klinenberg argued that any automatic assumption that a rise in single-person living reflected loneliness and social isolation was wrong: well-off people were increasingly *choosing* to live that way. He suggested that women's gains in independence in recent history were an important part of the trend. Women's earnings now meant that they could delay marriage, leave marriages that weren't working for them, and purchase their own homes on a scale that simply hadn't been possible fifty or sixty years previously. The digital and communications revolution had hugely impacted on sociability: it was easier than ever to live alone while maintaining a rich and active social life.[44]

Over the past few years, many women writers have launched a full-scale attack on the stereotype of single women or spinsters as sad or unfulfilled individuals. In the US, Kate Bolick, author of *Spinster: Making a Life of One's Own* (2015) and a contributing editor for *The Atlantic*, vigorously attacked recent portrayals of unmarried women in popular culture as 'either dating-obsessed shopaholics (Carrie Bradshaw) or binge-eating lonely hearts (Bridget Jones)'.[45] Bella DePaulo's *Singled Out: How Single Women Are Stereotyped, Stigmatized and Ignored and Still Live Happily Ever After* (2006) contended that social insularity was often a characteristic of coupledom rather than the single life.[46] Rebecca Traister's *All the Single Ladies: Unmarried Women and the Rise of an Independent Nation* (2016) quarried the past as well as contemporary experience to explore the lives of single women across divisions of class and ethnicity in order to reassess their importance in modern history.[47] Katherine Holden's study *The Shadow of Marriage: Singleness in England 1914–1960* (2007) brought more awareness of the history of unmarried women's lives in the UK.[48]

Those twenty-first-century women—and men—who turned to technology to find true love, soulmates, or merely interesting partners encountered a rapidly changing world. The proliferation of online dating agencies, and, after 2007–11, the ease with which smartphones could be used to hook up with location-based contacts, transformed the dating scene.[49] There is still a great deal of speculation about the impact of these changes, as studies such as Mark Brooks' 'How Has Internet Dating Changed Society?' (2011) or Dan Slater's *Love in The Time of Algorithms* (2013) have shown.[50] A central issue is that of *choice*. In the past people's choices of partner had to be made from limited groups: those randomly encountered in the locality or others one came across in the course of everyday social life. Now, choice seems infinite. At the touch of a screen it is possible to communicate with like-minded others anywhere in the world. 'Niche' dating sites allow for an extraordinary degree of specificity. Should you so want, you can search for partners who are pet lovers; who are pet lovers with ginger hair, Goths, military widows; who are already married; who have specific body measurements; who have unusual sexual preferences; who have certain medical conditions. You can shop for a husband or a bride in distant parts of the globe, in searches which some observers have found disconcertingly close to the processes and power relations of human trafficking.[51]

Many of us are inclined to celebrate this widening of choice. Expectations have risen and we can be more picky about who we choose to meet and potentially mate with. Mark Brooks' respondents pointed to an increase in interracial marriages and a growth in tolerance of gay, bisexual, and trans-inclusive relationships as liberating results of change.[52] But others have suggested that too much choice can confuse and bewilder, leading singles to trawl the internet on endless virtual shopping sprees in the search for the 'perfect' mate.[53] The odds become stacked against committing to someone, and the satisfaction and contentment that may come with that, because of a niggling feeling that there might be some-one just that bit better a click away. Comedian and writer Aziz Ansari joked that his father had spent less time deciding upon a wife (his parents had agreed to an arranged marriage) than he himself now spent on researching and selecting an electric citrus juicer or a protective case for his laptop.[54]

It is not yet clear whether the breathtaking expansion of choice now available to individuals will act to stabilize or to destabilize partnerships and commitment. Some of those questioned by Mark Brooks suggested that marriages might become more stable, because partners could be selected from a larger pool and people could make better, more discriminating and considered choices. Others believed that the internet facilitated cheating, and that fidelity was suffering. It was further suggested that low-quality, unhappy, and unfulfilling marriages were less likely to be toler-ated, given the ease of making new matches online. The expan-sion in use of digital social media sites generally has complicated issues of fidelity and commitment in other ways, too, as people check the profiles of new and older partners online—are their profiles still 'live' on dating sites? Do their Facebook profiles sug-gest continuing flirtation with other users?[55]

The rapid technological changes affecting the ways in which people meet and form relationships have taken place alongside a continuing blurring of gender expectations. It is easy to see why this can make for confusion. Women writers have described a conflict they feel in posting profiles that will attract attention, and record hesitancy in sticking to 'feminine' behaviour about not messaging men first or too often in case they come across as needy, desperate, or crazy. Writing in *Bust* Magazine, Oriana Asano, who described herself as a feminist long before she decided 'to jump into the man-infested waters of love and sex', found in internet dating a 'constant reminder of how suffocatingly confining gender roles are and how immobilizing male entitlement renders me in the dating game'.[56] She ruefully watched herself playing gender roles and felt out of control. It was hard to escape the frustration of what seemed a state of mandatory female passivity:

> I'm constantly in a state of waiting: waiting to be called, waiting to be asked out on a date, waiting to be kissed, waiting for a guy to make a decision for me and hope that he can read my mind and choose the thing I want.[57]

This kind of confession forces us to recognize the stubborn persistence of older values. Sherryl Lee Melnyk has also written wittily about the difficulties of internet dating protocol from a feminist point of view.[58] Problems came to a head when she crafted an internet profile describing herself as a serious-minded scholar. No one hit on her, and her male friends told her bluntly that her profile lacked sex appeal. So she tried 'sexing up' her profile to suggest someone 'fun and flirty' instead. It didn't come easily, since Melnyk confessed that she found this all rather humiliating and demeaning: 'the cyber equivalent of wearing leopard-skin spandex, donning red pumps and batting false eyelashes.'[59] Nonetheless, her inbox filled up. 'Feminists don't believe in frogs that turn into broad-shouldered men with a kiss, or wealthy princes who ride white stallions into a woman's life to save her from the drudgery of candidacy exams', Melnyk asserted, confessing that she didn't either—but, if it happened, she wouldn't be opposed to it. After all,

> Everyone wants love to end in a castle, even feminists like me...We want to believe that our soul-mate is out there, somewhere, and if I

just click on enough profiles, lose a couple of pounds, and put highlights in my hair, he would emerge from the Internet like a phoenix
to complete me.

But of course, as Melnyk knew too well, 'Love doesn't work that
way. It never has. Even on the Internet.'[60]

Over the past ten years, writing by younger women has shown
a renewed determination to challenge the romantic myths of love
and marriage which can still haunt female lives, leading to a sense
of inadequacy or failure in those whose experiences fall short of
the fairy tale. Some texts—such as Trinidadian-born British writer
Monique Roffey's *With the Kisses of His Mouth* (2011) and *The Tryst*
(2017), or Katherine Angel's *Unmastered: A Book on Desire, Most
Difficult to Tell* (2010)—have focused on the vagaries, intensities,
and unpredictable nature of female desire.[61] Roffey has written
perceptively about the problems which arise when sexual desire is
absent or separate from romantic, committed love. Angel's book
reminds us that it can still be difficult for women to find the courage and an appropriate voice in which to speak about desire. With
horizons no longer so limited by a desperate need to find and keep
husbands, more women have begun to explore alternatives to lifelong marriage and monogamy. This new confidence has fed into
the recent social and historical studies of singleness, for instance,
which were discussed above. A new boldness can also be dis-
cerned in works by young women exploring historical and contemporary patterns of dating and sexual arrangements such as
Moira Weigel's *Labor of Love: The Invention of Dating* and Emily Witt's
Future Sex: A New Kind of Free Love, both of which were first published in 2016.[62]

Both Weigel's and Witt's books incorporated personal, autobiographical details which offered a direct challenge to conventional

narratives of romance. Both writers tell us that they had begun writing their books when what they had believed to be significant love affairs went badly wrong. Both turned to internet dating and found themselves drawn into asking a series of searching questions about what love actually meant, particularly in the context of women's life ambitions. Weigel tells us that she was dumped by her older boyfriend. Pushing aside heartbreak and steeling herself to risk dating again, she suddenly realized that she had no idea what she really wanted: indeed, she didn't know *how to want*. Like many girls, she had grown up imagining that romance would shape her destiny. She had assumed that it was her job to make herself desirable to men, not to clarify her own particular desires and needs.[63]

Musing on these issues prompted Weigel to investigate the background to dating in America, and particularly its recent social history. She outlines the ways in which the challenges of HIV and AIDS in the 1980s had forced a new culture of explicitness about sex, since communication and openness were crucial if infection were to be avoided and contained.[64] The growth of the internet accentuated this opening up of discourse and communication. Alongside the proliferation of dating applications, it facilitated the popularity of chatrooms, online seduction, and cybersex. Many of those who participated in these new forms of dating felt pushed into 'roles which seemed to follow strictly gendered scripts that pitted them against their partners'.[65] Even so, courtship and sexual mores were transformed.

Weigel shows how the history of dating has been regularly punctured by moral panics about the impact of new technologies. When automobiles became widely available in the twentieth century, for instance, people fretted about the new opportunities cars

offered for young people to drive into the countryside and canoo-
dle unobserved in the back seats. Similarly, over recent decades,
women's freedoms have led to scaremongering over whether
career ambitions would cause them to wreck their lives by delaying having children until it was too late for them to do so 'natu-
rally'. Egg freezing can look like a desperate attempt to prolong
the search for a Prince Charming, Weigel suggests. Female bodies,
she contends, have been seen as 'time bombs'. It is as if 'at the
stroke of midnight, our eggs turn into dust'.[66] Cinderella stories
with their dark warnings still lurk in the imagination.

Emily Witt's *Future Sex* has a similar starting point, in that Witt
tells her readers that she was troubled when a relationship ended
and she found herself still single at thirty. Until then, she had
assumed that her experiences of love and sex were all leading up
to something, part of a journey towards an end, 'like a monorail
gliding to a stop at Epcot Centre'.[67] But what if this life-defining
love never happened? Reflecting on her love life so far, Witt realized that she lacked even a language with which to describe it
accurately. For her, periods of celibacy had been punctuated by
sporadic sexual engagement with a range of acquaintances. To
speak of 'being in a relationship' conveyed something of at least a
provisional commitment. To speak of a 'partner' or 'boyfriend'
also implied intention or commitment. Her own life was much
messier than this and, although she had experienced being in love,
it hadn't worked out.[68] Fully reciprocated love, she acknowledged
sadly, was a rare thing.

Witt was determined to embrace opportunities for sexual freedom, while confessing that at some profound level, she was still
planning for 'a monogamous destiny'. Her book is something
of a *Bildungsroman*. She gamely explores some of the quirkier

manifestations of sexual behaviour in modern San Francisco. Her investigations into 'orgasmic meditation', pornography, live web-cams and internet chatrooms, polyamory, and the Burning Man festival help her come to terms with her own sexuality. They encourage her to ask ever more searching questions about the narratives and values that have cramped women's lives. The book ends with Witt more firmly convinced than before that she wants 'to live in a world with a wider range of sexual identities', although beyond that she concedes uncertainty.[69]

Both Witt's book and Weigel's display courage in going 'off script', and they share an awareness of how traditional narratives have failed women. In pursuing the research that underlies both books, these authors acquire important knowledge about them-selves. In her oft-cited essay on 'Professions for Women' in 1931, Virginia Woolf had famously identified what she dubbed the 'Angel in the House' mentality as shackling and bedevilling wom-en's writing. The woman writer was haunted by the need to pre-serve feminine respectability, Woolf insisted, and it was near impossible to find the courage to speak the truth about her experi-ence as a body.[70] Forty years ago, and some half a century after Woolf's essay, literary scholar and writer Carolyn Heilbrun pub-lished a slim book titled *Writing a Woman's Life*, in which she explored the constraints which still hedged in women's autobiog-raphies and their imaginative writing.[71]

Heilbrun lamented that women's life stories were still domin-ated by courtship, a brief period when their subjects found them-selves in the limelight: 'it is the part of their lives most constantly and vividly enacted in a myriad of representations.' As often as not, this was an illusion, she insisted. Women saw finding the right man as quintessential, that is, 'the woman must entrap the man to ensure herself a centre for her life. The rest is aging and regret.'[72] The problem with such narratives was that 'safety and closure' were still held out to women as ideals of female destiny. And safety and closure were not 'places of adventure, or experience, or life'. [73]

Belief in happy endings, with the simple discovery of one's own True Love, dies hard. But there are signs that the culture is changing. Many of us enjoy romance, and some are still suckers for royal weddings and princess brides, but you'd be hard pushed to believe in girlhood innocence followed by the ineffably happy-ever-after any more. Though sexual double standards persist, many young women, like young men, now experiment with sexual relationships, seeing this as a sensible kind of research before deciding to settle with a partner. They may choose not to 'settle' at all. Divorce need no longer be seen as a mark of personal inadequacy or a terrible failing. Legislators set out to facilitate more effective and speedy 'no fault divorce' procedures in England and Wales in April 2019: public opinion had in the main come round to accepting that requiring evidence of 'unreasonable behaviour' or proof of blame in marital breakdown could often generate acrimony damaging both to former spouses and their children.[74] We are all too aware that even royal marriages can peter out in a welter of adulterous relationships, recriminations, divorce, and re-couplings, like any other marriage today. The belief that women need to have children to ensure lifelong happiness and fulfilment dies hard, but is nevertheless increasingly questioned. When Paul Dolan, a professor of behavioural science at Britain's London School of Economics, published a book called *Happy Ever After* in 2019, he received a storm of abuse for suggesting that evidence seemed to show many women were happier, healthier, and better off for remaining unmarried and childfree. Society invests heavily in traditional scripts and narratives. Challenges to such deeply held convictions are often met with hostility and incredulity.[75]

Yet as the status of women has improved, princesses are becoming more personable, even in Disney's world. They may not take well to being boxed up in pumpkins and palaces. The most recent Disney animations show a new generation of princesses bent on adventure. In *Frozen* (2013), Elsa is far too preoccupied with trying to deal with psychic forces and conflict in her own life to think about princes, while her devoted sister Anna has no hesitation in going for sisterly loyalty and adventure over a less than charming prince who turns out to be a dodgy character anyway.[76]

Frozen met with phenomenal success, becoming the highest grossing animated film in history and the fifth highest grossing film of all time. Maria Konnikova, writing in the *New Yorker*, succinctly described the film as having 'captured the culture'.[77] It appealed to adults as well as children. Viewers, critics, and journalists picked their brains as to why. In England, academics at the University of East Anglia devoted a whole conference to the study of the film ('Symfrozium', 2015).[78] Most have attributed its appeal to the film's celebration of girl power and sisterly love. *Frozen* clean broke away from the conventions of the romance plot. Elsa is no milk-and-water princess: she's somewhat screwed up as well as gorgeous, she's moody, she doesn't want to be beholden to others and she struggles with her own magical powers. She means well but does harm: she is certainly not perfect. Many people—not just girls—can identify with her, particularly when she runs away from it all and lets rip with her ice magic, seeking release in the wonderfully cathartic 'Let It Go' number. The story subverts stereotypes. The prince is handsome but a selfish creep. Elsa's little sister Anna is intrepid: her love for her sister propels her into bravery and adventure. Social class is no guarantee of noble behaviour: Kristoff, the humble iceman, has more integrity than Prince Hans—and, unlike Hans, he's no love rat. The patriarchal figures in the story are mostly decrepit, vain, and ineffectual.

There's no marriage in *Frozen* 1, nor any suggestion of happy ever after. Instead, we take away powerful messages about female courage, sisterly love, self-mastery, and the letting go of inhibition. What we *do* know is that Elsa and Anna will go on to have further adventures: the story hasn't yet ended for them.[79] Lucinda Everett, writing in the British newspaper *The Guardian* in 2016, found herself wondering whether the secret of the film's success lay in the fact that it represented 'the future that so many of us want'.[80] Castles in the air, maybe—but still a changing kind of dream.

Notes

1. Moran, Caitlin, *How to be a Woman* (London: Ebury Press, 2011), 134.
2. Ibid. 75.
3. Ibid.
4. Ibid. 78.
5. Ibid.
6. Ibid. 300–4.
7. Ibid. 302.
8. Perrick, P., 'A-Level or Glass Slipper?' *The Times*, 13 June 1983, www.gale.cengage.co.uk, accessed 3/08/2016.
9. Walter, Natasha, *Living Dolls: The Return of Sexism* (London: Virago, 2010); Toynbee, Polly, 'Girlification is Destroying all the Hope We Felt in 1968', *The Guardian*, 15 April 2008, 29.
10. Greenfield, Lauren, *Girl Culture* (San Francisco: Chronicle, 2002).
11. Orenstein, Peggy, 'What's Wrong with Cinderella?' *New York Times Magazine*, 24 December 2006, https://www.nytimes.com/2006/12/24/magazine/24princess.t.html, accessed 29/08/2018; Orenstein, P.,

Cinderella Ate My Daughter: Dispatches from the Front Lines of the New Girlie-Girl Culture (New York: HarperCollins, 2011).

12. Orenstein, 'What's Wrong with Cinderella?'

13. Ibid.

14. There's a fairly extensive literature on 'princess culture'. See, for instance, Hains, Rebecca, *The Princess Problem: Guiding Our Girls Through the Princess-Obsessed Years* (Naperville: Sourcebooks, 2014).

15. Purdum, Todd S., 'The Slipper Still Fits, Though the Style is New', *New York Times*, 2 November 1997, https://www.nytimes.com/1997/11/02/arts/television-the-slipper-still-fits-though-the-style-is-new.html, accessed 1/11/2018.

16. Giroux, Henry A., *The Mouse that Roared: Disney and the End of Innocence* (Lanham: Rowman and Littlefield, 1999); Brode, Douglas and Brode, Shea T., *Debating Disney: Pedagogical Perspectives on Commercial Cinema* (Lanham: Rowman and Littlefield, 2016).

17. Nguyen, Mimi, 'Who's Your Heroine? Negotiating Asian American Superpower in Disney's *Mulan*', PopPolitics.com, Identity Issue, 5 January 2001, https://web.archive.org/web/20080218080321/http://www.poppolitics.com/articles/2001/01/05/Whos-Your-Heroine, accessed 9/01/2018.

18. Maslin, Janet, 'A Warrior, She Takes on Huns and Stereotypes' (Review of Disney's *Mulan*), *New York Times*, Archives, 1998, 19 June 1998, https://www.nytimes.com, accessed 29/08/2018.

19. Nguyen, 'Who's Your Heroine?'.

20. Amador, Victoria, 'Fantasy Worlds and Disney Girls: Frozen, Brave and Reimagined Twenty-first-century Romance' in Brode, *Debating Disney*, 177–86.

21. Ibid. 180.

22. See, for instance, http://embracethechaos.squarespace.com/blog/2013/5/12/disneys-princess-merida-makeover-sparks-outrage-petition.html, accessed 29/08/2018; Child, Ben, 'Disney Retreats from Princess Merida Makeover after Widespread Criticism', *The Guardian*, 16 May 2013, https://www.theguardian.com/film/2013/may/16/disney-princess-merida-makeover, accessed 29/08/2018.

23. See for instance, Frost, John, Tangled Q&A: Meet the Directors (Nathan Greno, Bryan Howard), Disney Blog, 21/03/2011, https://thedisneyblog.com/2011/03/21/tangled-q-a-meet-the-directors/, accessed 29/08/2018.

24. Gillam, Ken and Wooden, Sharon R., 'Post-Princess Models of Gender: The New Man in Disney/Pixar', *Journal of Popular Film and Television*, vol. 36, no. 1, 7 August 2010, 2–8.

25. Blake Fitch, 'Dress Rehearsal'; see Kayle, Ellyn, 'Princess Culture: Portraits of Little Girls Dressed Up as their Favorite Disney Princesses', Feature shoot, 28 January 2015, https://www.featureshoot.com/2015/01/fascinating-portraits-of-little-girls-dressed-up-as-their-favorite-disney-princesses/, accessed 29/08/2018.

26. Ibid. See also http://blakefitchphotos.tumblr.com/, accessed 29/08/2018. See also Scheftel, Susan, 'Princess Culture: What Is it All About?', *Psychology Today*, 24 August 2015, https://www.psychologyto-day.com/gb/blog/evolving-minds/201508/princess-culture-what-is-it-all-about, accessed 29/08/2018.

27. See, for instance, Risman, Barbara, 'The Wedding Industrial Complex', *Huffpost*, 29 June 2012, https://www.huffingtonpost.com/barbara-risman/the-wedding-industrial-complex_b_1636120.html, accessed 30/08/2018; Ferguson, Sian, 'What the Wedding Industrial Complex is—and How It's Hurting Our Ideas of Love', *Everyday Feminism*, 13 April 2017, https://everydayfeminism.com/2017/04/wedding-industrial-complex/, accessed 30/08/2018.

28. The Knot, 2017 Real Weddings Study, XO Press Releases, 14 February 2018, https://xogroupinc.com/press-releases/the-knot-2017-real-weddings-study-wedding-spend/, accessed 30/08/2018.

29. Young, Sarah, 'Cost of Average British Wedding Hits All-Time High', *The Independent*, 9 September 2017, https://www.independent.co.uk/life-style/average-british-wedding-cost-uk-27000-hitched-venue-honeymoon-food-london-midlands-a7937551.html, accessed 30/08/2018.

30. https://www.disneyweddings.com/, accessed 30/08/2018.

31. Carter, Julia, 'Why Marry? The Role of Tradition in Women's Marital Aspirations', *Sociological Research Online*, 22, 1, 3, 28 February 2017, http://www.socresonline.org.uk/22/1/3.html, accessed 30/08/2018. Carter, Julia and Duncan, Simon, 'Wedding Paradoxes: Individualized Conformity and the "Perfect Day"', *Sociological Review*, vol. 65, no. 1, 1 January 2017, 3–20.

32. Otnes, Cele C. and Pleck, Elizabeth H., *Cinderella Dreams: The Allure of the Lavish Wedding* (Berkeley: University of California Press, 2003).

33. Ibid.

34. Ibid. 203.

35. Oxford English Dictionary entry for 'Bridezilla', added December 2009.

36. BBC News, 'News from Elsewhere: Japan: "Solo Weddings" for Single Women', https://www.bbc.co.uk/news/blogs-news-from-elsewhere-30574801; Harris, Naomi, 'Everything But the Groom: Why I Faked My

Own Wedding', *The Guardian*, 5 March 2016, https://www.theguardian.com/lifeandstyle/2016/mar/05/everything-but-the-groom-faked-own-wedding-naomi-harris, accessed 05/06/2018.

37. Ingraham, Chrys, *White Weddings: Romancing Heterosexuality in Popular Culture* (New York: Routledge, 1999), has an excellent list of films about weddings.

38. Fowler, Sarah, 'Where Did the Hen Party Explosion Come From?' *BBC News*, 21 July 2017, https://www.bbc.co.uk/news/magazine-22659227; Dysch, Hetti, 'A History of Hen Parties: The Hen Revolution', Wedmagazine, 2013, http://www.wedmagazine.co.uk/hen-parties-cornwall-devon-the-hen-revolution.html, accessed 30/08/2018.

39. https://www.vintageladybird.com/, accessed 30/08/2018; see also the recent series of parodies of Ladybird books by Jason Hazeley and Joel Morris, 'Ladybird Books for Grown-ups', https://www.penguin.co.uk/articles/book-talk/series/ladybird-books-for-grown-ups/, accessed 30/08/2018.

40. Burton, Neel, 'The Rise and Fall of Divorce', *Psychology Today*, 10 June 2017, https://www.psychologytoday.com/us/blog/hide-and-seek/201706/the-rise-and-fall-divorce, accessed 30/08/2018; DePaulo, Paula, 'What is the Divorce Rate, Really?' *Psychology Today*, 2 September 2017, https://www.psychologytoday.com/intl/blog/living-single/201702/what-is-the-divorce-rate-really, accessed 1/09/2018; Cain Miller, Claire, 'The Divorce Surge is Over But the Myth Lives On', *The New York Times*, 2 December 2014, https://www.nytimes.com/2014/12/02/upshot/the-divorce-surge-is-over-but-the-myth-lives-on.html, accessed 1/09/2018.

41. Hill, Amelia, 'Cohabiting Couples Fastest Growing Family Type, Says ONS', *The Guardian*, 7 August 2019, https://www.theguardian.com/uk-news/2019/aug/07/cohabiting-couples-fastest-growing-family-type-ons, accessed 8/08/2019.

42. Klinenberg, Eric, *Going Solo: The Extraordinary Rise and Surprising Appeal of Living Alone* (New York: Penguin, 2012); Stromberg, Joseph, 'Eric Klinenberg on Going Solo', *Smithsonian Magazine*, February 2012, https://www.smithsonianmag.com/science-nature/eric-klinenberg-on-going-solo-19299815/, accessed 1/09/2018.

43. Stromberg, 'Eric Klinenberg on Going Solo'.

44. Ibid.

45. Bolick, Kate, 'All the Single Ladies', *The Atlantic Magazine*, November 2011, https://www.theatlantic.com/magazine/archive/2011/11/all-the-single-ladies/308654/, accessed 1/09/2018.

46. DePaulo, Bella M., *Singled Out: How Singles are Stereotyped, Stigmatized and Ignored and Still Live Happily Ever After* (New York: St Martin's Press, 2006).

47. Traister, Rebecca, *All The Single Ladies: Unmarried Women and the Rise of an Independent Nation* (New York: Simon and Schuster, 2016).

48. Holden, Katherine, *The Shadow of Marriage: Singleness in England, 1914–1960* (Manchester: Manchester University Press, 2007).

49. Strimpel, Zoe, 'The Matchmaking Industry and Singles Culture in Britain, 1970–2000', thesis submitted for D. Phil., University of Sussex, 2017.

50. Brooks, Mark, 'How Has Internet Dating Changed Society? An Insider's Look', IDEA (Internet Dating Executive Alliance), January 2011, http://internetdating.typepad.com/courtland_brooks/2011/02/how-has-internet-dating-changed-society.html, accessed 1/09/2018; Slater, Dan, *Love in the Time of Algorithms: What Technology Does to Meeting and Mating* (New York: Current (Penguin Group), 2013).

51. Slater, 'Love in the Time of Algorithms', 167.

52. Brooks, 'How Has Internet Dating Changed Society?', 2.

53. Ibid.

54. Ansari, Aziz, *Modern Romance* (New York: Penguin/Allen Lane, 2015), 125.

55. Ibid. 195–6.

56. Asano, Oriana, 'Feminism v. Dating: Why are They at Odds?' *Bust Magazine*, 6/12/2014, https://bust.com/feminism/12384-feminism-vs-dating-why-are-they-at-odds.html, accessed 1/09/2018.

57. Ibid.

58. Melnyk, Sherryl Lee, 'Feminists Don't Date Online', *Journal of Integrated Studies*, vol.1, no. 3, 2012, http://jis.athabascau.ca/index.php/jis/article/view/115/81, accessed 1/09/2018.

59. Ibid.

60. Ibid.

61. Roffey, Monique, *With the Kisses of His Mouth: A Memoir* (London: Simon and Schuster, 2011); *The Tryst* (Dodo Ink, 2017); Angel, Katherine, *Unmastered: A Book on Desire, Most Difficult to Tell* (London: Penguin, 2012).

62. Weigel, Moira, *Labor of Love: The Invention of Dating* (New York: Farrar, Straus and Giroux, 2016); Witt, Emily, *Future Sex: A New Kind of Free Love* (London: Faber, 2016).

63. Weigel, *Labor of Love*, 4–6.

64. Ibid. 193–6.

65. Ibid. 262.

66. Ibid. 217.

67. Witt, *Future Sex*, 3.

68. Ibid. 4–8.

69. Ibid. 204, 210.

70. Showalter, Elaine, 'Killing the Angel in the House: The Autonomy of Women Writers', *The Antioch Review*, vol. 50, no. 1–2, Winter–Spring 1992, 207–20.

71. Heilbrun, Carolyn, *Writing a Woman's Life* (New York: Norton, 1988).

72. Heibrun, *Writing a Woman's Life* (this edition London: Women's Press, 1997), 21.

73. Ibid. 20.

74. Bowcott, Owen, 'No Fault Divorce Law Coming "As Soon as Parliamentary Time Allows"', *The Guardian*, 9 April 2019, https://www.theguardian.com/law/2019/apr/09/no-fault-divorce-law-coming-as-soon-as-parliamentary-time-allows, accessed 09/04/2019.

75. Dolan, P., *Happy Ever After: Escaping the Myth of the Perfect Life* (London: Allen Lane, 2019). For the controversy generated by Dolan's book and his talk at the Hay Literary Festival, see https://pauldolan.co.uk/category/happyeverafter.

76. *Frozen*, 2013 Disney animation directed by Jennifer Lee and Chris Buck.

77. Konnikova, Maria, 'How "Frozen" Took Over the World', *The New Yorker*, 25 June 2014, https://www.newyorker.com/science/maria-konnikova/how-frozen-took-over-the-world, accessed 3/09/2018.

78. Carolyn Rickards, Symfrozium, Conference Report, University of East Anglia Department of Film, Television and Media Studies Blog, posted 20 March 2015, https://filmtelevisionmediauea.wordpress.com/2015/05/20/symfrozium-conference-report/, accessed 3/09/2018.

79. *Frozen 2* (2019) does end with Anna's marriage to Kristoff, but this is clearly portrayed as a marriage which will preserve her—now Queenly—independence. And it comes after Anna and Elsa have rescued the kingdom of Arendelle and reversed the evils of colonialism.

80. Everett, Lucinda, 'Why Is Frozen So Popular?' *The Guardian*, 20 December 2016, https://www.theguardian.com/commentisfree/2016/dec/20/google-autocomplete-why-frozen-film-so-popular, accessed 3/09/2018.

AFTERWORD AND ACKNOWLEDGEMENTS

We rewrite our stories as we age. This is so for all of us, historians and non-historians alike. While this book spans the years of my own life, it isn't a personal story, although many of its themes have particular resonance for me. I grew up in the English Midlands, in a reasonably prosperous suburb, where my parents lived lives very characteristic of the 1950s. My father went out to work; my mother stayed at home.

My parents had met shortly after the War. They married in 1947 and spent their honeymoon in the Scilly Isles. I somehow think my father, a bit of a romantic, must have seen the Gainsborough film melodrama *Love Story* in 1944. Their honeymoon holiday snaps make them look disconcertingly like Margaret Lockwood and Stewart Granger in the film; they are even kitted out in similar clothes. I cannot know how much of my parents' marriage constituted a love story, although I believe they remained faithful to each other all their lives. Both endured disappointments, but there were also satisfactions. My father, a self-made man, prospered. My mother had chosen to marry someone with prospects, and she chose well. At the age of eighteen, she told me, she had known very clearly what she wanted: a good husband, four children, a nice home. She achieved all this. She worked hard at mothering. And over the next forty years she did an awful lot of—sometimes rather *driven*—housework.

20. *Love Story*, 1944: Margaret Lockwood and Stewart Granger find romance on the cliffs

As a child, I read voraciously. My first foray into authorship came when I started primary school. My mother kept this early literary effort and I have it still, a little booklet entitled *Cinderella*.[1] My spelling was almost entirely phonetic and quite original, which can scarcely be said of the plot. But I had certainly internalized the narrative. It was a script for the future: a girl grew up and met a boy. They married and had children (like my mother) and lived happily ever after. But as I grew to adolescence, and well before encountering 'second-wave feminism', I knew that I wanted something different. I didn't want to be a 'spinster', like many of the teachers at my grammar school. It seems rather shameful to me now, but we did tend to look upon our unmarried teachers as 'rejected', having 'missed out' on something desirable. But I didn't want to be a housewife either: that role lacked any allure and appeared insufferably boring. I hankered after something more adventurous, more significant—although I was not at all clear what that was.

Like so many girls of my generation in the UK, I was a beneficiary of the Butler Education Act, which extended secondary schooling to all, and of the expansion of university education in the 1960s. I went to a girls' grammar school and on to university. But it was hard to know where to go next. I remember the thin and dispiriting advice from the women's section of the university's Graduate Employment Service.[2] I was offered an apprenticeship at something called the Metal Box Company or, inevitably, teaching. I chose teaching. But at the time it seemed a let-down: didn't education open up any more options for women?

After many years working in higher education I now research and write full-time. Looking back, I can appreciate that education did indeed transform things for women, but it took time for society and culture—and for men—to begin to adjust. The educational opportunities made available to women in the post-war world reshaped their aspirations and prospects in a way that would mark out their experience as quite different from that of their mothers. I was fortunate that my husband, Nick von Tunzelmann, espoused feminist views, was a fellow academic, and was fully supportive of my own academic ambitions. He never looked upon parenting as anything other than our joint responsibility.

Those born during or after the 1970s took many of the changes associated with the sexual revolution of the 1960s and 1970s for granted. But some of the problems they faced about how to combine love and work, how to conduct relationships, or how to

21. *Cinderella*, by Carol Dyhouse, early 1950s

manage parenting and commitment were just as (if not more) challenging than those their mothers faced. What was incontrovertible was that the gender scripts of the 1950s, those fairy-tale narratives of love and marriage, no longer offered any useful guidance.

What have I learned since the 1950s? A great deal of history, certainly, which has allowed me to understand more about myself by seeing women's experiences, aspirations, and ideas about the good life; their notions about work, love, and romance, in a changing social context. As individuals, we craft our lives as best we can but we are nonetheless shaped by history. Our ideas of love and of work owe a great deal to the society and culture in which we grow up, although personal experience may lead us to question accepted values and attitudes. Finding love is not about reaching a destination. Love is multifaceted and comes in many different forms. Relationships aren't set in stone, and, even with the best will in the world, you cannot promise or guarantee to love someone forever. If marriages or loving partnerships flourish through several decades, giving stability and satisfying shape to individual lives, we are indeed blessed. But for many of us the odds are against this, and perhaps we would benefit from much more pragmatism in thinking about love and romance. Maybe the best we can do is to love as at a staging post, and to recognize this as at least in part the fulfilment of needs which will probably change as we journey on and grow older. What we do know is that for many—perhaps for most people—love matters a very great deal, giving both form and meaning to our lives as human beings.

Acknowledgements

My friends and former colleagues at the University of Sussex have been a vital source of encouragement and strength while I have worked on this book, and I owe a great deal to their generosity in having provided me with the resources to continue with my research and writing. Thanks particularly to Professor Liz James, until recently Head of the School of History, Art History and Philosophy, for her support in this respect, and to Head of Schools Coordinator, Ahmed Koyes. Conversations with younger historians working in similar areas have been a source of both inspiration and pleasure, and I have been fortunate indeed to have Claire Langhamer, Hester Barron, Lucy Robinson, Chris Warne, Sharon Webb, Vinita Damodaran, Tim Hitchcock, Maurice Howard and

Ian Gazeley working at various times in rooms nearby. Regular discussion of shared interests with Claire, Hester and Lucy have been invaluable, and that they are such wonderful friends, too, has been one of the blessings of my life in recent years. Chance meetings in corridors and discussions after the weekly work-in-progress sessions organised by historians at Sussex have often sent me off in enthusiastic pursuit of new ideas and sources. So, too, have symposia and day conferences organised by colleagues in the university. I learned a great deal from papers and discussions at an event dedicated to thinking about '1948: Seventy Years On', which was organised by Janice Winship for the Sussex Centre for Cultural Studies in November 2018. Laura Kounine's day symposium (part of a British Academy-funded Rising Star Engagement Award) on 'Subjectivity, Self-Narratives and the History of Emotions' in January 2019 was also a rich source of ideas. Discussions here at Sussex, at various times, with Kate Fisher and Jesse Olszynko-Gryn, were extremely helpful.

Friends and scholars elsewhere have also given generously of ideas and encouragement. It was a privilege to spend time in Belfast, where Queen's University hosts the Wiles lectures, which in the spring of 2019 allowed me to spend time talking about the twentieth century history of women with Amanda Vickery and other friends and colleagues. Thanks to Jenny Shaw, Marcia Pointon, June Purvis, Helen Taylor, Madge Dresser and Ulrike Meinhof for their friendship over many years – indeed, over decades. I am grateful, too, for the long-term friendship and support of Nigel Paris and Monica Collingham. Jeanne Openshaw is a friend of more recent times, but her anthropological insights, and her calm understanding of the trials and complexities of life and of writing have been invaluable. Tusia Werner and the members of our local book group have provided encouragement, critical ideas, and quantities of tea and cake. Vincent Quinn has been wise about the processes of thinking and writing, and his friendship and emotional intelligence, as we have both had to watch partners succumb to terrible illness over recent years, has been indispensable. Thanks to Pat Thane for her judicious and careful critique of this project: both her passion for social history and her understanding of women's lives in academia have continued to be inspirational. I owe a great deal to conversations with Owen Emmerson and Zoe Strimpel, both of whose intellectual energy and highly original insights have so often stimulated argument, mirth, and new ways of looking at things.

It should hardly need saying that the responsibility for the ideas purveyed here, though, is wholly mine. This is a wide-ranging and somewhat sprawling book, and I owe an enormous debt to the work of other scholars in the field. I am not going to attempt a full list of names here, but I hope that their research and writing is adequately acknowledged in the footnotes.

I must pay tribute to the many librarians and staff working in various archives who have made my research possible. I hope they will forgive me for not mentioning all of them by name, but especial thanks to the staff working in Sussex University Library, the British Library, and in the Mass Observation Collection at The Keep.

My agent, Maggie Hanbury, has been indispensable and I am hugely grateful to her, and to the staff at Oxford University Press and their extremely professional production team. Special thanks to Luciana O'Flaherty, Sandy Garel, and Kizzy Taylor-Richelieu. Kizzy Taylor-Richelieu in particular has shown sterling qualities of support and patience in steering this book through the press at a time when most of us were working at home owing to the ravages of Covid 19. My warm thanks to Kabilan Selvakumar, who has worked tirelessly to make the production process as smooth as possible.

My daughters, Alex and Eugénie von Tunzelmann, read versions of the text and made incisive and pertinent comments with tact and humour. They have both been generous and wonderful in so many ways that I cannot think that I could have gone on writing without them.

Carol Dyhouse, Autumn 2020

Notes

1. *Cinderella*, by Carol Dyhouse. (Spelling as it was.) 'One day a long time ago ther wos a lovey girl and her Mother did a long time and her Daddy marid a gan and she had a step Mother and to ugle sisdz thay made her do all the wirk and her ugle sisds did non and one day the ugeysisds wir invited to a ball and thay wir eveso icsited and thay mad Cinderella do them she put them clen jress is on them and then thay mad her do ther her and Cinderella did it and then thay went and cinderella started to crie and her fere god Mother came she sead you have bean a good girl you may go but Cinderella sead but I hav not a pritea jress and the fere sead you may hav one and Cinderella wos happy and and the Fere wavd her wond and chand her rags into a butful jress and the fere made a coch and Cinderella got into it and went at the ball the Prinss met her and danst with her and thay marid each uther and thay livd happy evir after.'

2. This was just before the impact of the 1975 Sex Discrimination Act. In these years most universities operated separate employment advisory services for men and women and almost all career opportunities and job advertisements were gender-coded.

PICTURE AND TEXT ACKNOWLEDGEMENTS

2: Cover image of The Story of Cinderella, illustrated by Evelyn Bowmar © Ladybird Books Ltd. 1944
3: Pictorial Press Ltd / Alamy Stock Photo
4: Shell Petroleum
5: Photo by Clive Limpkin/Express/ Hulton Archives /Getty Images
6: Moviestore Collection Ltd / Alamy Stock Photo
7: *Cinderella Love*, June 1955
8: 'Too Great a Risk!' Gillian Crampton Smith for FPA Birth Control advert
9: Photo by Joseph McKeown/Picture Post/Hulton Archive/Getty Images
10: Trinity Mirror / Mirrorpix / Alamy Stock Photo
11: Pfizer
12: Everett Collection Inc / Alamy Stock Photo
13: © British Library Board. All Rights Reserved / Bridgeman Images
14: © British Library Board
15: Peoples Collection Wales
16: Reproduced by kind permission of PRIVATE EYE magazine: private-eye.co.uk.
17: © Spencer Rowell
19: © Blake Fitch
20: ITV/Shutterstock
18; 21: Carol Dyhouse

We are grateful to reproduce extracts from the following material:
    'Replies to Women and Men Directive, 1991'.
    'Replies to Close Relationships Directive, 1990'.
    Reproduced with permission of Curtis Brown Group Ltd, London on behalf of The Trustees of the Mass Observation Archive © The Trustees of the Mass Observation Archive

SELECT BIBLIOGRAPHY

Adams, James Truslow, *The Epic of America* (Boston: Little, Brown and Company, 1931).

Allen, Anne Taylor, *Feminism and Motherhood in Western Europe, 1890–1970: The Maternal Dilemma* (New York: Palgrave Macmillan, 2005).

Angel, Katherine, *Unmastered: A Book on Desire, Most Difficult to Tell* (London: Penguin, 2012).

Ansari, Aziz, *Modern Romance* (New York: Penguin/Allen Lane, 2015).

Arnot, M., David, M., and Weiner, G., *Closing the Gender Gap: Postwar Education and Social Change* (Cambridge: Polity Press, 1999).

Attar, Dena, *Wasting Girls' Time: The History and Politics of Home Economics* (London: Virago, 1990).

Bailey, Beth L., *From Front Porch to Back Seat: Courtship in Twentieth-Century America* (Baltimore: Johns Hopkins University Press, 1989).

Barber, Lynn, *An Education* (London: Penguin, 2009).

Barker, M., *Rewriting the Rules: An Integrative Guide to Love, Sex and Relationships* (Abingdon: Routledge, 2012).

Barstow, S., *A Kind of Loving* (London: Michael Joseph, 1960).

Bauman, Zygmunt, *Liquid Love: On the Frailty of Human Bonds* (Cambridge: Polity, 2003).

Beck, Ulrich and Beck-Gernsheim, Elisabeth, *The Normal Chaos of Love* (Oxford: Polity, 1995).

Berkoff, S., *Free Association* (London: Faber & Faber,1996).

Bernard, Jessie, *The Future of Marriage* (New York: World Publishing, 1972).

Bettelheim, Bruno, *The Uses of Enchantment: The Meaning and Importance of Fairy Tales* (London: Thames and Hudson, 1976; Penguin edition, 1991).

Blume, Judy, *Forever* (London: Gollancz, 1976).

Bly, Robert, *Iron John: A Book about Men* (Boston: Addison Wesley, 1990).

Boston Women's Health Collective, *Our Bodies, Ourselves: A Book By and For Women* (New York: Simon and Schuster, 1973); British edition edited by Angela Phillips and Jill Rakusen (London: Penguin, 1978).

Bowlby, J., *Child Care and the Growth of Love* (London: Penguin, 1953).

Bradford, Barbara Taylor, *A Woman of Substance* (Bath: Chivers, 1979).

Brode, Douglas and Brode, Shea T., *Debating Disney: Pedagogical Perspectives on Commercial Cinema* (Lanham: Rowman and Littlefield, 2016).

Brookes, Barbara, *Abortion in England, 1900–1967* (London: Routledge, 1988).

Brown, Helen Gurley, *Sex and the Single Girl* (London: Frederick Mueller, 1963).

Brown, Helen Gurley, *Having It All: Love, Success, Sex, Money, Even If You're Starting with Nothing* (New York: Simon and Schuster, Linden Press, 1982).

Burgess, Adrienne, *Fatherhood Reclaimed: The Making of the Modern Father* (London: Vermilion, 1997).

Bushnell, Candace, *Sex and the City* (London: Abacus, 2008).

Butler, Judith, *Gender Trouble: Feminism and the Subversion of Identity* (New York and London: Routledge, 1990).

Cantu, Maya, *American Cinderellas on the Broadway Musical Stage: Imagining the Working Girl from Irene to Gypsy* (Palgrave Studies in Theatre and Performance History, Basingstoke: Palgrave Macmillan, 2015).

Chesser, Eustace, *The Sexual, Marital and Family Relationships of the English Woman* (London: Hutchinson's Medical Publications, 1956).

Clare, Anthony, *On Men: Masculinity in Crisis* (London: Chatto and Windus, 2000).

Cocks, H. G., *Classified: The Secret History of the Personal Column* (London: Random House, 2009).

Cohen, Deborah, *Family Secrets: Living with Shame from the Victorians to the Present Day* (London: Viking, 2013).

Collins, Marcus, *Modern Love: An Intimate History of Men and Women in Twentieth Century Britain* (London: Atlantic, 2003).

Comfort, Alex, *The Joy of Sex: A Gourmet Guide to Lovemaking* (London: Quartet, 1972).

Connolly, Cyril, *Enemies of Promise* (London: Routledge, 1938).

Conran, S., *Superwoman: Everywoman's Book of Household Management* (London: Sidgwick and Jackson, 1975).

Conran, Shirley, *Lace* (London: Sidgwick and Jackson, 1982).

Cornell, Drucilla (ed.), *Feminism and Pornography* (Oxford: Oxford University Press, 2000).

Cook, Hera, *The Long Sexual Revolution: English Women, Sex and Contraception, 1800–1975* (Oxford: Oxford University Press, 2004).

Coontz, S., *Marriage, A History: How Love Conquered Marriage* (New York: Penguin (USA), 2006).

Coontz, S., *A Strange Stirring: The Feminine Mystique and American Women at the Dawn of the 1960s* (New York: Basic Books, 2011).

Cusk, Rachel, *A Life's Work* (London: Fourth Estate, 2001).

Davidson, Caroline, *A Woman's Work is Never Done: A History of Housework in the British Isles 1650–1950* (London: Chatto and Windus, 1984).

Delap, Lucy, *Knowing Their Place: Domestic Service in Twentieth Century Britain* (Oxford: Oxford University Press, 2011).

DePaulo, Bella M., *Singled Out: How Singles are Stereotyped, Stigmatized and Ignored and Still Live Happily Ever After* (New York: St Martin's Press, 2006).

Dolan, P., *Happy Ever After: Escaping the Myth of the Perfect Life* (London: Allen Lane, 2019).

Dowling, Colette, *The Cinderella Complex: Women's Hidden Fear of Independence* (New York: Simon and Schuster, 1981).

Drabble, M., *A Summer Bird-Cage* (London: Weidenfeld and Nicolson, 1962).

Drabble, M., *The Millstone* (London: Weidenfeld and Nicolson, 1965).

Dunn, Nell, *Up the Junction* (London: MacGibbon and Kee, 1963).

Dunn, Nell, *Talking to Women* (London: Silver Press, 2018).

Dyhouse, C., *Feminism and the Family in England, 1880–1939* (Oxford: Blackwell, 1989).

Dyhouse, C., *Students: A Gendered History* (Abingdon: Routledge, 2006).

Dyhouse, C., *Glamour: Women, History, Feminism* (London: Zed Books, 2010).

Dyhouse, C., *Girl Trouble: Panic and Progress in the History of Young Women* (London: Zed Books, 2013).

Dyhouse, C., *Heartthrobs: A History of Women and Desire* (Oxford: Oxford University Press, 2017).

Dyhouse, Carol, *No Distinction of Sex? Women in British Universities 1870–1939* (London: UCL Press, 1995).

Easton, Dossie and Liszt, Catherine A. (Janet W. Hardy), *The Ethical Slut: A Guide to Infinite Sexual Possibilities* (Emeryville: Greenery Press, 1997).

Edwards, Elizabeth, *Women in Teacher Training Colleges: A Culture of Femininity* (London: Routledge, 2001).

Eisenmann, Linda, *Higher Education for Women in Postwar America, 1945–1965* (Baltimore: Johns Hopkins University Press, 2006).

Elwood, J., Maw, J., Epstein, D., and Hey, V. (eds), *Failing Boys? Issues in Gender and Achievement* (Milton Keynes: Open University Press, 1998).

Evans, Sara, *Personal Politics: The Roots of the Women's Liberation Movement in the Civil Rights Movement and the New Left* (New York: Alfred Knopf, 1979).

Faludi, Susan, *Backlash: The Undeclared War Against American Women* (London: Vintage, 1992).

Faludi, Susan, *Stiffed: The Betrayal of the American Man* (New York: W. Morrow and Co., 1999).

Fielding, Helen, *Bridget Jones's Diary* (London: Picador, 1996).

Figes, Kate, *Life after Birth* (London: Viking, 1998).

Firestone, S., *The Dialectic of Sex: The Case for Feminist Revolution* (London: The Women's Press, 1979).

Fisher, Kate, *Birth Control, Sex and Marriage in Britain, 1918–1960* (Oxford: Oxford University Press, 2006).

Fisher, K. and Szreter, S., *Sex before the Sexual Revolution: Intimate Life in England, 1918–1963* (Cambridge: Cambridge University Press, 2010).

Fisher, Kate and Toulalan, Sarah (eds), *Bodies, Sex and Desire from the Renaissance to the Present* (Basingstoke: Palgrave Macmillan, 2011).

Florey, Kenneth, *Women's Suffrage Memorabilia: An Illustrated Historical Study* (North Carolina: McFarland, 2013).

Francis, Becky, *Reassessing Gender and Achievement: Questioning Contemporary Key Debates* (Abingdon: Routledge, 2005).

Frankl, G., *The Failure of the Sexual Revolution* (London: Kahn and Averill, 1974).

Freedman, Estelle, *No Turning Back: The History of Feminism and the Future of Women* (New York: Ballantine, 2002).

French, Marilyn, *The Women's Room* (New York: Simon and Schuster, 1977).

Friday, N., *My Secret Garden: Women's Sexual Fantasies* (London: Quartet, 1975).

Friday, Nancy, *My Mother, Myself: The Daughter's Search for Identity* (London: Fontana, 1979).

Friedan, Betty, *The Feminine Mystique* (Harmondsworth: Penguin, 1965).

Galloway, Janice, *All Made Up* (London: Granta, 2011).

Gavron, Hannah, *The Captive Wife: Conflicts of Housebound Mothers* (London: Routledge and Kegan Paul, 1966).

Gerson, Kathleen, *No Man's Land: Men's Changing Commitments to Family and Work* (New York: Basic Books, 1993).

Gibson, Mel, *Remembered Reading: Memory, Comics and Post-War Constructions of British Girlhood* (Leuven: Leuven University Press, 2015).

Giddens, Anthony, *The Transformation of Intimacy: Sexuality, Love and Eroticism in Modern Societies* (Cambridge: Polity Press, 1992).

Giroux, Henry A., *The Mouse that Roared: Disney and the End of Innocence* (Lanham: Rowman and Littlefield, 1999).

Gorer, G., *Exploring English Character* (London: Cresset Press, 1955).

Gorer, G., *Sex and Marriage in England Today: A Study of the Views and Experience of the under 45s* (London: Nelson, 1971).

Grant, Linda, *Sexing the Millennium: Women and the Sexual Revolution* (New York: Grove Press, 1994).

Grant, Linda, *Remind Me Who I Am, Again* (London: Granta, 1998).

Gray, John, *Men are from Mars, Women are from Venus* (New York: HarperCollins, 1992).

Greenfield, Lauren, *Girl Culture* (San Francisco: Chronicle, 2002).

Greig, Charlotte, *A Girl's Guide to Modern European Philosophy* (London: Serpent's Tail, 2007).

Griswold, Robert L., *Fatherhood in America: A History* (New York: Basic Books, 1993).

Grossman, J., *Her Own Terms* (London: Grafton, 1988).

Haase, D. (ed.), *Fairy Tales and Feminism: New Approaches* (Detroit: Wayne State University Press, 2004).

Hains, Rebecca, *The Princess Problem: Guiding Our Girls Through the Princess-Obsessed Years* (Naperville: Sourcebooks, 2014).

Hall, Lesley A., *Hidden Anxieties: Male Sexuality 1900–1950* (Cambridge: Polity, 1991).

Hall, Ruth (ed.), *Dear Dr Stopes: Sex in the 1920s* (Harmondsworth: Penguin, 1981).

Haran, Maeve, *Having it All* (first published Harmondsworth: Penguin, 1991; this edition London: Pan, 2014).

Heilbrun, Carolyn, *Writing a Woman's Life* (New York: Norton, 1988).

Hinton, James, *The Mass Observers: A History, 1937–1949* (Oxford: Oxford University Press, 2013).

Hite, Shere, *The Hite Report: A Nationwide Study of Female Sexuality* (first edition 1976, this edition New York: Seven Stories Press, 2004).

Holden, Katherine, *The Shadow of Marriage: Singleness in England, 1914–1960* (Manchester: Manchester University Press, 2007).

Hough, M., *Rural Unwed Mothers: An American Experience, 1870–1950* (London: Pickering and Chatto, 2010).

Hubback, Judith, *Wives Who Went to College* (London: Heinemann, 1957).

Hubble, Nick, *Mass Observation and Everyday Life: Culture, History, Theory* (Basingstoke: Palgrave Macmillan, 2005).

Illouz, Eva, *Cold Intimacies: The Making of Emotional Capitalism* (Cambridge: Polity, 2007).

Ingham, Mary, *Now We Are Thirty: Women of the Breakthrough Generation* (London: Eyre Methuen, 1981).

Ingraham, Chrys, *White Weddings: Romancing Heterosexuality in Popular Culture* (New York: Routledge, 1999).

Jaffe, Rona, *The Best of Everything* (first published 1958, this edition London: Penguin, 2011).

Jeffreys, S., *Anticlimax: A Feminist Perspective on the Sexual Revolution* (London: The Woman's Press, 1990).

Jenkins, Elizabeth, *The Tortoise and the Hare* (London: Gollancz, 1954).

Jephcott, A. P., *Rising Twenty: Notes on Some Ordinary Girls* (London: Faber & Faber, 1945).

Jephcott, A. P., *Married Women Working* (London: George Allen and Unwin, 1962).

Jones, Dylan, *Manxiety: The Difficulties of Being Male* (London: Biteback Publishing, 2016).

Kiernan, K., Land, H., and Lewis, J., *Lone Motherhood in Twentieth Century Britain* (Oxford: Clarendon, 1998).

King, Laura, *Family Men: Fatherhood and Masculinity in Britain, c. 1914–1960* (Oxford: Oxford University Press, 2015).

Kinsey, Alfred C., Pomeroy, Wardell B., and Martin, Clyde E., *Sexual Behaviour in the Human Male* (Bloomington: Indiana University Press, 1948).

Kinsey, Alfred C., Pomeroy, Wardell B., Martin, Clyde E., and Gebhard, Paul H., *Sexual Behaviour in the Human Female* (Bloomington: Indiana University Press, 1953).

Klinenberg, Eric, *Going Solo: The Extraordinary Rise and Surprising Appeal of Living Alone* (New York: Penguin, 2012).

Komarovsky, Mirra, *The Unemployed Man and His Family* (New York: Dryden Press, 1940).

Krantz, Judith, *I'll Take Manhattan* (London: Bantam, 1986).

Kuhn, Annette, *An Everyday Magic: Cinema and Cultural Memory* (London: I. B. Tauris, 1998).

Kynaston, David, *Family Britain, 1951–1957* (London: Bloomsbury, 2010).

Ladd-Taylor, Molly and Umansky, Lauri, *'Bad Mothers': The Politics of Blame in Twentieth-Century America* (New York: New York University Press, 1998).

Langhamer, Claire, *Women's Leisure in England, 1920–1960* (Manchester: Manchester University Press, 2000).

Langhamer, Claire, *The English in Love: The Intimate Story of an Emotional Revolution* (Oxford: Oxford University Press, 2013).

LaRossa, Ralph, *The Modernization of Fatherhood: A Social and Political History* (Chicago: University of Chicago Press, 1997).

Lawson, Annette, *Adultery: An Analysis of Love and Betrayal* (Oxford: Blackwell, 1989).

Levin, Ira, *The Stepford Wives* (New York: Random House, 1972).

Levy, Ariel, *Female Chauvinist Pigs: Women and the Rise of Raunch Culture* (New York: Free Press, 2005).

Lewis, Jane, *The End of Marriage? Individualism and Intimate Relations* (Cheltenham: Edward Elgar, 2001).

Lodge, David, *Ginger, You're Barmy* (first published London: MacGibbon & Kee, 1962; this edition London: Vintage, 1982).

McCarthy, M., *The Group* (New York: Harcourt Brace, 1963).

McDonald, Ian, *Vindication! A Postcard History of the Women's Movement* (London: Bellew, 1989).

Makins, Peggy, *The Evelyn Home Story* (London: HarperCollins, 1975).

Malos, Ellen, *The Politics of Housework* (Cheltenham: New Clarion Press, 1995).

Masson, M. R. and Simonton, D. (eds), *Women and Higher Education: Past, Present and Future* (Aberdeen: Aberdeen University Press, 1996).

Masters, W. H., Johnson, Virginia E., and Kolodny, Robert C., *Masters and Johnson on Sex and Human Loving* (London: Macmillan, 1986).

Mills, Jane, *Make It Happy* (London: Virago, 1978).

Mohr, James C., *Abortion in America: The Origins and Evolution of National Policy* (New York: Oxford University Press, 1979).

Moran, Caitlin, *How to be a Woman* (London: Ebury Press, 2011).

Mortimer, Penelope, *Daddy's Gone A-Hunting* (London: Michael Joseph, 1958).

Mortimer, Penelope, *The Pumpkin Eater* (Harmondsworth: Penguin, 1964).

Motion, Andrew, *Philip Larkin: A Writer's Life* (London: Faber, 1993).

Munford, Rebecca and Waters, Melanie, *Feminism and Popular Culture: Investigating the Postfeminist Mystique* (New Brunswick: Rutgers University Press, 2014).

Munsch, Robert, *The Paper Bag Princess* (Toronto: Annick Press and Discus Books, 1980).

Myrdal, A. and Klein, V., *Women's Two Roles: Home and Work* (London: Routledge and Kegan Paul, 1956).

Newman, A., *A Share of the World* (London: Bodley Head, 1964).

Newman, A., *Alexa* (London: Triton, 1968).

Newsom, J., *The Education of Girls* (London: Faber, 1948).

Nolan, Michelle, *Love on the Racks: A History of American Romance Comics* (Jefferson: McFarland, 2008).

Nott, James, *Going to the Palais: A Social and Cultural History of Dancing and Dance Halls in Britain, 1918–1960* (Oxford: Oxford University Press, 2015).

Oakley, Ann, *Sex, Gender and Society* (Middlesex: Temple Smith, 1972).

Oakley, Ann, *Becoming a Mother* (Oxford: Martin Robertson, 1979).

Oakley, A., *Woman Confined: Towards a Sociology of Childbirth* (Oxford: Martin Robertson, 1980).

Oakley, A., *From Here to Maternity: Becoming a Mother* (Harmondsworth: Penguin, 1981).

O'Brien, Edna, *The Country Girls* (London: Hutchinson, 1960).

Ollerenshaw, K., *Education for Girls* (London: Faber & Faber, 1961).

Orenstein, P., *Cinderella Ate My Daughter: Dispatches from the Front Lines of the New Girlie-Girl Culture* (New York: HarperCollins, 2011).

Otnes, Cele C. and Pleck, Elizabeth H., *Cinderella Dreams: The Allure of the Lavish Wedding* (Berkeley: University of California Press, 2003).

Paasonen, Susanna, Nikunen, Kaarina, and Saarenmaa, Laura (eds), *Pornification: Sex and Sexuality in Media Culture* (Oxford: Berg, 2007).

Paintin, David, *Abortion Law Reform in Britain, 1964–2003: A Personal Account* (Stratford-on-Avon: BPAS, 2015).

Paul, Pamela, *Pornified: How Pornography is Transforming Our Lives, Our Relationships and our Families* (New York: Times Books, 2005).

Pearce, L. and Stacey, J. (eds), *Romance Revisited* (London: Lawrence and Wishart, 1995).

Pearson, Allison, *I Don't Know How She Does It* (London: Vintage, 2003).

Pearson, Allison, *How Hard Can It Be?* (London: Harper Collins, Borough Press, 2017).

Pedersen, S., *Family, Dependence and the Origins of the Welfare State: Britain and France 1914–1945* (Cambridge: Cambridge University Press, 1995).

Perel, Esther, *Mating in Captivity, Sex, Lies and Domestic Bliss* (New York: HarperCollins, 2006).

Perel, Esther, *The State of Affairs: Rethinking Infidelity* (New York: HarperCollins, 2017).

Pilgrim Trust, *Men without Work* (Cambridge: Cambridge University Press, 1938).

Private Eye, *Book of Wimmin* (London: Private Eye, 1986).

Reagan, Lesley J., *When Abortion was a Crime: Women, Medicine and the Law in the United States, 1867–1973* (Berkeley: University of California Press, 1998).

Rich, Adrienne, *Of Woman Born: Motherhood as Experience and Institution* (London: Virago, 1977).

Roffey, Monique, *With the Kisses of His Mouth: A Memoir* (London: Simon and Schuster, 2011).

Roffey, Monique, *The Tryst* (London: Dodo Ink, 2017).

Rowbotham, Sheila, *Promise of a Dream: Remembering the Sixties* (London: Allen Lane, 2000).

Ryan, Christopher and Jetha, Cacilda, *Sex at Dawn: The Prehistoric Origins of Modern Sexuality* (New York: HarperCollins, 2010).

Ryle, A., *Student Casualties* (London: Allen Lane, 1969).

Sage, Lorna, *Bad Blood* (London: Fourth Estate, 2000).

Schofield, M., in collaboration with Bynner, John, Lewis, Patricia, and Massie, Peter, *The Sexual Behaviour of Young People* (London: Longmans, 1965).

Schreiner, Olive, *Woman and Labour* (1911; London: Virago, 1978).

Scharff, C., *Repudiating Feminism: Young Women in a Neo-Liberal World* (Abingdon: Routledge, 2016).

Sharpe, S., *'Just Like a Girl': How Girls Learn to be Women* (London: Penguin, 1976).

Sillitoe, Alan, *Saturday Night and Sunday Morning* (London: W. H. Allan, 1958).

Simpson, Helen, *Hey Yeah Right Get a Life* (London: Jonathan Cape, 2000); published in United States as *Getting a Life* (New York: Alfred A Knopf, 2000).

Sinclair, Colette, *Man Hunt: The Search for Mr Right* (London: Sidgwick and Jackson, 1989).

Sinclair, May, *The Creators: A Comedy* (London: Hutchinson, 1910).

Slater, Dan, *Love in the Time of Algorithms: What Technology Does to Meeting and Mating* (New York: Current (Penguin Group), 2013).

Slater, Eliot and Woodside, Moya, *Patterns of Marriage: A Study of Marriage Relationships in the Urban Working Classes* (London: Cassell, 1951).

Solinger, Rickie, *Pregnancy and Power: A Short History of Reproductive Politics in America* (New York: New York University Press, 2005).

Sommers, Christina Hoff, *The War against Boys: How Misguided Feminism is Harming Our Young Men* (New York: Touchstone, 2000).

Spencer, Stephanie, *Gender, Work and Education in Britain in the 1950s* (Basingstoke: Palgrave Macmillan, 2005).

Stanley, L., *Sex Surveyed, 1949–1994; From Mass Observation's 'Little Kinsey' to the National Survey and the Hite Reports* (London: Taylor and Francis, 1995).

Stearns, Peter N., *Be a Man! Males in Modern Society* (New York: Holmes and Meier, 1979).

Steedman, Carolyn, *Landscape for a Good Woman: A Story of Two Lives* (London: Virago, 1986).

Stokes, Melvyn and Maltby, Richard (eds), *American Movie Audiences: From the Turn of the Century to the Early Sound Era* (London: BFI Publishing, 1999).

Stones, Rosemary (ed.), *More to Life than Mr Right: Stories for Young Feminists* (London: Piccadilly Press, 1985).

Stopes, M., *Mother England: A Contemporary History,* 'Self Written by those who have had no Historian' (London: John Bale, Sons and Danielsson, 1929).

Strasser, Susan, *Never Done: A History of American Housework* (New York: Henry Holt, 1982).

Sutherland, Daniel E., *Americans and Their Servants: Domestic Service in the United States from 1880–1920* (Baton Rouge: Louisiana State University Press, 1981).

Szreter, S. and Fisher, K., *Sex before the Sexual Revolution: Intimate Life in England, 1918–1963* (Cambridge: Cambridge University Press, 2010).

Tannen, Deborah, *You Just Don't Understand: Men and Women in Conversation* (New York: Morrow, 1990).

Thane, Pat and Evans, Tanya, *Sinners? Scroungers? Saints? Unmarried Motherhood in 20th-Century England* (Oxford: Oxford University Press, 2012).

Thwaite, Anthony, *Selected Letters of Philip Larkin, 1940–1985* (London: Faber and Faber, 1992).

Titmuss, R., *Essays on 'The Welfare State'* (London: Allen and Unwin, 1958).

Tosh, John, *Manliness and Masculinities in Nineteenth Century Britain: Essays on Gender, Family and Empire* (Harlow: Pearson, 2005).

Traister, Rebecca, *All the Single Ladies: Unmarried Women and the Rise of an Independent Nation* (New York: Simon and Schuster, 2016).

Tweedie, Jill, *In the Name of Love* (London: Macmillan, 1988).

Tyler May, Elaine, *America and the Pill: A History of Promise, Peril and Liberation* (New York: Basic Books, 2011).

Updike, John, *Couples* (New York: Alfred A. Knopf, 1968).

Vinen, Richard, *National Service: Conscription in Britain 1945–1963* (London: Allen Lane, 2014).

Walter, Natasha, *The New Feminism* (London: Little, Brown, 1998).

Walter, Natasha, *Living Dolls: The Return of Sexism* (London: Virago, 2010).

Warner, Marina, *From the Beast to the Blonde: On Fairy Tales and Their Tellers* (London: Vintage, 1995).

Warner, M., *Once Upon a Time: A Short History of Fairy Tales* (Oxford: Oxford University Press, 2016).

Weeks, Jeffrey, *The World We Have Won: The Remaking of Erotic and Intimate Life* (London: Routledge, 2007).

Weigel, Moira, *Labor of Love: The Invention of Dating* (New York: Farrar, Straus and Giroux, 2016).

Weldon, Fay, *Down Among the Women* (London: St Martin's Press, 1972).

Whitehorn, K., *Cooking In a Bedsitter* (Harmondsworth: Penguin, 1961).

Whitehorn, K., *Selective Memory: An Autobiography* (London: Virago, 2007).

Whyte, J., Kant, L., Deem, R., and Cruicksank, M. (eds), *Girl-Friendly Schooling* (London: Methuen, 1985).

Wilson, Sloan, *The Man in the Gray Flannel Suit* (London: Cassell, 1956).

Witt, Emily, *Futuresex: A New Kind of Free Love* (London: Faber, 2016).

Wolf, Naomi, *The Beauty Myth: How Images of Beauty are Used against Women* (London: Vintage, 1990).

Wolf, Naomi, *Misconceptions: Truth, Lies and the Unexpected on the Journey to Motherhood* (New York and London: Doubleday, 2001).

Wright, H., *The Sex Factor in Marriage: A Book for Those Who Are, or Are About to Be Married* (London: Williams and Norgate, 1937).

Wright, H., *More about the Sex Factor in Marriage* (London: Williams and Norgate, 1954).

Wright, Helena, *Sex and Society* (London: George Allen and Unwin, 1968).

Writers and Readers Publishing Co-Operative, *Sexism in Children's Books: Facts, Figures and Guidelines* (London: Writers and Readers Publishing Co-Operative, 1976).

Zipes, Jack (ed.), *Don't Bet on the Prince: Contemporary Feminist Fairy Tales in North America and England* (Aldershot: Gower, 1986).

Zipes, Jack, *Why Fairy Tales Stick: The Evolution and Relevance of a Genre* (Abingdon: Taylor and Francis, 2006).

Zipes, Jack, *The Irresistible Fairy Tales: The Cultural and Social History of a Genre* (Princeton: Princeton University Press, 2012).

Zweig, Ferdynand, *Women's Life and Labour* (London: Gollancz, 1952).

INDEX

Walt Disney Company 1–2, 218–19,
    222–3
Walter, Natasha 202–3, 214–15
    *Living Dolls: The Return of
      Sexism* 201–2
    New Feminism, The 201
wards of court 45–6
websites 203–5
'wedding-industrial complex' 222–3
weddings 41, 222–6
Weeks, Jeffrey
    *World We Have Won: The Remaking of
      Erotic and Intimate Life, The* 4–5
Weigel, Moira
    *Labor of Love: The Invention of
      Dating* 232–5
Weiner, Gaby *see* Arnot, Madeleine,
    David, Miriam and Weiner, Gaby
Weinstein, Harvey 204–5
Weldon, Fay
    Down Among the Women 149
Whitehorn, Katharine 46–7
    Cooking in a Bedsitter 65–6
white weddings 222–3
Wiig, Kristen 225
Wilder, Billy 86
Wilding, Michael 26–8
Wilson, Sloan
    Man in the Grey Flannel Suit, The 87–8
Winner, Michael 23–4
Witt, Emily
    *Future Sex: A New Kind of Free
      Love* 232–5
Wolf, Naomi
    Beauty Myth, The 200
    Misconceptions 141
Woman (magazine) 78
Woman's Own (magazine) 78
women's dependence 2–3, 6–7, 9–10,
    133–5

women's independence 136–8, 148–53,
    166, 227–8
'women's libbers' 8, 157–8
women's liberation movement 96–7,
    125f
Women's Press, The 119–20
women writers
    autobiographies 235–6
    on feminine helplessness 15
    and feminine respectability 235–6
    and internet dating 230–2
    on romantic myths of love and
      marriage 232–6
    on single women 228
Wooden, Shannon R. 220
Woods, Ilene 24–5
Woodside, Moya 54, 64–5, 83–4
Woolf, Virginia 113
    'Professions for Women' 235
working
    and domestic tasks 138–41
    and motherhood 137–8, 142–8
    new forms of identity 176
    wives 67, 69–73
    women 67
working class 71–2
    marriages 54, 87–8
    and unwanted pregnancies 41–2
    wives 83–5
    women 9–10
Wright, Helena
    Sex and Society 100
    Sex Factor in Marriage, The 82–3

Young Love (comic) 38
Young Romance (comic) 38

Zellweger, Renée 190
Zweig, Ferdynand 38–40, 69–70
    Women's Life and Labour 69–70